SUBJECT
AND
STRATEGY
A RHETORIC READER

Second Edition

SUBJECT
AND
STRATEGY
A RHETORIC READER

Second Edition

Editors

PAUL ESCHHOLZ
ALFRED ROSA
University of Vermont

St. Martin's Press   New York

ACKNOWLEDGMENTS

1. Narration

"How I Discovered Words: A Homemade Education" from *The Autobiography
of Malcolm X* by Malcolm X, with the assistance of Alex Haley. Copyright ©
1964 by Alex Haley and Malcolm X. Copyright © 1965 by Alex Haley and
Betty Shabazz. Reprinted by permission of Random House, Inc.

"Angels on a Pin" by Alexander Calandra. Copyright © 1968 by *Saturday
Review*. All rights reserved. Reprinted by permission.

"Assault on a Home in Brooklyn" by Joel Kramer. Copyright © 1980 by News
Group Publications, Inc. Reprinted with the permission of *New York* Magazine.

"Salvation" by Langston Hughes. Reprinted by permission of Farrar, Straus
and Giroux, Inc. From *The Big Sea* by Langston Hughes. Copyright 1940 by
Langston Hughes.

"Shooting an Elephant" by George Orwell. From *Shooting an Elephant and Other
Essays* by George Orwell. Copyright 1945, 1946, 1949, 1950 by Sonia Brownell
Orwell; renewed 1973, 1974 by Sonia Orwell. Reprinted by permission of
Harcourt Brace Jovanovich, Inc. By permission of A. M. Heath & Company,
Ltd. on behalf of Martin Secker & Warburg and Mrs. Sonia Brownell Orwell.

Acknowledgments and copyrights continue at the back of the book on pages
381–384, which constitute an extension of the copyright page.

Preface

Subject and Strategy: A Rhetoric Reader is an anthology of essays for college writing courses. The first eight sections focus on the strategies of narration, description, process analysis (a new section in this edition), definition, comparison and contrast, classification, cause and effect, and argumentation. A ninth section, "Essays for Further Analysis," offers additional essays chosen to illustrate these strategies working together in various combinations and provides an opportunity for students to apply their analytical skills without the assistance of editorial comment or questions. Finally, in a brief section called "Postscript," four professional writers offer practical advice on the qualities of good writing and on the writing process—getting started, revising, and editing.

Of the forty-six essays in this second edition, twenty-seven have been retained from the first edition and nineteen are new. The essays in *Subject and Strategy* represent a wide range of topics that students in our classes have found exciting and that we believe others will, too. A quick examination of the short quotations printed in the table of contents will suggest the variety of subjects, styles, and points of view far better than any description we could provide here. A new feature in this edition is an alternate table of contents that groups essays by subject. Such a classification is unavoidably a bit arbitrary, some essays fitting into subject categories more neatly than others and some appearing under more than one subject heading. We believe, nevertheless, that this listing will help to reveal opportunities for lively classroom discussion and student writing afforded both by the content of individual essays and also by the various rhetorical approaches to common themes.

In selecting the essays, we have continued to prize readability, whether in such classic and durable essays as George Orwell's "Shooting an Elephant," Langston Hughes's "Salvation," Thomas Jefferson's "Declaration of Independence," and E. B. White's "Once More to the Lake," or in such contemporary writing as Gay Talese's "New York," Joan Didion's "In Bed," and Lewis Thomas's "Death in the Open." We have also been conscious of the length of essays, generally preferring those that are brief, although a few longer ones have demanded to be included. Above all, we have chosen essays that are well written.

The arrangement of the sections in *Subject and Strategy* suggests one possible sequence for using the book: the movement from narration and description through exposition to argumentation. Each section is self-contained, however, so that an instructor may follow any sequence, omitting or emphasizing a section according to the special needs of the students. Most sections begin with a very brief selection. These short prose samples are especially helpful when beginning the study of each rhetorical strategy.

The essays in *Subject and Strategy* are followed by study questions of four kinds: "Questions on Subject," "Questions on Strategy," "Questions on Diction and Vocabulary," and "For Classroom Discussion." In addition, "Activities and Writing Suggestions" appear at the end of each section.

Questions on Subject are designed to focus the reader's attention on the content of the essay as well as on the author's purpose. These questions help students check their comprehension of the essays and are useful also as a basis for classroom discussion.

Questions on Strategy focus attention on the various rhetorical strategies the authors have employed in composing their essays. In answering these questions, students are encouraged to put themselves in the author's place and come to an awareness of how they may employ the same strategies effectively in their own writing.

Questions on Diction and Vocabulary emphasize the importance of each author's choice of appropriate words and phrases. We have tried always to remind students of the importance of the verbal context in which such choices are made. Each set of diction and vocabulary questions ends with an exercise in vocabulary building in which the reader is asked to use a desk dictionary to determine the meanings of words as they are used in the essay.

The *For Classroom Discussion* sections are designed to stimulate discussion of larger issues that grow out of the essays. Students are asked, for example, to question the validity of an argument, to compare their experiences with those of the writer, or to examine a principle developed in an essay in yet another context. We have found that these discussion topics produce lively and informative exchanges. In the course of these discussions, students often discover issues that they wish to pursue in their own writing.

Activities and Writing Suggestions appear at the end of each rhetorical section of the book. The "Activities" are brief exercises that enable students to work with each rhetorical strategy in the classroom, often collectively. They provide practice in, for example, brainstorming, using facts effectively, using examples to document a generalization, using strong action verbs, using figurative language, organizing sentences within paragraphs, classifying on the basis of distinctive characteristics, working with outlines for comparison and contrast, testing cause and effect relationships, and writing paragraphs or paragraph sequences in class. We have used all of these activities in our writing classes, and students have found them helpful and enjoyable. The "Writing Suggestions" offer students a wide range of topics suitable to the various rhetorical strategies.

In this edition we have added a "Glossary of Rhetorical Terms," located at the end of the book. This glossary provides students with concise definitions of terms useful for discussing the readings and their own writing. Wherever we have felt that information in the glossary might assist students in answering a study question, we have placed a cross-reference to the appropriate entry next to the question.

We have been deeply gratified by the acceptance of the first edition of *Subject and Strategy*. Our fellow teachers of composition in more than three hundred community colleges, liberal arts colleges, and universities have used the book. In preparing the second edition we have benefited inestimably from their comments and suggestions either directly to us or, more often, to the people from St. Martin's Press. We wish we could acknowledge individually all of our many debts, but to do so would be impossible. Among those who have helped us, however, we thank especially Edward P. J. Corbett, Ohio State University; Edward M. White, California State College, San Bernardino; Ronald W. Smith, Utah State University; Lynn Z. Bloom, College of William and Mary; Elaine Maimon, Beaver College; Donald M. Murray, University of New Hampshire; Richard Gebhardt, Findlay College; Virginia C. Edwards, West Virginia State College; Jim Saben, Portland Community College; Leo Rockas, University of Hartford; Keen Butterworth, University of South Carolina; Barbara Olive, Concordia College; John McCluskey, University of Tennessee at Martin; John W. Blair, Chaffey College; and Stacy Thompson, Central Michigan University. We would also like to express our appreciation to Thomas V. Broadbent and Nancy Perry of St. Martin's Press for their insightful editorial guidance. For the typing of the manuscript, we would like to thank Judy Cota. Finally, special thanks go to our students at the University of Vermont, whose enthusiasm for writing and responses to materials included in this book have been invaluable to us.

Paul Eschholz
Alfred Rosa

Contents

> "In the street, I had been the most articulate hustler out there—I had commanded attention when I said something. But now, trying to write simple English, I not only wasn't articulate, I wasn't even functional."

> "He was fed up with high school and college instructors trying to teach him how to think, to use the 'scientific method,' and to explore the deep inner logic of the subject in a pedantic way, as is often done in the new mathematics, rather than teaching him the structure of the subject."

> "The real terror began on March 20. My wife was at

"Name-calling can have a major impact on a child's
feelings about his identity, and it can sometimes be
devastating to his psychological development."

"When *you* hear a weasel word, you automatically hear
the implication. Not the real meaning, but the meaning
it wants *you* to hear."

"We can thus say that while the average human being
is a mixture, some people are mainly "digestion-
minded," some "muscle-minded," and some "brain-
minded," and correspondingly digestion-bodied,
muscle-bodied, or brain-bodied. The digestion-bodied
people look thick; the muscle-bodied people look wide;
and the brain-bodied people look long."

"Does culture shape language? Or does language shape
culture? This is as difficult a question as the old puzzler
of which came first, the chicken or the egg, because
there's no clear separation between language and culture."

"Each man was a mass culture hero to his generation,

but it tells us something of the difference between generations that each man's admirers would be hard-pressed to understand why the other could mean very much to his devotees."

"Two great Americans, Grant and Lee—very different yet under everything very much alike. Their encounter at Appomattox was one of the great moments of American history."

"The screams from the bowels of today's radio are not the birth cries of a new art form, but the death rattle of an old art medium. The death of silence is the death of sound broadcasting."

" 'Good morning, I'm Bill Beutel,' said Bill Beutel, his jacket flickering in alternating shades of green and yellow. 'The Westminster Kennel Club Show is opening in New York, and in a few moments we're going to be talking to you about that.' "

"But honesty is the best policy. Says who? Anyone willing to get laughed at. But the laugh is no laughing matter. It concerns the health and future of a nation."

"I make my living humping cargo for Seaboard World Airlines, one of the big international airlines at Kennedy Airport. They handle strictly all cargo. I was once told that one of the Rockefellers is the major stockholder for the airline, but I don't really think about that too much. I don't get paid to think."

are silent and you think them deserted, they will throng
with the returning hosts that once filled and still love
this beautiful land. The White Man will never be alone."

Alternate
Table of Contents
Arranged by Subject

WOMEN

WORK AND PLAY

THE MINORITY EXPERIENCE

HISTORY AND INSTITUTIONS

CONTEMPORARY SOCIAL ISSUES

ETHICS AND RELIGION

LANGUAGE AND WRITING

SUBJECT
AND
STRATEGY
A RHETORIC READER

Second Edition

1
NARRATION

To *narrate* is to tell a story, to tell what happened. Whenever you relate an incident or use an anecdote to make a point, you use narration. In its broadest sense, narration includes all writing that provides an account of an event or a series of events. While most often associated with novels and short fiction, narration is effective and useful in nonfiction as well. Consider, for example, the opening paragraph from Berton Roueché's "Eleven Blue Men":

At about eight o'clock on Monday morning, September 25, 1944, a ragged, aimless old man of eighty-two collapsed on the sidewalk on Dey Street, near the Hudson Terminal. Innumerable people must have noticed him, but he lay there alone for several minutes, dazed, doubled up with abdominal cramps, and in an agony of retching. Then a policeman came along. Until the policeman bent over the old man, he may have supposed that he had just a sick drunk on his hands; wanderers dropped by drink are common in that part of town in the early morning. It was not an opinion that he could have held for long. The old man's nose, lips, ears, and fingers were sky-blue. The policeman went to a telephone and put in an ambulance call to Beekman-Downtown Hospital, half a dozen blocks away. The old man was carried into the emergency room there at eight-thirty. By that time, he was unconscious and the blueness had spread over a large part of his body. The examining physician attributed the old man's morbid color to cyanosis, a condition that usually results from an insufficient supply of oxygen in the blood, and also noted that he was diarrheic and in a severe state of shock. The course of treatment prescribed by the doctor was conventional. It included an instant gastric lavage, heart stimulants, bed rest, and oxygen therapy. Presently, the old man recovered an encouraging, if painful, consciousness and demanded, irascibly and in the name of God, to know what had happened to him. It was a question that, at the moment, nobody could answer with much confidence.

Roueché has clearly (1) established a context for his narrative of medical detection, (2) selected his details with care, (3) placed the events in the order in which they occurred, and (4) chosen and maintained a consistent point of view. These four aspects of the narrative process are very important, and as a writer you must be concerned with each of them.

1. *Context.* A writer often begins a narrative by telling the reader when the action happened, where it happened, and to whom it happened. In the opening sentence Roueché tells us: "At about eight o'clock on Monday morning, September 25, 1944, a ragged, aimless old man of eighty-two collapsed on the sidewalk on Dey Street, near the Hudson Terminal." In this way he has provided the reader with a context, a common ground of understanding, before continuing with his story.

2. *Selection of details.* Good narrative makes effective use of details. In writing your own narrative, you should be careful to include sufficient detail—enough so that your reader knows what is happening but not so much that the reader becomes overwhelmed and confused. You should select your details with your reason for telling the story in mind and with the aim of creating a single theme. Roueché, instead of getting bogged down in descriptions of Dey Street, the policeman, the emergency room, or the examining physician, concentrates on the old man and the specifics of his peculiar condition.

3. *Organization.* A narrative, because it is a record of a complete action, should have a beginning, a middle, and an end. All narrative naturally lends itself to chronological ordering, but you do not necessarily have to start with the event that

occurred first. For example, you could start midway through the story with the event that is most important or most likely to arouse your reader's interest and then use flashbacks to fill in what happened earlier. Brief narratives like Roueché's, however, are usually best presented in chronological order. Whatever organizational pattern you select, you should avoid the needless repetition of conventional narrative transitions like *and, then,* and *next.* If you organize your narrative well, you will not need such obvious transitional devices.

4. *Point of view.* You should consider the point of view you wish to take in your narrative. Do you want a third-person narrative, one that provides a sense of objectivity and distance from the action, as in Roueché's story? Or would a first-person narrative, one that presents the events from the point of view of a participant in the action, be more appropriate? See, for example, Langston Hughes's "Salvation" in this section. Whatever your choice, you should maintain that same point of view throughout the narrative.

Always keep your purpose in mind when writing narration. Continually ask yourself *why* you are telling the story. Are you illustrating a concept or idea or developing a theme through your narration? Are you retelling a historical event to convince your reader of its significance? Whatever your purpose, you should remember the essential features of good narration: (1) a clear context, (2) well-chosen details, (3) a logical organizational pattern, and (4) an appropriate and consistent point of view.

In the essays in this section, the authors use narration to recount significant events that brought them to greater awareness of themselves and the complexities of life. For example, Malcolm X narrates how he came to an awareness of the power of words, Alexander Calandra tells a story that caused him to think about the meaning of education, and Joel Kramer recounts what it is like to have been the victim of a series of burglaries.

How I Discovered Words: A Homemade Education

MALCOLM X

On February 21, 1965, Malcolm X, the controversial Black Muslim leader, was showered with bullets and shotgun pellets' as he addressed an afternoon rally in Harlem. He was dead at the age of thirty-nine. He had begun his life in obscurity and had risen from the world of thievery, pimping, drug pushing, and prison to become one of the most articulate and powerful blacks in America during the early 1960s.

With the assistance of Alex Haley, who later wrote Roots, *Malcolm X told his story in* The Autobiography of Malcolm X *(1964), a moving and dramatic account of his search for personal and social fulfillment. In the following selection taken from the autobiography, Malcolm X narrates a major turning point in his life.*

It was because of my letters that I happened to stumble upon starting to acquire some kind of a homemade education. 1

I became increasingly frustrated at not being able to express 2 what I wanted to convey in letters that I wrote, especially those to Mr. Elijah Muhammad. In the street, I had been the most articulate hustler out there—I had commanded attention when I said something. But now, trying to write simple English, I not only wasn't articulate, I wasn't even functional. How would I sound writing in slang, the way I would *say* it, something such as, "Look, daddy, let me pull your coat about a cat. Elijah Muhammad—"

Many who today hear me somewhere in person, or on 3

television, or those who read something I've said, will think I
went to school far beyond the eighth grade. This impression
is due entirely to my prison studies.

It had really begun back in the Charlestown Prison, when   4
Bimbi first made me feel envy of his stock of knowledge. Bimbi
had always taken charge of any conversation he was in, and I
had tried to emulate him. But every book I picked up had few
sentences which didn't contain anywhere from one to nearly
all of the words that might as well have been in Chinese.
When I just skipped those words, of course, I really ended up
with little idea of what the book said. So I had come to the
Norfolk Prison Colony still going through only book-reading
motions. Pretty soon, I would have quit even these motions,
unless I had received the motivation that I did.

I saw that the best thing I could do was get hold of a   5
dictionary—to study, to learn some words. I was lucky enough
to reason also that I should try to improve my penmanship. It
was sad. I couldn't even write in a straight line. It was both
ideas together that moved me to request a dictionary along
with some tablets and pencils from the Norfolk Prison Colony
school.

I spent two days just riffling uncertainly through the diction-   6
ary's pages. I'd never realized so many words existed! I didn't
know *which* words I needed to learn. Finally, just to start some
kind of action, I began copying.

In my slow, painstaking, ragged handwriting, I copied into   7
my tablet everything printed on that first page, down to the
punctuation marks.

I believe it took me a day. Then, aloud, I read back, to   8
myself, everything I'd written on the tablet. Over and over,
aloud, to myself, I read my own handwriting.

I woke up the next morning, thinking about those words—   9
immensely proud to realize that not only had I written so
much at one time, but I'd written words that I never knew
were in the world. Moreover, with a little effort, I also could
remember what many of these words meant. I reviewed the
words whose meanings I didn't remember. Funny thing, from
the dictionary first page right now, that "aardvark" springs to
my mind. The dictionary had a picture of it, a long-tailed,

long-eared, burrowing African mammal, which lives off ter-
mites caught by sticking out its tongue as an anteater does
for ants.

I was so fascinated that I went on—I copied the dictionary's   10
next page. And the same experience came when I studied that.
With every succeeding page, I also learned of people and places
and events from history. Actually the dictionary is like a
miniature encyclopedia. Finally the dictionary's A section had
filled a whole tablet—and I went on into the B's. That was the
way I started copying what eventually became the entire
dictionary. It went a lot faster after so much practice helped
me to pick up handwriting speed. Between what I wrote in
my tablet, and writing letters, during the rest of my time in
prison I would guess I wrote a million words.

I suppose it was inevitable that as my word-base broadened,   11
I could for the first time pick up a book and read and now
begin to understand what the book was saying. Anyone who
has read a great deal can imagine the new world that opened.
Let me tell you something: from then until I left that prison,
in every free moment I had, if I was not reading in the library,
I was reading on my bunk. You couldn't have gotten me out
of books with a wedge. Between Mr. Muhammad's teachings,
my correspondence, my visitors—usually Ella and Reginald—
and my reading of books, months passed without my even
thinking about being imprisoned. In fact, up to then, I never
had been so truly free in my life.

FOR STUDY AND DISCUSSION

Questions on Subject

1. What motivated Malcolm X "to acquire some kind of a homemade
   education" (1)?
2. What does Malcolm X mean when he says that he was "going
   through only book-reading motions" (4)? How did he decide to
   solve this problem?
3. What does Malcolm X's essay suggest are the ultimate benefits
   of learning to read and write?

Questions on Strategy

1. What organizing principle does Malcolm X use in his narrative?
2. How do the first three paragraphs function in this essay?
3. What is the effect of the relative shortness of paragraphs 6 through 8? Could they be combined into a single paragraph? What would be gained or lost if they were to be combined?
4. The last sentence in this selection makes a dramatic and powerful statement about Malcolm X's passage from illiteracy to literacy. How does the narrative prepare the way for this dramatic ending? (Glossary: *Endings*)

Questions on Diction and Vocabulary

1. Why does Malcolm X use relatively simple vocabulary to narrate this particular experience? (Glossary: *Appropriateness*)
2. Refer to your desk dictionary to determine the meanings of the following words as they are used in this selection: *articulate* (2), *functional* (2), *emulate* (4), *tablets* (5), *inevitable* (11).

For Classroom Discussion

Malcolm X solved the problems of his own illiteracy by carefully studying the dictionary. Would this be a practical solution to the national problem of illiteracy? Are there any alternatives to Malcolm X's approach? What are they?

(Note: Activities and Writing Suggestions for Narration appear on pages 32–34.)

Angels on a Pin

ALEXANDER CALANDRA

Professor Alexander Calandra teaches physics at Washington University in St. Louis, specializing in statistical techniques in tests and measurements. He is a former editor of the Reporter, *a publication of the American Chemical Society.*

In the following essay, which first appeared in Saturday Review, *December 21, 1968, Calandra tells an amusing story about a student who had taken an exam. Calandra's essay provokes speculation about the purposes of education.*

Some time ago, I received a call from a colleague who asked if   1
I would be the referee on the grading of an examination
question. He was about to give a student a zero for his answer
to a physics question, while the student claimed he should
receive a perfect score and would if the system were not set up
against the student. The instructor and the student agreed to
submit this to an impartial arbiter, and I was selected.

I went to my colleague's office and read the examination   2
question: "Show how it is possible to determine the height of
a tall building with the aid of a barometer."

The student had answered: "Take the barometer to the top   3
of the building, attach a long rope to it, lower the barometer
to the street, and then bring it up, measuring the length of the
rope. The length of the rope is the height of the building."

I pointed out that the student really had a strong case for full   4
credit, since he had answered the question completely and
correctly. On the other hand, if full credit were given, it could
well contribute to a high grade for the student in his physics

course. A high grade is supposed to certify competence in physics, but the answer did not confirm this. I suggested that the student have another try at answering the question. I was not surprised that my colleague agreed, but I was surprised that the student did.

I gave the student six minutes to answer the question, with the warning that his answer should show some knowledge of physics. At the end of five minutes, he had not written anything. I asked if he wished to give up, but he said no. He had many answers to this problem; he was just thinking of the best one. I excused myself for interrupting him, and asked him to please go on. In the next minute, he dashed off his answer, which read:

"Take the barometer to the top of the building and lean over the edge of the roof. Drop the barometer, timing its fall with a stopwatch. Then, using the formula $S = \frac{1}{2} at^2$, calculate the height of the building."

At this point, I asked my colleague if *he* would give up. He conceded, and I gave the student almost full credit.

In leaving my colleague's office, I recalled that the student had said he had other answers to the problem, so I asked him what they were. "Oh, yes," said the student. "There are many ways of getting the height of a tall building with the aid of a barometer. For example, you could take the barometer out on a sunny day and measure the height of the barometer, the length of its shadow, and the length of the shadow of the building, and by the use of a simple proportion, determine the height of the building."

"Fine," I said. "And the others?"

"Yes," said the student. "There is a very basic measurement method that you will like. In this method, you take the barometer and begin to walk up the stairs. As you climb the stairs, you mark off the length of the barometer along the wall. You then count the number of marks, and this will give you the height of the building in barometer units. A very direct method.

"Of course, if you want a more sophisticated method, you can tie the barometer to the end of a string, swing it as a pendulum, and determine the value of 'g' at the street level and at the top of the building. From the difference between the two values of 'g,' the height of the building can, in principle, be calculated."

Finally he concluded, there are many other ways of solving the problem. "Probably the best," he said, "is to take the barometer to the basement and knock on the superintendent's door. When the superintendent answers, you speak to him as follows: 'Mr. Superintendent, here I have a fine barometer. If you will tell me the height of this building, I will give you this barometer.' "

At this point, I asked the student if he really did not know the conventional answer to this question. He admitted that he did, but said that he was fed up with high school and college instructors trying to teach him how to think, to use the "scientific method," and to explore the deep inner logic of the subject in a pedantic way, as is often done in the new mathematics, rather than teaching him the structure of the subject. With this in mind, he decided to revive scholasticism as an academic lark to challenge the Sputnik-panicked classrooms of America.

FOR STUDY AND DISCUSSION

Questions on Subject

1. What motivated the student to behave in the manner that he did? Why did he wish to avoid the "conventional answer" to the physics problem?

2. What is the point of Calandra's essay? (Glossary: *Thesis*) What makes the narrative more than a humorous story about a student and his physics exam?

3. There are three characters in this narrative, and each has a different attitude toward the problem. What is each character's attitude, and how is it related to the central problem? (Glossary: *Attitude*)

4. Why did the narrator's colleague concede to the student after receiving the answer given in paragraph 6?

Questions on Strategy

1. Calandra, like all good storytellers, indicates who, what, where, why, and when for his story. What are the answers to these five questions, and where is this information provided?
2. Would Calandra's narrative have been enhanced by a description of the student, the colleague, or the school? Why, or why not?
3. Calandra himself might have interpreted the incident for his readers. Why do you suppose that he chose instead to conclude with the student's comment on the incident? (Glossary: *Endings*)

Questions on Diction and Vocabulary

1. In order to present realistically the student's answers to the examination question, Calandra uses technical language commonly found in physics. Explain the meaning of the formula $S = \frac{1}{2} at^2$ and the symbol "g." (Glossary: *Technical Language*)
2. Refer to your desk dictionary to determine the meanings of the following words as they are used in this selection: *arbiter* (1), *sophisticated* (11), *pedantic* (13), *scholasticism* (13), *Sputnik* (13).

For Classroom Discussion

The title of Calandra's essay, "Angels on a Pin," refers to the almost legendary debate among scholastic philosophers in the Middle Ages about how many angels could stand on the head of a pin. Regarded seriously in its time, this debate is now associated with the trivial ends to which logic can be put. What does Calandra's title contribute to his narrative? Is his point about education still valid?

(Note: Activities and Writing Suggestions for Narration appear on pages 32–34.)

Assault on a Home in Brooklyn

JOEL KRAMER

*Joel Kramer was born in 1943 in New York City. Educated
at Queens College, the University of Michigan, and Wayne
State University, Kramer has taught public speaking and
acting at several universities. An actor by profession, he
has appeared in a number of Broadway plays and musicals.*

*The following narrative first appeared in New York
magazine in April 1980. In it Kramer recounts the terror he
and his wife experienced when they were the victims of
repeated burglaries.*

This morning I woke up in a bed in a stranger's apartment. The
few items of clothing I still had with me were in a shredding
shopping bag. As I am writing, I do not know where I will
sleep tonight. The transformation of my style of life from
middle-class coziness to itinerant shopping-bag person has
been sudden. It is a story of deliberate terrorism and official
impotence.

The street I lived on in Brooklyn is one of the most beautiful
urban residential blocks in existence. It is a street of attached
two-, three-, and four-story townhouses in brick and limestone,
none of which duplicates another—a perfect balance of variety
and cohesiveness. When I moved there six years ago, the area
was almost evenly divided ethnically into thirds: black, white,
and Hispanic. It was an area reputed to be low in crime, and
the neighborhood was actually improving. Young families were
moving in, renovating the townhouses, and becoming active
in block associations.

Then, during the summer of 1977, the blackout hit. Residents   3
became aware of a subtle change in the climate of the street.
Many of the stores along the avenue did not reopen, or they
reopened in altered form. Crimes against persons and property
were discussed more openly: a doctor on the block, knifed on
his doorstep by addicts; a ladder left by burglars across the
street. One of the townhouses was said to be a gang hangout;
this was clearly the case in a large, warren-like apartment house
on the next corner. People stayed in at night. Was this change
real or merely a modulation of perception? Several homeowners
did not wait to find out. Sales of homes on the block increased.
We, however, wanted to stay. We loved the stained-glass
skylights and the parquet floors, the fireplace and the beamed
dining room, the easy commute to midtown, the yard in which
our large dog could run. Most of all we loved the space: large
rooms and enough of them to allow ourselves the luxury of
specialization—a huge library for me and a conservatory for
my wife in which she could grow, among other exotica,
sugarcane and pineapples and fresh tomatoes. The house was
a great comfort to us and the envy of friends who lived in
studios in "the city" for higher rents than we were paying.

On March 1 of last year, while returning from work, my wife   4
was mugged in front of our house. She was followed by what
appeared to be a young couple. They accosted her and then
choked her and threw her to the ground. The thieves took her
purse with a week's wages, credit cards, identification, and
keys, but, more important, a bag in which was the majority of
research material for an important paper she had been working
on for several years. She had been preparing to return to college
this semester to complete her degree. We now had to go through
the rigmarole of calling all the department stores to cancel the
credit cards, replacing ID's, and all the attendant nuisances that
theft entails. The event was reported to the 71st Precinct, my
wife checked some mug shots at headquarters, the locks were
changed and the event put behind us. We counted ourselves
lucky that she had not been hurt seriously.

The real terror began on March 20. My wife was at work and   5
I had been out of town for the weekend delivering a lecture.
Nothing appeared to be wrong when I returned home at 9 P.M.

I made a cup of tea and went to turn on the stereo. Only it wasn't there. The sinking feeling of recognition hit at once. I ran to the cabinets; the silver was still there. A quick check of the walls showed all the art intact, nothing missing, no vandalism. I called my wife at work, called the police, and checked the house. The thieves had entered through a basement window and had been in every closet and drawer in the house. Thirteen closets and 46 drawers. And four trunks. They had meticulously replaced everything, much of it in the wrong places. Only street-salable items—electronic equipment, cameras, and jewels—were taken. Most of the jewelry was heirlooms, quite valuable, that had been left to my wife by two late aunts.

Every burglary victim knows the startling sense of violation that ensues when one's home is entered. In our case, two facts made the experience even more unsettling. First, the thieves had apparently not been in a rush. There were remnants of a meal they had eaten, a takeout Chinese meal: They knew they would not be interrupted, they knew our schedules. We had been watched. To me the ultimate slap was that they had ransacked the basement and found the ten-year-old cartons in which the stereo components had been packed, and they had disassembled the system and repacked it in the original containers.

A second and more direct piece of psychological warfare: They left a note. They called themselves "Rhythm" and "Blues." The note said that they would be back.

The next day the detectives arrived and dusted for fingerprints. They found a single print on the glass at the point of entry but told us that even if they were to capture a suspect in the act, they would be unable to fingerprint him if he was under sixteen. (I was fingerprinted, however, to make sure that the print was not mine.) When the police left, they assured us that the note, which they took for examination, was a bluff. R&B would not return. My landlord boarded up the basement windows and doors.

We awoke the next morning to find everything in apparent order once again. When I started to leave for work I could not find my wallet. The tension of the previous day caught up to me: I became distraught at the idea that, on top of everything else, I had stupidly lost my wallet, necessitating a cancellation of our replacement credit cards, some of which had already come. I needn't have blamed myself. My wallet had been where it always was, on the dresser by the bed. We had been robbed for the second time in two days. R&B hadn't been bluffing. They had come in through another window in the basement. This window was in a closet that had been nailed shut but that they had demolished with a crowbar.

They'd come upstairs into our room and gone over it again 10 while we lay in an exhausted sleep. There was a small black-and-white television missing from downstairs, and they had taken things from our room—a broken alarm clock, for example. But aside from my wallet, none of it had any value—and that was the most bizarre aspect of all. To me it was another message: "We can come and go as we please. We stole a clock inches from your head as you slept. Do you realize what we could have done if we had chosen to?"

This time the police attitude of solicitous non-involvement 11 was even more pronounced. They came to the house and made a perfunctory report. They did not look for the entry point—we found that later ourselves.

We were in an emotional shambles. We requested protection. 12 The police refused. We knew that R&B would return again. The police doubted it (strike three). In any case they could not, they said, spare someone to watch the house. We suggested that it might be a way of catching a criminal. They testily replied that if we were so sure of a repeat, I should go get a shotgun. Grand juries usually don't indict people who kill intruders, they said.

As that third night approached, I went through the house, 13 closing doors and nailing them shut. I felt as if I were in a frontier fort while the Indians were massing outside.

But R&B did not come back. That week. On Sunday, April 14 1, my wife boarded a plane for Detroit to return to her college. Because of a certain confluence of events and schedules this was to be her last chance to finish her degree. Things had apparently blown over, so she went. I spent my first night alone in the house. I felt somewhat more at ease. They had not come back for a while; everything easily fenced was gone; I'd had the basement windows bricked up and the ground floor barred.

The insurance investigator had pointed out that the second floor seemed vulnerable. It was.

At 5:30 A.M. on April 3, I awoke in my bedroom and got my first look at "Rhythm." Or "Blues." Or someone. I don't know for sure who he was, but he was in my room, approximately four feet from me. He had not been invited, save by the temptingly vulnerable window in the conservatory. He was tall and very thin. He was dressed in black and was moving stealthily, like a practiced cat burglar. 15

I wish that I could say I remained calm. I wish that I could have lain still and gotten a good description. I wish I hadn't screamed. 16

He ran out of my room, down the stairs, quickly opened the two locked front doors, and disappeared into the street. He knew his way around my house all right. He must have been a pro, because even in those brief seconds he managed to get a fur from my wife's closet. An experienced pro. He left the muskrat and took the mink. 17

When he left he stepped out of the front door right over the sleeping body of my imposing-looking Siberian husky. He must have known the dog wouldn't harm him. During the first robbery, they had beaten him viciously. 18

I called the movers the next day. 19

I do not live in my house anymore. I do not live anywhere really. Our furniture is in storage, our dog with my father, and until my wife returns from school to look for a new place, I'll probably go on staying with friends and relatives, schlepping around my three sets of underwear. 20

Until recently, I'd been riding the subways a lot. Even though the newspapers scream about subway-crime statistics, I feel safer there than in what was my home. What is more comforting is that I feel my wife is safe now with friends in Detroit. Detroit! At least I felt that way until last night when I called her. Someone had tried to break into her room. She couldn't speak with me at any length. She was with the police. 21

FOR STUDY AND DISCUSSION

Questions on Subject

1. What changes began to occur in the summer of 1977 in Kramer's Brooklyn neighborhood that indicated that the neighborhood was undergoing a transition?
2. What was the real terror of the Kramers' experiences with the thieves "Rhythm" and "Blues"? Why did the Kramers stay in their home as long as they did?
3. How would you characterize Kramer's attitude toward his experiences with the burglars and the police? Where specifically in the essay does he reveal his attitude? (Glossary: *Attitude*)

Questions on Strategy

1. Why do you suppose Kramer has chosen to write about his experiences, to share them with others? What sentence in particular most clearly reveals his purpose? (Glossary: *Purpose*)
2. How do paragraphs 2 and 3 relate to the narrative that follows?
3. Comment on Kramer's use of details to enhance the theme of terrorism that he wishes to convey. (Glossary: *Specific/General*)

Questions on Diction and Vocabulary

1. Kramer uses the phrase "solicitous non-involvement" (11) to characterize the attitude of the police to his problems. What does he mean by the phrase?
2. Refer to your desk dictionary to determine the meanings of the following words as they are used in this selection: *itinerant* (1), *rigmarole* (4), *meticulously* (5), *distraught* (9), *stealthily* (15).

For Classroom Discussion

In his essay, Kramer tells what it is like to be the victim of a series of crimes. His story is like the stories of thousands of other Americans who have had similar experiences. What insights into the problem of crime in America does Kramer's essay afford you? Are there any defenses against crime, or are we all as vulnerable as the Kramers?

(Note: Activities and Writing Suggestions for Narration appear on pages 32–34.)

Salvation

LANGSTON HUGHES

*Born in Joplin, Missouri, Langston Hughes (1902–1967)
wrote poetry, fiction, and drama and regularly contributed
a column to the* New York Post. *An important figure in
the Harlem Renaissance, he is best known for* Weary Blues,
The Negro Mother, Shakespeare in Harlem, *and* Ask
Your Mama, *volumes of poetry which reflect his racial
pride, his familiarity with the traditions of black people,
and his knowledge of jazz rhythms.*

In this selection taken from his autobiography, The Big
Sea, *Hughes narrates his experiences at a church revival
meeting he attended when he was twelve years old.*

I was saved from sin when I was going on thirteen. But not
really saved. It happened like this. There was a big revival at
my Auntie Reed's church. Every night for weeks there had
been much preaching, singing, praying, and shouting, and
some very hardened sinners had been brought to Christ, and
the membership of the church had grown by leaps and bounds.
Then just before the revival ended, they held a special meeting
for children, "to bring the young lambs to the fold." My aunt
spoke of it for days ahead. That night I was escorted to the
front row and placed on the mourners' bench with all the other
young sinners, who had not yet been brought to Jesus.

My aunt told me that when you were saved you saw a light,
and something happened to you inside! And Jesus came into
your life! And God was with you from then on! She said you
could see and hear and feel Jesus in your soul. I believed her.
I have heard a great many old people say the same thing and
it seemed to me they ought to know. So I sat there calmly in
the hot, crowded church, waiting for Jesus to come to me.

The preacher preached a wonderful rhythmical sermon, all 3
moans and shouts and lonely cries and dire pictures of hell,
and then he sang a song about the ninety and nine safe in
the fold, but one little lamb was left out in the cold. Then he
said: "Won't you come? Won't you come to Jesus? Young
lambs, won't you come?" And he held out his arms to all us
young sinners there on the mourners' bench. And the little
girls cried. And some of them jumped up and went to Jesus
right away. But most of us just sat there.

A great many old people came and knelt around us and 4
prayed, old women with jet-black faces and braided hair, old
men with work-gnarled hands. And the church sang a song
about the lower lights are burning, some poor sinners to be
saved. And the whole building rocked with prayer and song.

Still I kept waiting to *see* Jesus. 5

Finally all the young people had gone to the altar and were 6
saved, but one boy and me. He was a rounder's son named
Westley. Westley and I were surrounded by sisters and deacons
praying. It was very hot in the church, and getting late now.
Finally Westley said to me in a whisper: "God damn! I'm tired
o' sitting here. Let's get up and be saved." So he got up and
was saved.

Then I was left all alone on the mourners' bench. My aunt 7
came and knelt at my knees and cried, while prayers and songs
swirled all around me in the little church. The whole congre-
gation prayed for me alone, in a mighty wail of moans and
voices. And I kept waiting serenely for Jesus, waiting, waiting—
but he didn't come. I wanted to see him, but nothing happened
to me. Nothing! I wanted something to happen to me, but
nothing happened.

I heard the songs and the minister saying: "Why don't you 8
come? My dear child, why don't you come to Jesus? Jesus is
waiting for you. He wants you. Why don't you come? Sister
Reed, what is this child's name?"

"Langston," my aunt sobbed. 9

"Langston, why don't you come? Why don't you come and 10
be saved? Oh, Lamb of God! Why don't you come?"

Now it was really getting late. I began to be ashamed of 11
myself, holding everything up so long. I began to wonder

what God thought about Westley, who certainly hadn't seen Jesus either, but who was now sitting proudly on the platform, swinging his knickerbockered legs and grinning down at me, surrounded by deacons and old women on their knees praying. God had not struck Westley dead for taking his name in vain or for lying in the temple. So I decided that maybe to save further trouble, I'd better lie, too, and say that Jesus had come, and get up and be saved.

So I got up.   12

Suddenly the whole room broke into a sea of shouting, as   13
they saw me rise. Waves of rejoicing swept the place. Women leaped in the air. My aunt threw her arms around me. The minister took me by the hand and led me to the platform.

When things quieted down, in a hushed silence, punctuated   14
by a few ecstatic "Amens," all the new young lambs were blessed in the name of God. Then joyous singing filled the room.

That night, for the last time in my life but one—for I was a   15
big boy twelve years old—I cried. I cried, in bed alone, and couldn't stop. I buried my head under the quilts, but my aunt heard me. She woke up and told my uncle I was crying because the Holy Ghost had come into my life, and because I had seen Jesus. But I was really crying because I couldn't bear to tell her that I had lied, that I had deceived everybody in the church, that I hadn't seen Jesus, and that now I didn't believe there was a Jesus any more, since he didn't come to help me.

FOR STUDY AND DISCUSSION

Questions on Subject

1. Why does the young Langston expect to be saved at the revival meeting? Once the children are in church, what appeals are made to them to encourage them to seek salvation?

2. Trace the various pressures working on Hughes that lead to his decision to "get up and be saved" (11). What important realization finally convinces him to lie about being saved?

3. Even though Hughes's account of the events at the revival is at points humorous, the experience was nonetheless painful for

him. Why does he cry on the night of his "salvation"? Why does his aunt think he is crying? What significance is there in the disparity between their views?

Questions on Strategy

1. What paradox or apparent contradiction does Hughes present in the first two sentences of the narrative? Why do you suppose he uses this device? (Glossary: *Paradox*)
2. What is the function of the third sentence, "It happened like this"?
3. Hughes consciously varies the structure and length of his sentences to create different effects. What effect does he create through the short sentences in paragraphs 2 and 3 and the long sentence which concludes the final paragraph? How do the short, one-sentence paragraphs aid him in telling his story?
4. Although Hughes tells most of his story himself, he allows Auntie Reed, the minister, and Westley to speak for themselves. What does Hughes gain by having his characters speak for themselves?

Questions on Diction and Vocabulary

1. How does Hughes's choice of words help to establish a realistic atmosphere for a religious revival meeting? Does he use any traditional religious figures of speech? (Glossary: *Figures of Speech*)
2. Why does Hughes italicize the word *see* in paragraph 5? What do you think he means by *see*? What do you think his aunt means by *see* (2)? Explain.
3. Refer to your desk dictionary to determine the meanings of the following words as they are used in this selection: *dire* (3), *gnarled* (4), *vain* (11), *punctuated* (14), *ecstatic* (14).

For Classroom Discussion

Like the young Langston Hughes, we sometimes find ourselves in situations in which, for the sake of conformity, we do things we do not believe in. Consider one such experience you have had. What is it about human nature that makes us occasionally act in ways that contradict our inner feelings?

(Note: Activities and Writing Suggestions for Narration appear on pages 32–34.)

Shooting an Elephant

GEORGE ORWELL

George Orwell is the pen name of Eric Blair, an English novelist and essayist and one of the most brilliant satirists of the twentieth century. Born in Bengal, India, in 1903, Orwell was educated at Eton in England and served for five years with the Imperial Police in Burma. He returned to Europe in the 1930s, began his writing career, and served with the Loyalist forces in the Spanish Civil War. Seeing firsthand the destructive power of war, he developed a fierce hatred of totalitarianism. Settling finally in England, Orwell wrote his most famous books: Animal Farm, *published in 1945, and* 1984, *a futuristic novel published in 1949, both masterful satires on totalitarianism. Orwell died of a lung ailment in 1950.*

In "Shooting an Elephant," taken from an essay collection of the same title, Orwell narrates an incident which proved to be a turning point in his political thinking.

In Moulmein, in lower Burma, I was hated by large numbers 1
of people—the only time in my life that I have been important
enough for this to happen to me. I was sub-divisional police
officer of the town, and in an aimless, petty kind of way anti-
European feeling was very bitter. No one had the guts to raise
a riot, but if a European woman went through the bazaars
alone somebody would probably spit betel juice over her dress.
As a police officer I was an obvious target and was baited
whenever it seemed safe to do so. When a nimble Burman
tripped me up on the football field and the referee (another
Burman) looked the other way, the crowd yelled with hideous
laughter. This happened more than once. In the end the

sneering yellow faces of young men that met me everywhere, the insults hooted after me when I was at a safe distance, got badly on my nerves. The young Buddhist priests were the worst of all. There were several thousands of them in the town and none of them seemed to have anything to do except stand on street corners and jeer at Europeans.

All this was perplexing and upsetting. For at that time I had already made up my mind that imperialism was an evil thing and the sooner I chucked up my job and got out of it the better. Theoretically—and secretly, of course—I was all for the Burmese and all against their oppressors, the British. As for the job I was doing, I hated it more bitterly than I can perhaps make clear. In a job like that you see the dirty work of Empire at close quarters. The wretched prisoners huddling in the stinking cages of the lock-ups, the grey, cowed faces of the long-term convicts, the scarred buttocks of the men who had been flogged with bamboos—all these oppressed me with an intolerable sense of guilt. But I could get nothing into perspective. I was young and ill-educated and I had had to think out my problems in the utter silence that is imposed on every Englishman in the East. I did not even know that the British Empire is dying, still less did I know that it is a great deal better than the younger empires that are going to supplant it. All I knew was that I was stuck between my hatred of the empire I served and my rage against the evil-spirited little beasts who tried to make my job impossible. With one part of my mind I thought of the British Raj as an unbreakable tyranny, as something clamped down, in *saecula saeculorum*, upon the will of prostrate peoples; with another part I thought that the greatest joy in the world would be to drive a bayonet into a Buddhist priest's guts. Feelings like these are the normal by-products of imperialism; ask any Anglo-Indian official, if you can catch him off duty.

One day something happened which in a roundabout way was enlightening. It was a tiny incident in itself, but it gave me a better glimpse than I had had before of the real nature of imperialism—the real motives for which despotic governments act. Early one morning the sub-inspector at a police station the other end of the town rang me up on the 'phone and said that an elephant was ravaging the bazaar. Would I please come and do something about it? I did not know what I could do, but I wanted to see what was happening and I got on to a pony and started out. I took my rifle, an old .44 Winchester and much too small to kill an elephant, but I thought the noise might be useful *in terrorem.* Various Burmans stopped me on the way and told me about the elephant's doings. It was not, of course, a wild elephant, but a tame one which had gone "must." It had been chained up, as tame elephants always are when their attack of "must" is due, but on the previous night it had broken its chain and escaped. Its mahout, the only person who could manage it when it was in that state, had set out in pursuit, but had taken the wrong direction and was now twelve hours' journey away, and in the morning the elephant had suddenly reappeared in the town. The Burmese population had no weapons and were quite helpless against it. It had already destroyed somebody's bamboo hut, killed a cow and raided some fruit-stalls and devoured the stock; also it had met the municipal rubbish van and, when the driver jumped out and took to his heels, had turned the van over and inflicted violences upon it.

The Burmese sub-inspector and some Indian constables were 4 waiting for me in the quarter where the elephant had been seen. It was a very poor quarter, a labyrinth of squalid bamboo huts, thatched with palm-leaf, winding all over a steep hillside. I remember that it was a cloudy, stuffy morning at the beginning of the rains. We began questioning the people as to where the elephant had gone and, as usual, failed to get any definite information. That is invariably the case in the East; a story always sounds clear enough at a distance, but the nearer you get to the scene of events the vaguer it becomes. Some of the people said that the elephant had gone in one direction, some said that he had gone in another, some professed not even to have heard of any elephant. I had almost made up my mind that the whole story was a pack of lies, when we heard yells a little distance away. There was a loud, scandalized cry of "Go away, child! Go away this instant!" and an old woman with a switch in her hand came round the corner of a hut, violently shooing away a crowd of naked children. Some more women followed, clicking their tongues and exclaiming; evidently there was something that the children ought not to have seen. I rounded the hut and saw a man's dead body sprawling in the mud. He was an Indian, a black Dravidian coolie, almost naked, and he could not have been dead many minutes. The people said that the elephant had come suddenly upon him round the corner of the hut, caught him with its trunk, put its foot on his back and ground him into the earth. This was the rainy season and the ground was soft, and his face had scored a trench a foot deep and a couple of yards long. He was lying on his belly with arms crucified and head sharply twisted to one side. His face was coated with mud, the eyes wide open, the teeth bared and grinning with an expression of unendurable agony. (Never tell me, by the way, that the dead look peaceful. Most of the corpses I have seen looked devilish.) The friction of the great beast's foot had stripped the skin from his back as neatly as one skins a rabbit. As soon as I saw the dead man I sent an orderly to a friend's house nearby to borrow an elephant rifle. I had already sent back the pony, not wanting it to go mad with fright and throw me if it smelt the elephant.

The orderly came back in a few minutes with a rifle and five cartridges, and meanwhile some Burmans had arrived and told us that the elephant was in the paddy fields below, only a few hundred yards away. As I started forward practically the whole population of the quarter flocked out of the houses and followed me. They had seen the rifle and were all shouting excitedly that I was going to shoot the elephant. They had not shown much interest in the elephant when he was merely ravaging their homes, but it was different now that he was going to be shot. It was a bit of fun to them, as it would be to an English crowd; besides they wanted the meat. It made me vaguely uneasy. I had no intention of shooting the elephant—I had merely sent for the rifle to defend myself if necessary—and it is always unnerving to have a crowd following you. I marched down the hill, looking and feeling a fool, with the rifle over my shoulder and an ever-growing army of people jostling at my heels. At the bottom, when you got away from the huts, there was a metalled road and beyond that a miry

5

waste of paddy fields a thousand yards across, not yet ploughed but soggy from the first rains and dotted with coarse grass. The elephant was standing eight yards from the road, his left side towards us. He took not the slightest notice of the crowd's approach. He was tearing up bunches of grass, beating them against his knees to clean them and stuffing them into his mouth.

I had halted on the road. As soon as I saw the elephant I 6 knew with perfect certainty that I ought not to shoot him. It is a serious matter to shoot a working elephant—it is comparable to destroying a huge and costly piece of machinery—and obviously one ought not to do it if it can possibly be avoided. And at that distance, peacefully eating, the elephant looked no more dangerous than a cow. I thought then and I think now that his attack of "must" was already passing off; in which case he would merely wander harmlessly about until the mahout came back and caught him. Moreover, I did not in the least want to shoot him. I decided that I would watch him for a little while to make sure that he did not turn savage again, and then go home.

But at that moment I glanced round at the crowd that had 7 followed me. It was an immense crowd, two thousand at the least and growing every minute. It blocked the road for a long distance on either side. I looked at the sea of yellow faces above the garish clothes—faces all happy and excited over this bit of fun, all certain that the elephant was going to be shot. They were watching me as they would watch a conjurer about to perform a trick. They did not like me, but with the magical rifle in my hands I was momentarily worth watching. And suddenly I realized that I should have to shoot the elephant after all. The people expected it of me and I had got to do it; I could feel their two thousand wills pressing me forward, irresistibly. And it was at this moment, as I stood there with the rifle in my hands, that I first grasped the hollowness, the futility of the white man's dominion in the East. Here was I, the white man with his gun, standing in front of the unarmed native crowd—seemingly the leading actor of the piece; but in reality I was only an absurd puppet pushed to and fro by the will of those yellow faces behind. I perceived in this moment that when the white man turns tyrant it is his own freedom that he destroys. He becomes a sort of hollow, posing dummy, the conventionalized figure of a sahib. For it is the condition of his rule that he shall spend his life in trying to impress the "natives," and so in every crisis he has got to do what the "natives" expect of him. He wears a mask, and his face grows to fit it. I had got to shoot the elephant. I had committed myself to doing it when I sent for the rifle. A sahib has got to act like a sahib; he has got to appear resolute, to know his own mind and do definite things. To come all that way, rifle in hand, with two thousand people marching at my heels, and then to trail feebly away, having done nothing— no, that was impossible. The crowd would laugh at me. And my whole life, every white man's life in the East, was one long struggle not to be laughed at.

But I did not want to shoot the elephant. I watched him beating his bunch of grass against his knees, with that preoccupied grandmotherly air that elephants have. It seemed to me that it would be murder to shoot him. At that age I was not squeamish about killing animals, but I had never shot an elephant and never wanted to. (Somehow it always seems worse to kill a *large* animal.) Besides, there was the beast's owner to be considered. Alive, the elephant was worth at least a hundred pounds; dead, he would only be worth the value of his tusks, five pounds, possibly. But I had got to act quickly. I turned to some experienced-looking Burmans who had been there when we arrived, and asked them how the elephant had been behaving. They all said the same thing: he took no notice of you if you left him alone, but he might charge if you went too close to him.

It was perfectly clear to me what I ought to do. I ought to walk up to within, say, twenty-five yards of the elephant and test his behavior. If he charged, I could shoot; if he took no notice of me, it would be safe to leave him until the mahout came back. But also I knew that I was going to do no such thing. I was a poor shot with a rifle and the ground was soft mud into which one would sink at every step. If the elephant charged and I missed him, I should have about as much chance as a toad under a steam-roller. But even then I was not thinking particularly of my own skin, only of the watchful yellow faces behind. For at that moment, with the crowd watching me, I was not afraid in the ordinary sense, as I would have been if I had been alone. A white man mustn't be frightened in front of "natives"; and so, in general, he isn't frightened. The sole thought in my mind was that if anything went wrong those two thousand Burmans would see me pursued, caught, trampled on and reduced to a grinning corpse like that Indian up the hill. And if that happened it was quite probable that some of them would laugh. That would never do. There was only one alternative. I shoved the cartridges into the magazine and lay down on the road to get a better aim.

The crowd grew very still, and a deep, low, happy sigh, as ⓘ⁰ of people who see the theatre curtain go up at last, breathed from innumerable throats. They were going to have their bit of fun after all. The rifle was a beautiful German thing with cross-hair sights. I did not then know that in shooting an elephant one would shoot to cut an imaginary bar running from ear-hole to ear-hole. I ought, therefore, as the elephant was sideways on, to have aimed straight at his ear-hole; actually I aimed several inches in front of this, thinking the brain would be further forward.

When I pulled the trigger I did not hear the bang or feel ⓘⁱ the kick—one never does when a shot goes home—but I heard the devilish roar of glee that went up from the crowd. In that instant, in too short a time, one would have thought, even for the bullet to get there, a mysterious, terrible change had come over the elephant. He neither stirred nor fell, but every line of his body had altered. He looked suddenly stricken, shrunken, immensely old, as though the frightful impact of the bullet had paralysed him without knocking him down. At last, after what seemed a long time—it might have been five seconds, I dare say—he sagged flabbily to his knees. His mouth slobbered. An enormous senility seemed to have settled upon him. One could have imagined him thousands of years old. I fired again into the same spot. At the second shot he did not collapse but climbed with desperate slowness to his feet and stood weakly upright, with legs sagging and head drooping. I fired a third time. That was the shot that did for him. You could see the agony of it jolt his whole body and knock the last remnant of strength from his legs. But in falling he seemed for a moment to rise, for as his hind legs collapsed beneath him he seemed to tower upward like a huge rock toppling, his trunk reaching skywards like a tree. He trumpeted, for the first and only time. And then down he came, his belly towards me, with a crash that seemed to shake the ground even where I lay.

I got up. The Burmans were already racing past me across the mud. It was obvious that the elephant would never rise again, but he was not dead. He was breathing very rhythmically with long rattling gasps, his great mound of a side painfully rising and falling. His mouth was wide open—I could see far down into caverns of pale pink throat. I waited a long time for him to die, but his breathing did not weaken. Finally I fired my two remaining shots into the spot where I thought his heart must be. The thick blood welled out of him like red velvet, but still he did not die. His body did not even jerk when the shots hit him, the tortured breathing continued without a pause. He was dying, very slowly and in great agony, but in some world remote from me where not even a bullet could damage him further. I felt that I had got to put an end to that dreadful noise. It seemed dreadful to see the great beast lying there, powerless to move and yet powerless to die, and not even to be able to finish him. I sent back for my small rifle and poured shot after shot into his heart and down his throat. They seemed to make no impression. The tortured gasps continued as steadily as the ticking of a clock.

In the end I could not stand it any longer and went away. I heard later that it took him half an hour to die. Burmans were bringing dahs and baskets even before I left, and I was told they had stripped his body almost to the bones by the afternoon.

Afterwards, of course, there were endless discussions about the shooting of the elephant. The owner was furious, but he was only an Indian and could do nothing. Besides, legally I had done the right thing, for a mad elephant has to be killed, like a mad dog, if its owner fails to control it. Among the Europeans opinion was divided. The older men said I was right, the younger men said it was a damn shame to shoot an elephant for killing a coolie, because an elephant was worth more than any damn Coringhee coolie. And afterwards I was very glad that the coolie had been killed; it put me legally in the right and it gave me a sufficient pretext for shooting the elephant. I often wondered whether any of the others grasped that I had done it solely to avoid looking a fool.

FOR STUDY AND DISCUSSION

Questions on Subject

1. "Shooting an Elephant" takes place in the British colony of Burma in the 1920s, when anti-imperialistic feelings were running strong. Why is the setting of this narrative significant?
2. What is imperialism, and why is it important in this narrative?
3. How does the narrator view himself? Why does he feel that he should get out of his job as a subdivisional police officer for the British government?
4. What pressures exerted on the narrator lead him to shoot the elephant? How does he regard these pressures?
5. How does the narrator justify shooting the elephant? How comfortable is he with his rationalizations for the shooting? What does the statement "I was very glad that the coolie had been killed" (14) reveal about the narrator and his situation after shooting the elephant?
6. In your opinion, what is the point of the story Orwell tells? (Glossary: *Thesis*) Does the shooting of the elephant confirm the narrator's suspicions about imperialism, expressed in paragraphs 1 and 2?
7. Although in paragraph 2 Orwell says, "I could get nothing into perspective," does he come to a greater awareness of himself, of social structures, and of political systems as a result of killing the elephant? Does the narrator have his life in perspective at the end of the essay? Explain.

Questions on Strategy

1. The narrative of the elephant-shooting incident actually begins in paragraph 3 and ends with paragraph 13. How do paragraphs 1, 2, and 14 relate to this narrative? (Glossary: *Beginnings/Endings*)
2. What is the function of the second sentence in paragraph 3?

3. Study paragraphs 3 through 13 carefully. How does Orwell organize his narrative? How does he ensure continuity in his story? What transitional devices does he use between paragraphs? (Glossary: *Transitions*)
4. A good narrative usually has an attention-grabbing opening and a thought-provoking closing. Is this true of Orwell's essay? Explain. (Glossary: *Beginnings/Endings*)
5. The most memorable part of Orwell's essay for many readers is the actual shooting of the elephant. Discuss Orwell's use of concrete and specific words in paragraphs 11 and 12 as well as elsewhere in the essay. (Glossary: *Concrete/Abstract* and *Specific/ General*)

Questions on Diction and Vocabulary

1. From the context of paragraph 3, what do you think an attack of "must" is? Since this usage is not included in most desk dictionaries, consult an unabridged dictionary such as *Webster's Third New International Dictionary* for its precise meaning in this context.
2. Refer to your desk dictionary to determine the meanings of the following words as they are used in this selection: *baited* (1), *squalid* (4), *conventionalized* (7), *resolute* (7), *senility* (11), *remnant* (11), *caverns* (12).

For Classroom Discussion

Orwell discovers that he must kill the elephant in order to "act like a sahib" and avoid being laughed at by the crowd. Consider situations in which you have been the leader, like Orwell, or a part of a crowd, like the Burmans. As a leader, what was your attitude toward your followers? As a follower, how did you feel about your leader? On the basis of your experiences, what conclusions can you draw about leader-follower relationships? To what extent are such relationships controlled by one party pressuring the other to conform to established expectations?

(Note: Activities and Writing Suggestions for Narration appear on pages 32–34.)

Activities and Writing Suggestions for Narration

ACTIVITIES

1. Narrative depends on a sense of continuity or flow, a logical ordering of events and ideas. The following sentences, which make up the first paragraph of E. B. White's essay "Once More to the Lake (August 1941)," have been rearranged. Place the sentences in what seems to be a coherent sequence based on language signals such as transitions, repeated words, pronouns, and temporal references. Be prepared to explain your reasons for the placement of each sentence.

   a. I have since become a salt-water man, but sometimes in summer there are days when the restlessness of the tides and the fearful cold of sea water and the incessant wind that blows across the afternoon and into the evening make me wish for the placidity of a lake in the woods.

   b. We all got ringworm from some kittens and had to rub Pond's Extract on our arms and legs night and morning, and my father rolled over in a canoe with all his clothes on; but outside of that the vacation was a success and from then on none of us ever thought there was any place in the world like that lake in Maine.

   c. A few weeks ago this feeling got so strong I bought myself a couple of bass hooks and a spinner and returned to the lake where we used to go, for a week's fishing and to revisit old haunts.

   d. One summer, along about 1904, my father rented a camp on a lake in Maine and took us all there for the month of August.

   e. We returned summer after summer—always on August 1st for one month.

2. Effective narrations use strong verbs—verbs which contribute significantly to the action of a story. Sportswriters, because they must repeatedly describe similar situations, are acutely aware of the need for action verbs. It is not enough for them to say that a team wins or loses; they must describe the type of win or loss precisely. Thus, such verbs as *beats, buries, edges, shocks,* and *trounces* are common in the headlines on the sports page. Each of these verbs not only describes a victory but also makes a statement about the quality of

the victory. Like sportswriters, all of us write about actions that are performed daily. If we were restricted to the verbs *eat, drink, sleep,* and *work* for these activities, our writing would be repetitious and monotonous. List as many verbs as you can to describe these four actions. What connotative (subjective) differences do you find in your list of alternatives? What is the importance of these connotative differences for you as a writer?

3. Any narrative requires that the writer gather information concerning a particular incident from his or her own experience or from the people involved in that event. Interview a member of your class so as to obtain enough information to write a brief narrative about an interesting event in that person's life. Write your narrative in the third person.

WRITING SUGGESTIONS

1. Narrate an experience that gave you a new awareness of yourself. Use enough telling detail in your narrative to allow your reader to visualize that experience and understand its significance for you. You may find the following suggestions helpful in choosing an experience to narrate in the first person.

   a. my biggest failure
   b. my greatest success
   c. my most embarrassing moment
   d. my first truly frightening experience
   e. an experience that turned my hero or idol into an ordinary person
   f. an experience that turned an ordinary person I know into a hero

2. Like Malcolm X, Joel Kramer, Langston Hughes, and George Orwell, each of us can tell of an experience that has been unusually significant for us. Think about your past, identify one experience that has been especially important for you, and write an essay about it. In preparing to write your narrative, you may find it helpful to ask such questions as: Why is the experience important for me? What details are necessary for me to re-create the experience in an interesting and engaging way? How can my narrative of the experience be most effectively organized? What point of view will work best?

3. Reports of events emphasize facts and are usually narrated in the third person. Carefully observe a fairly brief event on your campus (for example, an athletic contest, a concert, a laboratory demon-

stration, or a public debate). Note significant facts about that event, and then write an objective account of it.

4. Sometimes the little, insignificant, seemingly trivial experiences in our daily lives can provide the material for very entertaining personal narratives—narratives that reveal something about ourselves and the world we live in. Select one of the following experiences, or one of your own choosing, and write an essay in which you narrate that experience and its significance for you.

   a. having your name misspelled and/or mispronounced
   b. being confused with another person in your family
   c. rushing to keep an appointment, only to find that you are a day early or a day late
   d. dialing the wrong number more than once
   e. moving to avoid someone who is moving to avoid you and bumping into that person
   f. walking to class one morning
   g. sleeping through the alarm clock
   h. not being able to find a parking space
   i. familiar greetings ("Hi." "How are you?" "Just fine." "What's up?")
   j. getting "ripped off" by a vending machine

2

DESCRIPTION

To describe is to paint a verbal picture of something—a person, a place, or a thing. Even an idea or a state of mind can be made vividly concrete, as in, "The old woman was as silent as a ghost." Although descriptive writing can stand alone, description is often used with other rhetorical strategies; for instance, description can make examples more interesting, explain the complexities of a process, or clarify a definition or comparison.

It is useful to distinguish between objective description and subjective or impressionistic description. *Objective description* emphasizes the *object* itself and is factual without resorting to such scientific extremes that the reader cannot understand the facts. For example, Roger Angell describes many facts about a baseball without sacrificing readability. *Subjective* or *impressionistic description*, on the other hand, emphasizes the *observer* and gives a personal interpretation of the subject matter through language rich in modifiers and figures of speech. For example, you could objectively describe a race car as "traveling at a speed of 135 miles per hour"; somewhat more impressionistically you could write that the car was "traveling very fast"; even more impressionistically you could write that it "streaked past." Each description is different, each accurate, and each useful in its own way.

Writing any description requires, first of all, that you gather a great many details about a subject, relying not merely on what your eyes see but also on what your fingertips, tongue, nose, and ears tell you. From this catalogue of details you select those which will be most helpful in developing a *dominant impression*—the single mood, atmosphere, or quality you wish to emphasize. In this section, for example, Agnes De Mille portrays the passionate artistry of the ballerina Pavlova, and Gay Talese conveys to his readers a sense of the activity, both noticed and usually unnoticed, that characterizes New York City. The selection of details for a dominant impression is influenced by the nature of the subject and your intended or assumed audience as well as your purpose. As you determine the dominant impression and select significant details to vivify it, you begin to re-create an image or series of images. During this process, you truly begin to exert control over your material.

Like your choice of details, the order in which you present them depends on your subject and your reason for describing it. The important thing is to arrange the details in a pattern that is easy to follow and fits the subject of the description naturally. For example, details can be arranged spatially from left to right, top to bottom, near to far, or just the reverse of these. Other possible arrangements are from general to specific, smallest to largest, least significant to most significant, and most unusual to least unusual. And these are but a few of the many patterns available to you. If you keep your reader and the purpose of your description firmly in mind, chances are that you will choose an appropriate pattern.

Finally, remember that overloading a description with details—or, more precisely, with insignificant details—can distract the reader and weaken the dominant impression you are trying to create. The quality and the proper selection of the details matter more than mere quantity.

In the essays in this section, each author uses description to present a verbal picture of a particular person, place, or thing. By means of vivid language and carefully selected details, each author re-creates a memorable aspect of our world.

On the Ball

ROGER ANGELL

Roger Angell was born in New York City in 1920. After graduating from Harvard University, he became an editor at Holiday *magazine. He is currently an editor at* The New Yorker *and regularly contributes short fiction, humor and parody, light verse, and sportswriting to that magazine. His books include* The Stone Arbor, A Day in the Life of Roger Angell, The Summer Game, *and* Five Seasons.

In this selection, the opening paragraph of Five Seasons *(1977), Angell describes one of the marvels and mysteries of the game of baseball, the ball itself.*

It weighs just over five ounces and measures between 2.86 and 2.94 inches in diameter. It is made of a composition-cork nucleus encased in two thin layers of rubber, one black and one red, surrounded by 121 yards of tightly wrapped blue-gray wool yarn, 45 yards of white wool yarn, 53 more yards of blue-gray wool yarn, 150 yards of fine cotton yarn, a coat of rubber cement, and a cowhide (formerly horsehide) exterior, which is held together with 216 slightly raised red cotton stitches. Printed certifications, endorsements, and outdoor advertising spherically attest to its authenticity. Like most institutions, it is considered inferior in its present form to its ancient archetypes, and in this case the complaint is probably justified; on occasion in recent years it has actually been known to come apart under the demands of its brief but rigorous active career. Baseballs are assembled and hand-stitched in Taiwan (before this year the work was done in Haiti, and before 1973 in Chicopee, Massachusetts), and contemporary pitchers claim that there is a tangible variation in the size and feel of the balls that now come into play in a single game; a true peewee is treasured by hurlers, and its departure from the premises, by fair means or foul, is secretly mourned. But never mind: any baseball is beautiful. No other small package comes as close to the ideal in design and utility. It is a perfect object for a man's hand. Pick it up and it instantly suggests its purpose; it is meant to be thrown a considerable distance— thrown hard and with precision. Its feel and heft are the beginning of the sport's critical dimensions; if it were a fraction of an inch larger or smaller, a few centigrams heavier or lighter, the game of baseball would be utterly different. Hold a baseball in your hand. As it happens, this one is not brand-new. Here, just to one side of the curved surgical welt of stitches, there is a pale-green grass smudge, darkening on one edge almost to black—the mark of an old infield play, a tough grounder now lost in memory. Feel the ball, turn it over in your hand; hold it across the seam or the other way, with the seam just to the side of your middle finger. Speculation stirs. You want to get outdoors and throw this spare and sensual object to somebody or, at the very least, watch somebody else throw it. The game has begun.

FOR STUDY AND DISCUSSION

Questions on Subject

1. According to Angell, what makes a baseball beautiful?
2. How does Angell reveal the purpose of the ball?
3. What kinds of information do you learn about a baseball from Angell's paragraph? What do these facts add to his description?

Questions on Strategy

1. Why, in your opinion, does Angell begin with *It* rather than *The ball*?
2. Angell's description of a baseball moves from the objective to the impressionistic. At what point does the description become impressionistic? Why do you think Angell has organized his description in this way? (Glossary: *Objective/Subjective*)

3. At several points Angell addresses his reader directly: "Pick it up. . . . Hold a baseball in your hand. . . . Feel the ball, turn it over in your hand." What is the effect of this strategy? Explain.

Questions on Diction and Vocabulary

1. What is the effect of Angell's use of such words as *peewee, hurlers, infield play,* and *tough grounder?*
2. Comment on the appropriateness of the italicized words in each of the following excerpts from "On the Ball" (Glossary: *Appropriateness*):

   a. Like most *institutions,* it is considered inferior in its present form to its ancient *archetypes*
   b. there is a *tangible* variation in the size
   c. the beginning of the sport's *critical dimensions*
   d. curved *surgical welt* of stitches
   e. this *spare* and *sensual* object

3. Refer to your desk dictionary to determine the meanings of the following words as they are used in this selection: *certifications, endorsements, attest, heft.*

For Classroom Discussion

Baseball has long been considered our national sport, and from spring training to the World Series it attracts the attention of millions of people. In your opinion, what accounts for our national fascination with this particular sport?

(Note: Activities and Writing Suggestions for Description appear on pages 58–62.)

Pavlova

AGNES DE MILLE

Agnes De Mille, choreographer, dancer, and creator of the ballet Rodeo, *was born in New York City in 1908. She was raised in the world of the theater; her father was a New York theatrical producer, and her uncle was the famous Hollywood film producer Cecil B. De Mille. As a result, she came to know the great stage performers of her time, many of whom she wrote about in her autobiographical book* Dance to the Piper *(1952).*

In this selection from her book, De Mille describes a performance of the great Russian ballerina Anna Pavlova and her reactions to that memorable experience.

Anna Pavlova! My life stops as I write that name. Across the daily preoccupation of lessons, lunch boxes, tooth brushings and quarrelings with Margaret flashed this bright, unworldly experience and burned in a single afternoon a path over which I could never retrace my steps. I had witnessed the power of beauty, and in some chamber of my heart I lost forever my irresponsibility. I was as clearly marked as though she had looked me in the face and called my name. For generations my father's family had loved and served the theater. All my life I had seen actors and actresses and had heard theater jargon at the dinner table and business talk of box-office grosses. I had thrilled at Father's projects and watched fascinated his picturesque occupations. I took a proprietary pride in the profitable and hasty growth of "The Industry." But nothing in his world or my uncle's prepared me for theater as I saw it that Saturday afternoon.

Since that day I have gained some knowledge in my trade

40

and I recognize that her technique was limited; tha arabesques were not as pure or classically correct as Markov, that her jumps and batterie were paltry, her turns not to b. compared in strength and number with the strenuous durability of Baronova or Toumanova. I know that her scenery was designed by second-rate artists, her music was on a level with restaurant orchestrations, her company definitely inferior to all the standards we insist on today, and her choreography mostly hack. And yet I say that she was in her person the quintessence of theatrical excitement.

As her little bird body revealed itself on the scene, either 3 immobile in trembling mystery or tense in the incredible arc which was her lift, her instep stretched ahead in an arch never before seen, the tiny bones of her hands in ceaseless vibration, her face radiant, diamonds glittering under her dark hair, her little waist encased in silk, the great tutu balancing, quickening and flashing over her beating, flashing, quivering legs, every man and woman sat forward, every pulse quickened. She never appeared to rest static, some part of her trembled, vibrated, beat like a heart. Before our dazzled eyes, she flashed with the sudden sweetness of a hummingbird in action too quick for understanding by our gross utilitarian standards, in action sensed rather than seen. The movie cameras of her day could not record her allegro. Her feet and hands photographed as a blur.

Bright little bird bones, delicate bird sinews! She was all fire 4 and steel wire. There was not an ounce of spare flesh on her skeleton, and the life force used and used her body until she died of the fever of moving, gasping for breath, much too young.

She was small, about five feet. She wore a size one and a 5 half slipper, but her feet and hands were large in proportion to her height. Her hand could cover her whole face. Her trunk was small and stripped of all anatomy but the ciphers of adolescence, her arms and legs relatively long, the neck extraordinarily long and mobile. All her gestures were liquid and possessed of an inner rhythm that flowed to inevitable completion with the finality of architecture or music. Her arms seemed to lift not from the elbow or the arm socket, but from the base of the spine. Her legs seemed to function from the waist. When she bent her head her whole spine moved and the motion was completed the length of the arm through the elongation of her slender hand and the quivering reaching fingers. I believe there has never been a foot like hers, slender, delicate and of such an astonishing aggressiveness when arched as to suggest the ultimate in human vitality. Without in any way being sensual, being, in fact, almost sexless, she suggested all exhilaration, gaiety and delight. She jumped, and we broke bonds with reality. We flew. We hung over the earth, spread in the air as we do in dreams, our hands turning in the air as in water—the strong forthright taut plunging leg balanced on the poised arc of the foot, the other leg stretched to the horizon like the wing of a bird. We lay balancing, quivering, turning, and all things were possible, even to us, the ordinary people.

I have seen two dancers as great or greater since, Alicia Markova and Margot Fonteyn, and many other women who have kicked higher, balanced longer or turned faster. These are poor substitutes for passion. In spite of her flimsy dances, the bald and blatant virtuosity, there was an intoxicated rapture, a focus of energy, Dionysian in its physical intensity, that I have never seen equaled by a performer in any theater of the world. Also she was the *first* of the truly great in our experience.

I sat with the blood beating in my throat. As I walked into the bright glare of the afternoon, my head ached and I could scarcely swallow. I didn't wish to cry. I certainly couldn't speak. I sat in a daze in the car oblivious to the grownups' ceaseless prattle. At home I climbed the stairs slowly to my bedroom and, shutting myself in, placed both hands on the brass rail at the foot of my bed, then rising laboriously to the tips of my white buttoned shoes I stumped the width of the bed and back again. My toes throbbed with pain, my knees shook, my legs quivered with weakness. I repeated the exercise. The blessed, relieving tears stuck at last on my lashes. Only by hurting my feet could I ease the pain in my throat.

Death came to Anna Pavlova in 1931, when she was fifty. She had not stopped touring for a single season. Her knees had sustained some damage, but she would not rest, and she was in a state of exhaustion when the train that was carrying her to Holland was wrecked. She ran out into the snow in her nightgown and insisted on helping the wounded. When she reached The Hague she had double pneumonia. Her last spoken words were, "Get the *Swan* dress ready."

Standing on Ninth Avenue under the El, I saw the headlines on the front page of the *New York Times.* It did not seem possible. She was in essence the denial of death. My own life was rooted to her in a deep spiritual sense and had been during the whole of my growing up. It mattered not that I had only spoken to her once and that my work lay in a different direction. She was the vision and the impulse and the goal.

FOR STUDY AND DISCUSSION

Questions on Subject

1. What dominant impression of Anna Pavlova does De Mille create in this essay? (Glossary: *Dominant Impression*)
2. Why is De Mille's estimate of Pavlova as a dancer so high even though she recognizes that her technique was limited?
3. Why is Pavlova important to De Mille personally? What did Pavlova represent for De Mille?

Questions on Strategy

1. How does De Mille use the extended metaphor of the "little bird" (3) to develop her description of Pavlova? How appropriate and useful is this metaphor? Explain. (Glossary: *Figures of Speech*)
2. In paragraph 6 De Mille contrasts Pavlova with other dancers. How does this contrast enhance De Mille's description of Pavlova? (Glossary: *Comparison/Contrast*)
3. In paragraph 7 De Mille describes her own actions after seeing Pavlova perform. Explain how she conveys the intensity of this very personal and emotional experience.

Questions on Diction and Vocabulary

1. In the first paragraph De Mille acknowledges that she had heard theater jargon while she was growing up. Point out technical ballet terms that she uses. Does this language help or hinder her description of Pavlova? Explain. (Glossary: *Technical Language*)

2. Comment on the effectiveness of the description "She was all fire and steel wire" (4). (Glossary: *Figures of Speech*)
3. Refer to your desk dictionary to determine the meanings of the following words as they are used in this selection: *proprietary* (1), *paltry* (2), *quintessence* (2), *utilitarian* (3), *exhilaration* (5), *taut* (5), *blatant* (6).

For Classroom Discussion

Pavlova was a cultural hero for De Mille and others of her generation. As De Mille says, Pavlova "was the vision and the impulse and the goal." Who are today's cultural heroes, and what influence are they having on our society?

(Note: Activities and Writing Suggestions for Description appear on pages 58–62.)

New York

GAY TALESE

Born in 1932, Gay Talese began his career as a reporter for
The New York Times. Along with other young journalists
like Tom Wolfe, he has rejuvenated the reporter's craft. He
is best known for The Kingdom and the Power, *a "bi-*
ography" of The New York Times; Honor Thy Father,
a study of organized crime; and Thy Neighbor's Wife, *an*
investigation of sexual practices and attitudes in America.

In this selection, first published in 1960 in Esquire, *Talese*
describes New York as "a city of things unnoticed."

New York is a city of things unnoticed. It is a city with cats   1
sleeping under parked cars, two stone armadillos crawling up
St. Patrick's Cathedral, and thousands of ants creeping on top
of the Empire State Building. The ants probably were carried
up there by wind or birds, but nobody is sure; nobody in
New York knows any more about the ants than they do about
the panhandler who takes taxis to the Bowery; or the dapper
man who picks trash out of Sixth Avenue trash cans; or the
medium in the West Seventies who claims, "I am clairvoyant,
clairaudient and clairsensuous."

New York is a city for eccentrics and a center for odd bits   2
of information. New Yorkers blink twenty-eight times a minute,
but forty when tense. Most popcorn chewers at Yankee Stadium
stop chewing momentarily just before the pitch. Gumchewers
on Macy's escalators stop chewing momentarily just before
they get off—to concentrate on the last step. Coins, paper clips,
ball-point pens, and little girls' pocketbooks are found by
workmen when they clean the sea lion's pool at the Bronx Zoo.

A Park Avenue doorman has parts of three bullets in his   3
head—there since World War I. Several young gypsy daughters,

influenced by television and literacy, are running away from home because they don't want to grow up and become fortune-tellers. Each month a hundred pounds of hair is delivered to Louis Feder on 545 Fifth Avenue, where blond hairpieces are made from German women's hair; brunette hairpieces from Italian women's hair; but no hairpieces from American women's hair which, says Mr. Feder, is weak from too frequent rinses and permanents.

Some of New York's best informed men are elevator operators, who rarely talk, but always listen—like doormen. Sardi's doormen listen to the comments made by Broadway's first-nighters walking by after the last act. They listen closely. They listen carefully. Within ten minutes they can tell you which shows will flop and which will be hits. 4

On Broadway each evening a big, dark, 1948 Rolls-Royce pulls into Forty-sixth Street—and out hop two little ladies armed with Bibles and signs reading, "The Damned Shall Perish." These ladies proceed to stand on the corner screaming at the multitudes of Broadway sinners, sometimes until three A.M., when their chauffeur in the Rolls picks them up and drives them back to Westchester. 5

By this time Fifth Avenue is deserted by all but a few strolling insomniacs, some cruising cabdrivers, and a group of sophisticated females who stand in store windows all night and day wearing cold, perfect smiles. Like sentries they line Fifth Avenue—these window mannequins who gaze onto the quiet street with tilted heads and pointed toes and long rubber fingers reaching for cigarettes that aren't there. 6

At five A.M. Manhattan is a town of tired trumpet players and homeward-bound bartenders. Pigeons control Park Avenue and strut unchallenged in the middle of the street. This is Manhattan's mellowest hour. Most *night* people are out of sight—but the *day* people have not yet appeared. Truck drivers and cabs are alert, yet they do not disturb the mood. They do not disturb the abandoned Rockefeller Center, or the motionless night watchmen in the Fulton Fish Market, or the gas-station attendant sleeping next to Sloppy Louie's with the radio on. 7

At five A.M. the Broadway regulars either have gone home or to all-night coffee shops where, under the glaring light, you 8 see their whiskers and wear. And on Fifty-first Street a radio press car is parked at the curb with a photographer who has nothing to do. So he just sits there for a few nights, looks through the windshield, and soon becomes a keen observer of life after midnight.

"At one A.M.," he says, "Broadway is filled with wise guys and with kids coming out of the Astor Hotel in white dinner jackets—kids who drive to dances in their fathers' cars. You also see cleaning ladies going home, always wearing kerchiefs. By two A.M. some of the drinkers are getting out of hand, and this is the hour for bar fights. At three A.M. the last show is over in the nightclubs, and most of the tourists and out-of-town buyers are back in hotels. And small-time comedians are criticizing big-time comedians in Hanson's Drugstore. At four A.M., after the bars close, you see the drunks come out—and also the pimps and prostitutes who take advantage of drunks. At five A.M., though, it is mostly quiet. New York is an entirely different city at five A.M."

At six A.M. the early workers begin to push up from the subways. The traffic begins to move down Broadway like a river. And Mrs. Mary Woody jumps out of bed, dashes to her office and phones dozens of sleepy New Yorkers to say in a cheerful voice, rarely appreciated: "Good morning. Time to get up." For twenty years, as an operator of Western Union's Wake-Up Service, Mrs. Woody has gotten millions out of bed.

By seven A.M. a floridly robust little man, looking very Parisian in a blue beret and turtleneck sweater, moves in a hurried step along Park Avenue visiting his wealthy lady friends—making certain that each is given a brisk, before-breakfast rubdown. The uniformed doormen greet him warmly and call him either "Biz" or "Mac" because he is Biz Mackey, a ladies' masseur *extraordinaire*. He never reveals the names of his customers, but most of them are middle-aged and rich. He visits each of them in their apartments, and has special keys to their bedrooms; he is often the first man they see in the morning, and they lie in bed waiting for him.

The doormen that Biz passes each morning are generally an obliging, endlessly articulate group of sidewalk diplomats who list among their friends some of Manhattan's most powerful men, most beautiful women and snootiest poodles. More often than not, the doormen are big, slightly Gothic in design, and the possessors of eyes sharp enough to spot big tippers a block away in the year's thickest fog. Some East Side doormen are as proud as grandees, and their uniforms, heavily festooned, seem to come from the same tailor who outfitted Marshal Tito.

Shortly after seven-thirty each morning hundreds of people 13 are lined along Forty-second Street waiting for the eight A.M. opening of the ten movie houses that stand almost shoulder-to-shoulder between Times Square and Eighth Avenue. Who are these people who go to the movies at eight A.M.? They are the city's insomniacs, night watchmen, and people who can't go home, do not want to go home, or have no home. They are derelicts, homosexuals, cops, hacks, truck drivers, cleaning ladies and restaurant men who have worked all night. They are also alcoholics who are waiting at eight A.M. to pay forty cents for a soft seat and to sleep in the dark, smoky theatre. And yet, aside from being smoky, each of Times Square's theatres has a special quality, or lack of quality, about it. At the Victory Theatre one finds horror films, while at the Times Square Theatre they feature only cowboy films. There are first-run films for forty cents at the Lyric, while at the Selwyn there are always second-run films for thirty cents. But if you go to the Apollo Theatre you will see, in addition to foreign films, people in the lobby talking with their hands. These are deaf-and-dumb movie fans who patronize the Apollo because they read the subtitles. The Apollo probably has the biggest deaf-and-dumb movie audience in the world.

New York is a city of 38,000 cabdrivers, 10,000 bus drivers, 14 but only one chauffeur who has a chauffeur. The wealthy chauffeur can be seen driving up Fifth Avenue each morning, and his name is Roosevelt Zanders. He earns $100,000 a year, is a gentleman of impeccable taste and, although he owns a $23,000 Rolls-Royce, does not scorn his friends who own Bentleys. For $150 a day, Mr. Zanders will drive anyone anywhere in his big, silver Rolls. Diplomats patronize him, models pose next to him, and each day he receives cables from around the world urging that he be waiting at Idlewild, on the docks, or outside the Plaza Hotel. Sometimes at night, however, he is too tired to drive anymore. So Bob Clarke, his chauffeur, takes over and Mr. Zanders relaxes in the back.

New York is a town of 3,000 bootblacks whose brushes and   15
rhythmic rag-snaps can be heard up and down Manhattan from midmorning to midnight. They dodge cops, survive rainstorms, and thrive in the Empire State Building as well as on the Staten Island Ferry. They usually wear dirty shoes.

New York is a city of headless men who sit obscurely in   16
subway booths all day and night selling tokens to people in a hurry. Each weekday more than 4,500,000 riders pass these money changers who seem to have neither heads, faces, nor personalities—only fingers. Except when giving directions, their vocabulary consists largely of three words: "How many, please?"

In New York there are 200 chestnut vendors, and they average   17
$25 on a good day peddling soft, warm chestnuts. Like many vendors, the chestnut men do not own their own rigs—they borrow or rent them from pushcart makers such as David Amerman.

Mr. Amerman, with offices opposite a defunct public bath-   18
house on the Lower East Side, is New York's master builder of pushcarts. His father and grandfather before him were pushcart makers, and the family has long been a household word among the city's most discriminating junkmen, fruit vendors and hot-dog peddlers.

In New York there are 500 mediums, ranging from semi-   19
trance to trance to deep-trance types. Most of them live in New York's West Seventies and Eighties, and on Sundays some of these blocks are communicating with the dead, vibrating to trumpets, and solving all problems.

The Manhattan Telephone Directory has 776,300 names, of   20
which 3,316 are Smith, 2,835 are Brown, 2,444 are Williams, 2,070 are Cohen—and one is Mike Krasilovsky. Anyone who doubts this last fact has only to look at the top of page 876 where, in large black letters, is this sign: "There is only one Mike Krasilovsky. Sterling 3-1990."

In New York the Fifth Avenue Lingerie shop is on Madison   21
Avenue; The Madison Pet Shop is on Lexington Avenue; the Park Avenue Florist is on Madison Avenue; and the Lexington

Hand Laundry is on Third Avenue. New York is the home of 120 pawnbrokers and it is where Bishop Sheen's brother, Dr. Sheen, shares an office with one Dr. Bishop.

New York is a town of thirty tattooists where interest in mankind is skin-deep, but whose impressions usually last a lifetime. Each day the tattooists go pecking away over acres of anatomy. And in downtown Manhattan, Stanley Moskowitz, a scion of a distinguished family of Bowery skin-peckers, does a grand business. 22

When it rains in Manhattan, automobile traffic is slow, dates are broken and, in hotel lobbies, people slump behind newspapers or walk aimlessly about with no place to sit, nobody to talk to, nothing to do. Taxis are harder to get; department stores do between fifteen and twenty-five percent less business, and the monkeys in the Bronx Zoo, having no audience, slouch grumpily in their cages looking more bored than the lobby-loungers. 23

While some New Yorkers become morose with rain, others prefer it, like to walk in it, and say that on rainy days the city's buildings seem somehow cleaner—washed in an opalescence, like a Monet painting. There are fewer suicides in New York when it rains. But when the sun is shining, and New Yorkers seem happy, the depressed person sinks deeper into depression, and Bellevue Hospital gets more suicide calls. 24

New York is a town of 8,485 telephone operators, 1,364 Western Union messenger boys, and 112 newspaper copyboys. An average baseball crowd at Yankee Stadium uses over ten gallons of liquid soap per game—an unofficial high mark for cleanliness in the major leagues; the stadium also has the league's top number of ushers (360), sweepers (72), and men's rooms (34). 25

New York is a town in which the brotherhood of Russian Bath Rubbers, the only union advocating sweatshops, appears to be heading for its last rubdown. The union has been going in New York City for years, but now most of the rubbers are pushing seventy and are deaf—from all the water and the hot temperatures. 26

Each afternoon in New York a rather seedy saxophone player, his cheeks blown out like a spinnaker, stands on the sidewalk 27

playing *Danny Boy* in such a sad, sensitive way that he soon
has half the neighborhood peeking out of windows tossing
nickels, dimes and quarters at his feet. Some of the coins roll
under parked cars, but most of them are caught in his out-
stretched hand. The saxophone player is a street musician
named Joe Gabler; for the past thirty years he has serenaded
every block in New York and has sometimes been tossed as
much as $100 a day in coins. He is also hit with buckets of
water, empty beer cans and eggs, and chased by wild dogs.
He is believed to be the last of New York's ancient street
musicians.

New York is a town of nineteen midget wrestlers. They all 28
can squeeze into the Hotel Holland's elevator, six can sleep in
one bed, eight can be comfortably transported to Madison
Square Garden in the chauffeur-driven Cadillac reserved for
the midget wrestlers.

In New York from dawn to dusk to dawn, day after day, 29
you can hear the steady rumble of tires against the concrete
span of George Washington Bridge. The bridge is never completely still. It trembles with traffic. It moves in the wind. Its
great veins of steel swell when hot and contract when cold;
its span often is ten feet closer to the Hudson River in summer
than in winter. It is an almost restless structure of graceful
beauty which, like an irresistible seductress, withholds secrets
from the romantics who gaze upon it, the escapists who jump
off it, the chubby girl who lumbers across its 3,500-foot span
trying to reduce, and the 100,000 motorists who each day cross
it, smash into it, shortchange it, get jammed up on it.

When street traffic dwindles and most people are sleeping 30
in New York, some neighborhoods begin to crawl with cats.
They move quickly through the shadows of buildings; night
watchmen, policemen, garbage collectors and other nocturnal
wanderers see them—but never for long.

There are 200,000 stray cats in New York. A majority of 31
them hang around the fish market, or in Greenwich Village,
and in the East and West Side neighborhoods where garbage
cans abound. No part of the city is without its strays, however,
and all-night garage attendants in such busy neighborhoods
as Fifty-fourth Street have counted as many as twenty of them

around the Ziegfeld Theatre early in the morning. Troops of cats patrol the waterfront piers at night searching for rats. Subway trackwalkers have discovered cats living in the darkness. They seem never to get hit by trains, though some are occasionally liquidated by the third rail. About twenty-five cats live seventy-five feet below the west end of Grand Central Terminal, are fed by the underground workers, and never wander up into the daylight.

New York is a city in which large, cliff-dwelling hawks cling to skyscrapers and occasionally zoom to snatch a pigeon over Central Park, or Wall Street, or the Hudson River. Bird watchers have seen these peregrine falcons circling lazily over the city. They have seen them perched atop tall buildings, even around Times Square. About twelve of these hawks patrol the city, sometimes with a wingspan of thirty-five inches. They have buzzed women on the roof of the St. Regis Hotel, have attacked repairmen on smokestacks, and, in August, 1947, two hawks jumped women residents in the recreation yard of the Home of the New York Guild for the Jewish Blind. Maintenance men at the Riverside Church have seen hawks dining on pigeons in the bell tower. The hawks remain there for only a little while. And then they fly out to the river, leaving pigeons' heads for the Riverside maintenance men to clean up. When the hawks return, they fly in quietly—*unnoticed,* like the cats, the headless men, the ants, the ladies' masseur, the doorman with three bullets in his head, and most of the other offbeat wonders in this town without time.

32

FOR STUDY AND DISCUSSION

Questions on Subject

1. What is Talese's purpose in describing New York? Specifically, which sentence controls the entire essay? (Glossary: *Purpose* and *Thesis*)

2. What is Talese's attitude toward New York? How do you know? Is it consistent throughout the essay or does it change? How can you tell? (Glossary: *Attitude*)

3. What is the dominant impression of New York that you get from Talese's description of the city? What, specifically, helps to create this dominant impression? (Glossary: *Dominant Impression*)

Questions on Strategy

1. Talese presents a wealth of factual data in this essay. What is it about these facts that engages the reader's interest? Explain.
2. When presenting such a large collection of statistics, facts, and events, organization becomes a major concern for the writer. How has Talese organized his materials? Does he use more than one organizational pattern? Explain.
3. In an essay in which the writer presents seemingly disconnected or unrelated information in rather brief paragraphs, achieving unity can be a problem. What specific devices does Talese use to unify his essay? (Glossary: *Unity*)
4. What important functions does the final sentence of the essay serve? (Glossary: *Endings*)

Questions on Diction and Vocabulary

1. Talese's essay is particularly rich in metaphors and similes. For example, he calls the doormen "sidewalk diplomats" (12) and describes the saxophone player's cheeks as "blown out like a spinnaker" (27). Point out four other metaphors or similes, and comment on their contributions to the description. (Glossary: *Figures of Speech*)
2. Study the verbs in paragraph 29. How would you characterize them? What kinds of verbs seem to be most effective in descriptions? Find other examples of particularly effective verbs in this essay.
3. Refer to your desk dictionary to determine the meanings of the following words as they are used in this selection: *panhandler* (1), *patronize* (14), *vendors* (17), *defunct* (18), *morose* (24), *nocturnal* (30).

For Classroom Discussion

Cities, like people, have different personalities. Select a city that you know well, and describe the impression that it made on you. What in particular gave you this impression? How do your feelings compare with those of classmates who have also been to that city?

(Note: Activities and Writing Suggestions for Description appear on pages 58–62.)

The Turtle

JOHN STEINBECK

*California novelist John Steinbeck (1902–1968) dropped out
of Stanford University to become a reporter and later began
a literary career. His concern for the problems of landless
migrant laborers and factory workers is reflected in his
novels* Tortilla Flat, Of Mice and Men, The Grapes of
Wrath, *and* East of Eden. *He won the Pulitzer Prize in
1940 and the Nobel Prize in 1962.*

"The Turtle" is an early chapter from The Grapes of
Wrath, *a novel about the painful migration of farmers to
California from the Oklahoma dust bowl. This highly
descriptive passage is an allegory of the struggle for survival
that the farmers faced as they traveled west.*

The concrete highway was edged with a mat of tangled, broken, 1
dry grass, and the grass heads were heavy with oat beards to
catch on a dog's coat, and foxtails to tangle in a horse's fetlocks,
and clover burrs to fasten in sheep's wool; sleeping life waiting
to be spread and dispersed, every seed armed with an appliance
of dispersal, twisting darts and parachutes for the wind, little
spears and balls of tiny thorns, and all waiting for animals and
for the wind, for a man's trouser cuff or the hem of a woman's
skirt, all passive but armed with appliances of activity, still, but
each possessed of the anlage of movement.

The sun lay on the grass and warmed it, and in the shade 2
under the grass the insects moved, ants and ant lions to set
traps for them, grasshoppers to jump into the air and flick their
yellow wings for a second, sow bugs like little armadillos,
plodding restlessly on many tender feet. And over the grass at
the roadside a land turtle crawled, turning aside for nothing,

dragging his high-domed shell over the grass. His hard legs and yellow-nailed feet threshed slowly through the grass, not really walking, but boosting and dragging his shell along. The barley beards slid off his shell, and the clover burrs fell on him and rolled to the ground. His horny beak was partly open, and his fierce, humorous eyes, under brows like fingernails, stared straight ahead. He came over the grass leaving a beaten trail behind him, and the hill, which was the highway embankment, reared up ahead of him. For a moment he stopped, his head held high. He blinked and looked up and down. At last he started to climb the embankment. Front clawed feet reached forward but did not touch. The hind feet kicked his shell along, and it scraped on the grass, and on the gravel. As the embankment grew steeper and steeper, the more frantic were the efforts of the land turtle. Pushing hind legs strained and slipped, boosting the shell along, and the horny head protruded as far as the neck could stretch. Little by little the shell slid up the embankment until at last a parapet cut straight across its line of march, the shoulder of the road, a concrete wall four inches high. As though they worked independently the hind legs pushed the shell against the wall. The head upraised and peered over the wall to the broad smooth plain of cement. Now the hands, braced on top of the wall, strained and lifted, and the shell came slowly up and rested its front end on the wall. For a moment the turtle rested. A red ant ran into the shell, into the soft skin inside the shell, and suddenly head and legs snapped in, and the armored tail clamped in sideways. The red ant was crushed between body and legs. And one head of wild oats was clamped into the shell by a front leg. For a long moment the turtle lay still, and then the neck crept out and the old humorous frowning eyes looked about and the legs and tail came out. The back legs went to work, straining like elephant legs, and the shell tipped to an angle so that the front legs could not reach the level cement plain. But higher and higher the hind legs boosted it, until at last the center of balance was reached, the front tipped down, the front legs scratched at the pavement, and it was up. But the head of wild oats was held by its stem around the front legs.

Now the going was easy, and all the legs worked, and the ₃

shell boosted along, waggling from side to side. A sedan driven by a forty-year-old woman approached. She saw the turtle and swung to the right, off the highway, the wheels screamed and a cloud of dust boiled up. Two wheels lifted for a moment and then settled. The car skidded back onto the road, and went on, but more slowly. The turtle had jerked into its shell, but now it hurried on, for the highway was burning hot.

And now a light truck approached, and as it came near the driver saw the turtle and swerved to hit it. His front wheel struck the edge of the shell, flipped the turtle like a tiddly-wink, spun it like a coin, and rolled it off the highway. The truck went back to its course along the right side. Lying on its back, the turtle was tight in its shell for a long time. But at last its legs waved in the air, reaching for something to pull it over. Its front foot caught a piece of quartz and little by little the shell pulled over and flopped upright. The wild oat head fell out and three of the spearhead seeds stuck in the ground. And as the turtle crawled on down the embankment, its shell dragged dirt over the seeds. The turtle entered a dust road and jerked itself along, drawing a wavy shallow trench in the dust with its shell. The old humorous eyes looked ahead, and the horny beak opened a little. His yellow toe nails slipped a fraction in the dust.

4

FOR STUDY AND DISCUSSION

Questions on Subject

1. The story of the turtle is more than a description of the turtle and his crossing of a highway; it is an effective description of life's processes, the struggle for existence. What is Steinbeck's attitude toward these life processes? (Glossary: *Attitude*)
2. What dominant impression of the turtle does Steinbeck create? (Glossary: *Dominant Impression*)
3. In Steinbeck's description of the turtle's struggle for existence, what roles are played by the woman driver and the man driver?
4. In your opinion, does the turtle get to the other side of the highway? What evidence supports your opinion?

Questions on Strategy

1. Within the context of the entire essay, how does Steinbeck's introductory paragraph function? What would have been gained or lost had Steinbeck introduced the turtle in paragraph 1? (Glossary: *Beginnings*)
2. List six striking details that Steinbeck selects to describe the turtle. Why has he chosen these details from among the many that he could have used?
3. In paragraph 2 Steinbeck's description makes the turtle appear mechanistic. Carefully reread the paragraph, and then explain how Steinbeck has created this impression.

Questions on Diction and Vocabulary

1. Identify three similes that Steinbeck uses, and explain how each figure of speech strengthens his description. (Glossary: *Figures of Speech*)
2. Comment on the appropriateness of the italicized words and phrases in the following excerpts from this essay (Glossary: *Appropriateness*):

   a. *sleeping* life waiting to be spread (1)
   b. *appliance* of dispersal (1)
   c. concrete *wall* four inches high (2)
   d. a cloud of dust *boiled* up (3)
   e. *jerked* itself along (4)

3. Refer to your desk dictionary to determine the meanings of the following words as they are used in this selection: *anlage* (1); *threshed* (2); *horny* (2); *parapet* (2).

For Classroom Discussion

What is your reaction to Steinbeck's allegory of the turtle? Did you find the essay tedious, mildly interesting, or very interesting? What has Steinbeck gained by putting his beliefs in the form of an allegory? How else could he have expressed these same beliefs?

(Note: Activities and Writing Suggestions for Description appear on pages 58–62.)

Activities and Writing Suggestions for Description

ACTIVITIES

1. An objective description seeks to present an accurate and impersonal picture of the thing described. Exactness of detail is, therefore, essential to its effectiveness. Furthermore, such a description usually is organized according to a plan based on space, time, or function. Test your ability to convey objectively a verbal picture of a geometric drawing such as this one.

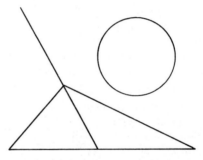

   Make a drawing about as complex as the diagram above, and write a description of your diagram. Test the adequacy of your description by seeing whether, based on what you have written, another student can reproduce your diagram. Adjust your wording until the only possible rendering of your description is the diagram you devised.

2. Factual material can often be used to advantage in descriptive writing. One common characteristic of many of the facts in Gay Talese's essay about New York City is that they surprise us. For example, in paragraph 1 he notes that there are "thousands of ants creeping on top of the Empire State Building" and points to "the panhandler who takes taxis to the Bowery" and "the dapper man who picks trash out of Sixth Avenue trash cans." In each of these examples Talese brings together two things that are not usually associated with each other, and their conjunction surprises us. There is no trick in what Talese has done; he has merely trained himself to *see* what is there for us all to see.

To sharpen your powers of observation, record any surprising incongruities that you notice as you go about your daily activities. Once you have recorded your observations, try to re-create each one in several sentences that convey accurately to your reader your initial surprise when you observed the incongruity. Then discuss your observations with other members of your class.

3. Most menus use connotative language to lead patrons to believe they are having an unusual eating experience. On menus, phrases like the following are common: "skillfully seasoned and basted with butter," "festive red cranberry sauce," "a bed of shredded lettuce," "coffee by candlelight." Write a menu in which you use connotative language to describe the following basic foods, making them both attractive and inviting for the diner:

   a. juice
   b. soup
   c. ground beef
   d. sole
   e. peas
   f. potatoes
   g. salad
   h. bread and butter
   i. tea
   j. cake

4. The writer of a description usually does more than compile a catalogue or inventory, listing everything from left to right or from top to bottom; instead, the writer plans the description around a dominant impression. Most writers begin with an abundance of information but end with only that which is significant. Make an extensive list of specific details about one of the following places:

   a. lecture hall
   b. dentist's office
   c. record store
   d. drugstore
   e. courtroom
   f. hospital emergency room

   Carefully consider the items on your list. Does a dominant impression emerge from your list, or are there several strong impressions? Select one impression, and mark all details on your list that suggest it. Add any other details that now come to mind. Write a paragraph making selective use of the specific details that create the dominant impression you wish to communicate.

5. Figurative language, particularly metaphors and similes, is especially helpful to the writer of description. A *metaphor*, according to a widely used handbook of literary terms, is "an implied analogy which imaginatively identifies one object with another and ascribes to the first one or more of the qualities of the second or invests the first with emotional or imaginative qualities associated with the second." The same handbook defines a *simile* as "a figure of speech

in which a similarity between two objects is directly expressed. . . . Most similes are introduced by *as* or *like*." Write a metaphor or simile that would be helpful in describing each item in the following list.

a. a skyscraper
b. the sound of an explosion
c. an intelligent student
d. a crowded bus
e. a slow-moving car

f. a pillow
g. a narrow alley
h. a loved one
i. the hot sun
j. a sharp knife

Compare your metaphors and similes with those written by other members of your class. Which metaphors and similes for each item on the list seem to work best? Why?

6. Many writers consciously use the sounds of words to reinforce their intended meanings. For example, notice how the sounds of the words in each of the following sentences convey a sense of or a feeling for the thing described:

SUBJECT	SENTENCES
	The bees buzzed in the blossoming crabapple trees.
Bees	
	The murmuring of innumerable bees could be heard as we approached the hives.

For each of the following items, write a descriptive sentence that uses appropriate-sounding words:

a. running water
b. burning candle
c. heavy rainfall
d. braking car
e. gunshot

f. dry cereal
g. alarm clock
h. sweater
i. hammering
j. nervous laughter

Compare your descriptive sentences with those written by other members of your class.

7. Write a paragraph of description using one of the following short introductory sentences to focus and control the descriptive details you select:

a. It was the noisiest place I had ever visited.
b. The woman was very excited.
c. I was terribly frightened.

d. Signs of the strike were evident everywhere.
e. I had never eaten in such a dirty restaurant.

WRITING SUGGESTIONS

1. Most description is predominantly visual; that is, it appeals to the eyes. Good description, however, goes beyond the visual; it appeals as well to one or more of the other senses—hearing, smelling, tasting, and touching. One way to heighten your awareness of these other senses is purposefully to deemphasize the visual impressions you receive. For example, while standing on a busy street corner, sitting in a classroom, or shopping in a supermarket, carefully note what you hear, smell, taste, or feel. (It may help actually to close your eyes to eliminate visual distraction as you carry out this experiment.) Use these sense impressions to write a brief description of the street corner, the classroom, or the supermarket.

2. Select one of the following topics, and write an objective description of it. Remember that your task in writing objective description is to inform the reader about the object, not to convey to the reader the mood or feeling that the object evokes in you.

   a. a pine tree
   b. a pocket calculator
   c. a bake shop
   d. a dictionary
   e. a fast-food restaurant

   f. a football field
   g. the layout of your campus
   h. a stereo system
   i. a house plant
   j. your room

3. Writers of description often rely on factual information to give substance and interest to their writing. Using facts, statistics, or other information found in standard reference works in your college library (encyclopedias, dictionaries, almanacs, atlases, biographical dictionaries, or yearbooks), write an essay of several paragraphs describing one of the people, places, or things from the list below. Be sure that you focus your description, that you have a purpose for your description, and that you present your facts in an interesting manner.

   a. the Statue of Liberty
   b. the telephone
   c. Ronald Reagan
   d. Niagara Falls
   e. Death Valley

   f. Walter Cronkite
   g. Muhammad Ali
   h. the Washington Monument
   i. the sun
   j. the Chicago stockyards

4. Select one of the places listed below, and write a multiparagraph description which captures your subjective sense impressions of that particular place.

   a. a busy downtown intersection
   b. a bakery
   c. an auction
   d. a factory

   e. a service station
   f. a zoo
   g. a cafeteria
   h. a farmers' market

5. A new or interesting point of view can be the key to a successful description. Consider for a moment the many viewpoints from which a car can be described. It can, for example, be described from the point of view of the

   a. manufacturer
   b. salesman
   c. owner
   d. repairman
   e. passenger
   f. victim of an auto accident
   g. insurance adjuster
   h. hitchhiker

   i. car thief
   j. used-car dealer
   k. car-wash attendant
   l. toll collector
   m. parking-lot attendant
   n. carhop at a fast-food restaurant
   o. teenage car buff
   p. muffler repairman

   Are there any other viewpoints which you think would make for an interesting description? Choose one viewpoint, and write a description of a car. Be sure that the purpose of your description is clear.

6. Select one of the following topics, and write a subjective or impressionistic description of it. Remember the importance of creating a dominant impression by selecting those details which best convey to the reader the mood or feeling that the subject evokes in you.

   a. a certain classroom
   b. a flower shop
   c. your favorite movie
   d. a crowded elevator

   e. a wedding
   f. your favorite sandwich
   g. Thanksgiving dinner
   h. a college party

3

PROCESS ANALYSIS

When you give directions to your house, tell how to make ice cream, or explain how a president is elected, you are using *process analysis*. Magazines and newspapers are filled with "how to" articles as well as regular columns about such subjects as how to invest your money, how to improve your health, how to cope with social problems, how to care for your pet, and how to make home repairs. People simply want to know how things work and how to do things for themselves, so it is not surprising that process analysis is one of the most popular forms of writing today.

Process analysis usually orders a series of events and relates them to one another. In this respect, process analysis resembles both narration and cause and effect, but it should not be confused with these other types of writing. Narration tells *what* happens, and cause and effect tells *why* it happens; process analysis tells *how* it happens.

There are two types of process analysis: directional and informational. The *directional* type provides instructions on how to do something. These instructions can be as brief as the directions for making instant coffee printed on a label or as complex as the directions in a manual for building your own home computer. The purpose of directional process analysis is simple: the reader can follow the directions and achieve the desired results.

Consider, for example, the following directions for building a fire in a fireplace taken from Bernard Gladstone's *The New York Times Complete Manual of Home Repair.*

> Though "experts" differ as to the best technique to follow when building a fire, one generally accepted method consists of first laying a generous amount of crumpled newspaper on the hearth between the andirons. Kindling wood is then spread generously over this layer of newspaper and one of the thickest logs is placed across the back of the andirons. This should be as close to the back of the fireplace as possible, but not quite touching it. A second log is then placed an inch or so in front of this, and a few additional sticks of kindling are laid across these two. A third log is then placed on top to form a sort of pyramid with air space between all logs so that flames can lick freely up between them.
>
> A mistake frequently made is in building the fire too far forward so that the rear wall of the fireplace does not get properly heated. A heated back wall helps increase the draft and tends to suck smoke and flames rearward with less chance of sparks or smoke spurting out into the room.
>
> Another common mistake often made by the inexperienced fire-tender is to try to build a fire with only one or two logs, instead of using at least three. A single log is difficult to ignite properly, and even two logs do not provide an efficient bed with adequate fuel-burning capacity.
>
> Use of too many logs, on the other hand, is also a common fault and can prove hazardous. Building too big a fire can create more smoke and draft than the chimney can safely handle, increasing the possibility of sparks or smoke being thrown out into the room. For best results, the homeowner should start with three medium-size logs as described above, then add additional logs as needed if the fire is to be kept burning.

Gladstone has (1) clearly described a sequence of six steps for building a fire in a fireplace, (2) described each step in enough detail for the reader both to understand the individual steps and to follow his overall directions, and (3) provided explanations of what can go wrong if these directions are not followed precisely. His description of the process is clear, simple, and orderly, and any reader who so desires can follow the directions step by step and successfully build a fire.

The *informational* type of process analysis, on the other hand, tells how something works, how something is made, or how something occurred. You would use informational process analysis if you wanted to explain to a reader how the human heart functions, how hailstones are formed, how an atomic bomb works, how iron ore is made into steel, how you selected the college you are attending, or how the Salk polio vaccine was developed. Rather than giving specific directions, the informational type of process analysis has the purpose of explaining and informing.

Clarity is vital for successful process analysis, for just one unclear or misplaced step may render the entire process meaningless. In order to ensure clarity, you must pay attention to the exact sequence of the steps involved, being careful that no step is inadequately described or, worse yet, omitted. On occasion you might also have to explain why a certain step is needed, especially if the reason is not immediately apparent. And in describing an especially intricate, abstract, or difficult-to-follow step, you might use an analogy or a comparison to clarify it for your reader. For example, if you were explaining how rugby is played, you might compare it to the game of football.

Furthermore, you must maintain a consistent point of view in a process analysis so as to avoid confusing and annoying shifts from the imperative *you* to the personal *I* to the objective *he* or *she*. Finally, transitional words and phrases such as *then*, *next*, and *after doing this* can both emphasize and clarify a sequence of steps, but you should be careful not to overuse them.

In the essays in this section, each author uses process analysis to explain how something has happened or continues to happen. For example, Laurence J. Peter and Raymond Hull explain how the Peter Principle works, that is, how people reach a level of incompetence in their jobs; Roy C. Selby, Jr., describes the intricate steps involved in a delicate operation to remove a brain tumor; and Lewis Thomas discusses death as a natural process.

The Peter Principle

LAURENCE J. PETER

AND RAYMOND HULL

Laurence J. Peter is currently professor of education at the University of Southern California, where he coordinates programs for emotionally disturbed children. Born in 1919 in Canada, Peter is a prolific writer and is perhaps best known for his books Prescriptive Teaching, The Peter Principle, *and* The Peter Plan. *He is described by his co-worker Raymond Hull as "the Newton of incompetence theory."*

Raymond Hull was born in England in 1919 and since 1947 has resided in Canada. A playwright by profession, Hull has written plays for television as well as many articles for popular magazines. In 1969, he collaborated with Laurence Peter on The Peter Principle, *a book which has enjoyed great popularity since its publication.*

In the following selection from The Peter Principle, *Peter and Hull analyze the process by which people are promoted within hierarchies. From their study they derive the theory of occupational incompetence known as the Peter Principle.*

When I was a boy I was taught that the men upstairs knew what they were doing. I was told, "Peter, the more you know, the further you go." So I stayed in school until I graduated from college and then went forth into the world clutching firmly these ideas and my new teaching certificate. During the first year of teaching I was upset to find that a number of teachers, school principals, supervisors and superintendents appeared to be unaware of their professional responsibilities and incompetent in executing their duties. For example my principal's main concerns were that all window shades be at the same level, that classrooms should be quiet and that no one step on or near the rose beds. The superintendent's main concerns were that no minority group, no matter how fanatical, should ever be offended and that all official forms be submitted on time. The children's education appeared farthest from the administrator mind.

At first I thought this was a special weakness of the school 2 system in which I taught so I applied for certification in another province. I filled out the special forms, enclosed the required documents and complied willingly with all the red tape. Several weeks later, back came my application and all the documents!

No, there was nothing wrong with my credentials; the forms 3 were correctly filled out; an official departmental stamp showed that they had been received in good order. But an accompanying letter said, "The new regulations require that such forms cannot be accepted by the Department of Education unless they have been registered at the Post Office to ensure safe delivery. Will you please remail the forms to the Department, making sure to register them this time?"

I began to suspect that the local school system did not have 4 a monopoly on incompetence.

As I looked further afield, I saw that every organization 5 contained a number of persons who could not do their jobs.

A Universal Phenomenon

Occupational incompetence is everywhere. Have you noticed 6 it? Probably we all have noticed it.

We see indecisive politicians posing as resolute statesmen 7 and the "authoritative source" who blames his misinformation on "situational imponderables." Limitless are the public servants who are indolent and insolent; military commanders whose behavioral timidity belies their dreadnought rhetoric, and governors whose innate servility prevents their actually governing. In our sophistication, we virtually shrug aside the immoral cleric, corrupt judge, incoherent attorney, author who cannot write and English teacher who cannot spell. At universities we see proclamations authored by administrators whose own office communications are hopelessly muddled; and droning lectures from inaudible or incomprehensible instructors.

Seeing incompetence at all levels of every hierarchy—political, legal, educational and industrial—I hypothesized that the cause was some inherent feature of the rules governing the placement of employees. Thus began my serious study of the ways in which employees move upward through a hierarchy, and of what happens to them after promotion.

For my scientific data hundreds of case histories were collected. Here are three typical examples.

MUNICIPAL GOVERNMENT FILE, CASE NO. 17. J. S. Minion* was a maintenance foreman in the public works department of Excelsior City. He was a favorite of the senior officials at City Hall. They all praised his unfailing affability.

"I like Minion," said the superintendent of works. "He has good judgment and is always pleasant and agreeable."

This behavior was appropriate for Minion's position: he was not supposed to make policy, so he had no need to disagree with his superiors.

The superintendent of works retired and Minion succeeded him. Minion continued to agree with everyone. He passed to his foreman every suggestion that came from above. The resulting conflicts in policy, and the continual changing of plans, soon demoralized the department. Complaints poured in from the Mayor and other officials, from taxpayers and from the maintenance-workers' union.

Minion still says "Yes" to everyone, and carries messages briskly back and forth between his superiors and his subordinates. Nominally a superintendent, he actually does the work of a messenger. The maintenance department regularly exceeds its budget, yet fails to fulfill its program of work. In short,

---

* Some names have been changed, in order to protect the guilty.

Minion, a competent foreman, became an incompetent super-intendent.

SERVICE INDUSTRIES FILE, CASE NO. 3.   E. Tinker was exception-   15
ally zealous and intelligent as an apprentice at G. Reece Auto
Repair Inc., and soon rose to journeyman mechanic. In this job
he showed outstanding ability in diagnosing obscure faults,
and endless patience in correcting them. He was promoted to
foreman of the repair shop.

But here his love of things mechanical and his perfectionism   16
become liabilities. He will undertake any job that he thinks
looks interesting, no matter how busy the shop may be. "We'll
work it in somehow," he says.

He will not let a job go until he is fully satisfied with it.   17

He meddles constantly. He is seldom to be found at his desk.   18
He is usually up to his elbows in a dismantled motor and while
the man who should be doing the work stands watching, other
workmen sit around waiting to be assigned new tasks. As a
result the shop is always overcrowded with work, always in a
muddle, and delivery times are often missed.

Tinker cannot understand that the average customer cares   19
little about perfection—he wants his car back on time! He
cannot understand that most of his men are less interested in
motors than in their pay checks. So Tinker cannot get on with
his customers or with his subordinates. He was a competent
mechanic, but is now an incompetent foreman.

MILITARY FILE, CASE NO. 8.   Consider the case of the late   20
renowned General A. Goodwin. His hearty, informal manner,
his racy style of speech, his scorn for petty regulations and his
undoubted personal bravery made him the idol of his men. He
led them to many well-deserved victories.

When Goodwin was promoted to field marshal he had to   21
deal, not with ordinary soldiers, but with politicians and allied
generalissimos.

He would not conform to the necessary protocol. He could   22
not turn his tongue to the conventional courtesies and flatteries.
He quarreled with all the dignitaries and took to lying for days

at a time, drunk and sulking, in his trailer. The conduct of the war slipped out of his hands into those of his subordinates. He had been promoted to a position that he was incompetent to fill.

An Important Clue!

In time I saw that all such cases had a common feature. The employee had been promoted from a position of competence to a position of incompetence. I saw that, sooner or later, this could happen to every employee in every hierarchy.

HYPOTHETICAL CASE FILE, CASE NO. 1.   Suppose you own a pill-rolling factory, Perfect Pill Incorporated. Your foreman-pill roller dies of a perforated ulcer. You need a replacement. You naturally look among your rank-and-file pill rollers.

Miss Oval, Mrs. Cylinder, Mr. Ellipse and Mr. Cube all show various degrees of incompetence. They will naturally be ineligible for promotion. You will choose—other things being equal—your most competent pill roller, Mr. Sphere, and promote him to foreman.

Now suppose Mr. Sphere proves competent as foreman. Later, when your general foreman, Legree, moves up to Works Manager, Sphere will be eligible to take his place.

If, on the other hand, Sphere is an incompetent foreman, he will get no more promotion. He has reached what I call his "level of incompetence." He will stay there till the end of his career.

Some employees, like Ellipse and Cube, reach a level of incompetence in the lowest grade and are never promoted. Some, like Sphere (assuming he is not a satisfactory foreman), reach it after one promotion.

E. Tinker, the automobile repair-shop foreman, reached his level of incompetence on the third stage of the hierarchy. General Goodwin reached his level of incompetence at the very top of the hierarchy.

So my analysis of hundreds of cases of occupational incompetence led me on to formulate *The Peter Principle:*

In a Hierarchy Every Employee Tends to Rise to His Level of Incompetence

A New Science!

Having formulated the Principle I discovered that I had inad- 31
vertently founded a new science, hierarchiology, the study of
hierarchies.

The term "hierarchy" was originally used to describe the 32
system of church government by priests graded into ranks. The
contemporary meaning includes any organization whose members or employees are arranged in order of rank, grade or class.

Hierarchiology, although a relatively recent discipline, ap- 33
pears to have great applicability to the fields of public and
private administration.

This Means You!

My Principle is the key to an understanding of all hierarchal 34
systems, and therefore to an understanding of the whole
structure of civilization. A few eccentrics try to avoid getting
involved with hierarchies, but everyone in business, industry,
trade-unionism, politics, government, the armed forces, religion and education is so involved. All of them are controlled
by the Peter Principle

Many of them, to be sure, may win a promotion or two, 35
moving from one level of competence to a higher level of
competence. But competence in that new position qualifies
them for still another promotion. For each individual, for *you,*
for *me,* the final promotion is from a level of competence to a
level of incompetence.

So, given enough time—and assuming the existence of 36
enough ranks in the hierarchy—each employee rises to, and
remains at, his level of incompetence. Peter's Corollary states:

In time, every post tends to be occupied by an employee who is 37
incompetent to carry out its duties.

Who Turns the Wheels?

You will rarely find, of course, a system in which *every* employee has reached his level of incompetence. In most instances, something is being done to further the ostensible purposes for which the hierarchy exists.

Work is accomplished by those employees who have not yet reached their level of incompetence.

FOR STUDY AND DISCUSSION

Questions on Subject

1. The Peter Principle describes a process which, according to Peter and Hull, operates in all hierarchies. Briefly explain how the process of the Peter Principle works.
2. Peter and Hull argue that "occupational incompetence is every-where." They ask, "Have you noticed it?" (6) Briefly discuss several examples of occupational incompetence that you are familiar with, and consider whether or not the Peter Principle applies.
3. Peter and Hull claim, *"In time, every post tends to be occupied by an employee who is incompetent to carry out its duties"* (37). If this is true, who does the work in any organization?
4. Why do employees in an organization allow themselves to be promoted, or even strive to be promoted, if the end result is that they achieve a level of incompetence?

Questions on Strategy

1. Explain how Peter and Hull's use of examples is effective in explaining the process involved in the Peter Principle. (Glossary: *Example*)
2. Peter and Hull use a case study from their Municipal Government File, one from their Service Industries File, and another from their Military File. Why, in your opinion, did they choose case studies from three different files, and why did they choose the particular case histories that they did?
3. Peter and Hull claim they had hundreds of actual case histories available to them. Why, then, did they include a "Hypothetical Case File"?

4. Peter and Hull wait until paragraph 23 before giving a statement of the Peter Principle. What would have been gained or lost if they had presented this statement earlier?

Questions on Diction and Vocabulary

1. Peter and Hull coin the term *hierarchiology.* What does the term mean? By what process did they invent the term?
2. Explain the choice of names that Peter and Hull use for the people in each of the case histories. In what ways are the names appropriate?
3. Refer to your desk dictionary to determine the meanings of the following words as they are used in this selection: *indolent* (7), *inherent* (8), *affability* (10), *zealous* (15), *journeyman* (15), *meddles* (18), *protocol* (22), *corollary* (36), *ostensible* (38).

For Classroom Discussion

One obvious solution to the problem described by the Peter Principle would be to abolish hierarchies. Assuming that this is unlikely, what changes within hierarchical structures can you suggest that would eliminate or minimize the negative effects of promoting people to their levels of incompetence?

(Note: Activities and Writing Suggestions for Process Analysis appear on pages 92–95.)

A Delicate Operation

ROY C. SELBY, JR.

Roy C. Selby, Jr., was born in 1930 in Arkansas. He graduated from Louisiana State University and the University of Arkansas Medical School, where he specialized in neurology and neurosurgery. The author of numerous professional articles in his field of specialization, Selby currently has a private practice in the Chicago area.

"A Delicate Operation" first appeared in the December 1975 issue of Harper's *magazine. In an essay filled with drama, Selby uses descriptive details to capture the intricate process of operating on and removing a brain tumor.*

In the autumn of 1973 a woman in her early fifties noticed, upon closing one eye while reading, that she was unable to see clearly. Her eyesight grew slowly worse. Changing her eyeglasses did not help. She saw an ophthalmologist, who found that her vision was seriously impaired in both eyes. She then saw a neurologist, who confirmed the finding and obtained X rays of the skull and an EMI scan—a photograph of the patient's head. The latter revealed a tumor growing between the optic nerves at the base of the brain. The woman was admitted to the hospital by a neurosurgeon.

Further diagnosis, based on angiography, a detailed X-ray study of the circulatory system, showed the tumor to be about two inches in diameter and supplied by many small blood vessels. It rested beneath the brain, just above the pituitary gland, stretching the optic nerves to either side and intimately close to the major blood vessels supplying the brain. Removing it would pose many technical problems. Probably benign and slow-growing, it may have been present for several years. If left alone it would continue to grow and produce blindness and

74

might become impossible to remove completely. Removing it, however, might not improve the patient's vision and could make it worse. A major blood vessel could be damaged, causing a stroke. Damage to the undersurface of the brain could cause impairment of memory and changes in mood and personality. The hypothalamus, a most important structure of the brain, could be injured, causing coma, high fever, bleeding from the stomach, and death.

The neurosurgeon met with the patient and her husband and discussed the various possibilities. The common decision was to operate. 3

The patient's hair was shampooed for two nights before surgery. She was given a cortisonelike drug to reduce the risk of damage to the brain during surgery. Five units of blood were cross-matched, as a contingency against hemorrhage. At 1:00 P.M. the operation began. After the patient was anesthetized her hair was completely clipped and shaved from the scalp. Her head was prepped with an organic iodine solution for ten minutes. Drapes were placed over her, leaving exposed only the forehead and crown of the skull. All the routine instruments were brought up—the electrocautery used to coagulate areas of bleeding, bipolar coagulation forceps to arrest bleeding from individual blood vessels without damaging adjacent tissues, and small suction tubes to remove blood and cerebrospinal fluid from the head, thus giving the surgeon a better view of the tumor and surrounding areas. 4

A curved incision was made behind the hairline so it would be concealed when the hair grew back. It extended almost from ear to ear. Plastic clips were applied to the cut edges of the scalp to arrest bleeding. The scalp was folded back to the level of the eyebrows. Incisions were made in the muscle of the right temple, and three sets of holes were drilled near the temple and the top of the head because the tumor had to be approached from directly in front. The drill, powered by nitrogen, was replaced with a fluted steel blade, and the holes were connected. The incised piece of skull was pried loose and held out of the way by a large sponge. 5

Beneath the bone is a yellowish leatherlike membrane, the dura, that surrounds the brain. Down the middle of the head 6 the dura carries a large vein, but in the area near the nose the vein is small. At that point the vein and dura were cut, and clips made of tantalum, a hard metal, were applied to arrest and prevent bleeding. Sutures were put into the dura and tied to the scalp to keep the dura open and retracted. A malleable silver retractor, resembling the blade of a butter knife, was inserted between the brain and skull. The anesthesiologist began to administer a drug to relax the brain by removing some of its water, making it easier for the surgeon to manipulate the retractor, hold the brain back, and see the tumor. The nerve tracts for smell were cut on both sides to provide additional room. The tumor was seen approximately two-and-one-half inches behind the base of the nose. It was pink in color. On touching it, it proved to be very fibrous and tough. A special retractor was attached to the skull, enabling the other retractor blades to be held automatically and freeing the surgeon's hands. With further displacement of the frontal lobes of the brain, the tumor could be seen better, but no normal structures—the carotid arteries, their branches, and the optic nerves—were visible. The tumor obscured them.

A surgical microscope was placed above the wound. The surgeon had selected the lenses and focal length prior to the operation. Looking through the microscope, he could see some of the small vessels supplying the tumor and he coagulated them. He incised the tumor to attempt to remove its core and thus collapse it, but the substance of the tumor was too firm to be removed in this fashion. He then began to slowly dissect the tumor from the adjacent brain tissue and from where he believed the normal structures to be.

Using small squares of cotton, he began to separate the tumor from very loose fibrous bands connecting it to the brain and to the right side of the part of the skull where the pituitary gland lies. The right optic nerve and carotid artery came into view, both displaced considerably to the right. The optic nerve had a normal appearance. He protected these structures with cotton compresses placed between them and the tumor. He began to raise the tumor from the skull and slowly to reach the point of its origin and attachment—just in front of the pituitary gland and medial to the left optic nerve, which still could not be seen.

The small blood vessels entering the tumor were cauterized. The upper portion of the tumor was gradually separated from the brain, and the branches of the carotid arteries and the branches to the tumor were coagulated. The tumor was slowly and gently lifted from its bed, and for the first time the left carotid artery and optic nerve could be seen. Part of the tumor adhered to this nerve. The bulk of the tumor was amputated, leaving a small bit attached to the nerve. Very slowly and carefully the tumor fragment was resected.

The tumor now removed, a most impressive sight came into view—the pituitary gland and its stalk of attachment to the hypothalamus, the hypothalamus itself, and the brainstem, which conveys nerve impulses between the body and the brain. As far as could be determined, no damage had been done to these structures or other vital centers, but the left optic nerve, from chronic pressure of the tumor, appeared gray and thin. Probably it would not completely recover its function. 9

After making certain there was no bleeding, the surgeon closed the wounds and placed wire mesh over the holes in the skull to prevent dimpling of the scalp over the points that had been drilled. A gauze dressing was applied to the patient's head. She was awakened and sent to the recovery room. 10

Even with the microscope, damage might still have occurred to the cerebral cortex and hypothalamus. It would require at least a day to be reasonably certain there was none, and about seventy-two hours to monitor for the major postoperative dangers—swelling of the brain and blood clots forming over the surface of the brain. The surgeon explained this to the patient's husband, and both of them waited anxiously. The operation had required seven hours. A glass of orange juice had given the surgeon some additional energy during the closure of the wound. Though exhausted, he could not fall asleep until after two in the morning, momentarily expecting a call from the nurse in the intensive care unit announcing deterioration of the patient's condition. 11

At 8:00 A.M. the surgeon saw the patient in the intensive care unit. She was alert, oriented, and showed no sign of additional damage to the optic nerves or the brain. She appeared to be in better shape than the surgeon or her husband. 12

FOR STUDY AND DISCUSSION

Questions on Subject

1. What series of events led to the decision to operate?
2. What might have happened if the patient had not chosen to have the operation? What risks did the operation itself involve?
3. What are the major stages of the operation that Selby describes?
4. Once the operation itself was completed, what dangers were still present?

Questions on Strategy

1. What type of process analysis is this essay?
2. What is the relationship between the first three paragraphs and the remainder of the essay? (Glossary: *Beginnings*)
3. For what audience was this essay written? What specific evidence do you find in the essay to support your conclusion?
4. In paragraph 10 Selby briefly describes the process of concluding the operation—closing and dressing the wounds. Why do you suppose his description of this stage of the operation is so brief?
5. This process analysis is remarkable for the care with which Selby recounts the individual steps in the process and the sequence in which they occurred. Selby also uses descriptive detail to enhance his analysis of the operation. Where specifically in paragraphs 5 and 6 does he do this? Why is such descriptive detail appropriate in this type of process analysis?

Questions on Diction and Vocabulary

1. At several points Selby uses technical terminology which he briefly defines. Does any other technical terminology need to be defined? Explain. (Glossary: *Technical Language*)
2. Describe the tone of this essay. How does Selby's diction establish this tone? Is the tone appropriate for Selby's subject and purpose? Explain. (Glossary: *Tone*)
3. Refer to your desk dictionary to determine the meanings of the following words as they are used in this selection: *ophthalmologist* (1), *coagulate* (4), *fluted* (5), *incised* (7), *compresses* (8), *resected* (8), *chronic* (9).

For Classroom Discussion

"A Delicate Operation" was originally published in *Harper's* magazine, a widely read popular magazine. What does the decision of the editors of *Harper's* to publish this article reveal about American attitudes toward health care, the practice of medicine, disease, the use of drugs, and knowledge of our bodies?

(Note: Activities and Writing Suggestions for Process Analysis appear on pages 92–95.)

The Spider and the Wasp

ALEXANDER PETRUNKEVITCH

*Alexander Petrunkevitch (1875–1964), a Russian-born zo-
ologist, was a leading authority on spiders. He published
his first important work,* The Index Catalogue of Spiders
of North, Central, and South America, *in 1911. In addition
to his scientific research, Petrunkevitch was widely recognized for his accomplished translations of English and
Russian poetry.*

In this essay, first published in 1952 in Scientific American, *Petrunkevitch describes the way in which the "intelligence" of digger wasps is pitted against the "instincts"
of tarantula spiders.*

topic

In the feeding and safeguarding of their progeny insects and   1
spiders exhibit some interesting analogies to reasoning and
some crass examples of blind instinct. The case I propose to
describe here is that of the tarantula spiders and their arch-
enemy, the digger wasps of the genus Pepsis. It is a classic
example of what looks like intelligence pitted against instinct—
thesis ⟨ a strange situation in which the victim, though fully able to
defend itself, submits unwittingly to its destruction.

Most tarantulas live in the tropics, but several species occur   2
in the temperate zone and a few are common in the southern
U.S. Some varieties are large and have powerful fangs with
which they can inflict a deep wound. These formidable looking
spiders do not, however, attack man; you can hold one in
your hand, if you are gentle, without being bitten. Their bite
is dangerous only to insects and small mammals such as mice;
for man it is no worse than a hornet's sting.

Tarantulas customarily live in deep cylindrical burrows, from   3 which they emerge at dusk and into which they retire at dawn. Mature males wander about after dark in search of females and occasionally stray into houses. After mating, the male dies in a few weeks, but a female lives much longer and can mate several years in succession. In a Paris museum is a tropical specimen which is said to have been living in captivity for 25 years.

A fertilized female tarantula lays from 200 to 400 eggs at a 4 time; thus it is possible for a single tarantula to produce several thousand young. She takes no care of them beyond weaving a cocoon of silk to enclose the eggs. After they hatch, the young walk away, find convenient places in which to dig their burrows and spend the rest of their lives in solitude. The eyesight of tarantulas is poor, being limited to a sensing of change in the intensity of light and to the perception of moving objects. They apparently have little or no sense of hearing, for a hungry tarantula will pay no attention to a loudly chirping cricket placed in its cage unless the insect happens to touch one of its legs.

But all spiders, and especially hairy ones, have an extremely 5 delicate sense of touch. Laboratory experiments prove that tarantulas can distinguish three types of touch: pressure against the body wall, stroking of the body hair, and riffling of certain very fine hairs on the legs called trichobothria. Pressure against the body, by the finger or the end of a pencil, causes the tarantula to move off slowly for a short distance. The touch excites no defensive response unless the approach is from above where the spider can see the motion, in which case it rises on its hind legs, lifts its front legs, opens its fangs and holds this threatening posture as long as the object continues to move.

The entire body of a tarantula, especially its legs, is thickly 6 clothed with hair. Some of it is short and wooly, some long and stiff. Touching this body hair produces one of two distinct reactions. When the spider is hungry, it responds with an immediate and swift attack. At the touch of a cricket's antennae the tarantula seizes the insect so swiftly that a motion picture taken at the rate of 64 frames per second shows only the result and not the process of capture. But when the spider is not hungry, the stimulation of its hairs merely causes it to shake the touched limb. An insect can walk under its hairy belly unharmed.

The trichobothria, very fine hairs growing from dislike membranes on the legs, are sensitive only to air movement. A light breeze makes them vibrate slowly, without disturbing the common hair. When one blows gently on the trichobothria, the tarantula reacts with a quick jerk of its four front legs. If the front and hind legs are stimulated at the same time, the spider makes a sudden jump. This reaction is quite independent of the state of its appetite.

These three tactile responses—to pressure on the body wall, to moving of the common hair, and to flexing of the trichobothria—are so different from one another that there is no possibility of confusing them. They serve the tarantula adequately for most of its needs and enable it to avoid most annoyances and dangers. But they fail the spider completely when it meets its deadly enemy, the digger wasp Pepsis.

These solitary wasps are beautiful and formidable creatures. Most species are either a deep shiny blue all over, or deep blue with rusty wings. The largest have a wing span of about four inches. They live on nectar. When excited, they give off a pungent odor—a warning that they are ready to attack. The sting is much worse than that of a bee or common wasp, and the pain and swelling last longer. In the adult stage the wasp lives only a few months. The female produces but a few eggs, one at a time at intervals of two or three days. For each egg the mother must provide one adult tarantula, alive but paralyzed. The mother wasp attaches the egg to the paralyzed spider's abdomen. Upon hatching from the egg, the larva is many hundreds of times smaller than its living but helpless victim. It eats no other food and drinks no water. By the time it has finished its single Gargantuan meal and become ready for wasphood, nothing remains of the tarantula but its indigestible chitinous skeleton.

The mother wasp goes tarantula-hunting when the egg in her ovary is almost ready to be laid. Flying low over the ground late on a sunny afternoon, the wasp looks for its victim or for the mouth of a tarantula burrow, a round hole edged by a bit of silk. The sex of the spider makes no difference, but the mother is highly discriminating as to species. Each species of Pepsis requires a certain species of tarantula, and the wasp will not attack the wrong species. In a cage with a tarantula which is not its normal prey, the wasp avoids the spider and is usually killed by it in the night.

Yet when a wasp finds the correct species, it is the other way about. To identify the species the wasp apparently must explore the spider with her antennae. The tarantula shows an amazing tolerance to this exploration. The wasp crawls under it and walks over it without evoking any hostile response. The molestation is so great and so persistent that the tarantula often rises on all eight legs, as if it were on stilts. It may stand this way for several minutes. Meanwhile the wasp, having satisfied itself that the victim is of the right species, moves off a few inches to dig the spider's grave. Working vigorously with legs and jaws, it excavates a hole 8 to 10 inches deep with a diameter slightly larger than the spider's girth. Now and again the wasp pops out of the hole to make sure that the spider is still there. 11

When the grave is finished, the wasp returns to the tarantula to complete her ghastly enterprise. First she feels it all over once more with her antennae. Then her behavior becomes more aggressive. She bends her abdomen, protruding her sting, and searches for the soft membrane at the point where the spider's legs join its body—the only spot where she can penetrate the horny skeleton. From time to time, as the exasperated spider slowly shifts ground, the wasp turns on her back and slides along with the aid of her wings, trying to get under the tarantula for a shot at the vital spot. During all this maneuvering, which can last for several minutes, the tarantula makes no move to save itself. Finally the wasp corners it against some obstruction and grasps one of its legs in her powerful jaws. Now at last the harassed spider tries a desperate but vain defense. The two contestants roll over and over on the ground. It is a terrifying sight and the outcome is always the same. The wasp finally manages to thrust her sting into the soft spot and holds it there for a few seconds while she pumps in the poison. Almost immediately the tarantula falls 12 paralyzed on its back. Its legs stop twitching; its heart stops beating. Yet it is not dead, as is shown by the fact that if taken from the wasp it can be restored to some sensitivity by being kept in a moist chamber for several months.

After paralyzing the tarantula, the wasp cleans herself by dragging her body along the ground and rubbing her feet, sucks the drop of blood oozing from the wound in the spider's abdomen, then grabs a leg of the flabby, helpless animal in her jaws and drags it down to the bottom of the grave. She stays there for many minutes, sometimes for several hours, and what she does all that time in the dark we do not know. Eventually she lays her egg and attaches it to the side of the spider's abdomen with a sticky secretion. Then she emerges, fills the grave with soil carried bit by bit in her jaws, and finally tramples the ground all around to hide any trace of the grave from prowlers. Then she flies away, leaving her descendant safely started in life. 13

In all this the behavior of the wasp evidently is qualitatively different from that of the spider. The wasp acts like an intelligent animal. This is not to say that instinct plays no part or that she reasons as man does. But her actions are to the point; they are not automatic and can be modified to fit the situation. We do not know for certain how she identifies the tarantula—probably it is by some olfactory or chemo-tactile sense—but she does it purposefully and does not blindly tackle a wrong species. 14

On the other hand, the tarantula's behavior shows only confusion. Evidently the wasp's pawing gives it no pleasure, for it tries to move away. That the wasp is not simulating sexual stimulation is certain because male and female tarantulas react in the same way to its advances. That the spider is not anesthetized by some odorless secretion is easily shown by blowing lightly at the tarantula and making it jump suddenly. What, then, makes the tarantula behave as stupidly as it does? 15

No clear, simple answer is available. Possibly the stimulation by the wasp's antennae is masked by a heavier pressure on the spider's body, so that it reacts as when prodded by a pencil. But the explanation may be much more complex. Initiative in attack is not in the nature of tarantulas; most 16 species fight only when cornered so that escape is impossible. Their inherited patterns of behavior apparently prompt them to avoid problems rather than attack them. For example, spiders always weave their webs in three dimensions, and when a spider finds that there is insufficient space to attach certain threads in the third dimension, it leaves the place and seeks another, instead of finishing the web in a single plane. This urge to escape seems to arise under all circumstances, in all phases of life, and to take the place of reasoning. For a spider to change the pattern of its web is as impossible as for an inexperienced man to build a bridge across a chasm obstructing his way.

In a way the instinctive urge to escape is not only easier but often more efficient than reasoning. The tarantula does exactly what is most efficient in all cases except in an encounter with a ruthless and determined attacker dependent for the existence of her own species on killing as many tarantulas as she can lay eggs. Perhaps in this case the spider follows its usual pattern of trying to escape, instead of seizing and killing the wasp, because it is not aware of its danger. In any case, the survival of the tarantula species as a whole is protected by the fact that the spider is much more fertile than the wasp. 17

FOR STUDY AND DISCUSSION

Questions on Subject

1. What is Petrunkevitch's purpose in this essay? Where is his purpose revealed? (Glossary: *Purpose*)
2. Petrunkevitch contrasts the behavior of the tarantula with that of the wasp. What significant differences does he note? How are these differences related to his overall purpose in the essay?
3. Briefly describe the process that the mother wasp follows in hunting a tarantula.

Questions on Strategy

1. Petrunkevitch describes the way the wasp hunts the tarantula in order to use it as food for its young. How is the description of this process related to his overall purpose in the essay?

2. How has Petrunkevitch organized his essay? You may find it helpful to outline the essay in answering this question.
3. In paragraphs 10 through 13 Petrunkevitch describes what happens when the wasp encounters the tarantula. How has Petrunkevitch organized this process analysis? What transitional or linking devices has he used to give coherence to his description of the process? (Glossary: *Transitions*)

Questions on Diction and Vocabulary

1. Identify some examples of informal or colloquial expressions (for example, "pitted against" [1] and impressionistic words and phrases (for example, "ghastly enterprise" [12]), which, while not appropriate in a technical report, engage the nonscientific reader. What specifically do they add to Petrunkevitch's essay?
2. Refer to your desk dictionary to determine the meanings of the following words as they are used in this selection: *progeny* (1), *crass* (1), *unwittingly* (1), *fangs* (2), *riffling* (5), *tactile* (8), *qualitatively* (14).

For Classroom Discussion

In his essay Petrunkevitch closely examines the interdependent relationship between the tarantula and the digger wasp. Discuss any other interdependent relationship that you know of in the natural world. What do these relationships tell us about life itself?

(Note: Activities and Writing Suggestions for Process Analysis appear on pages 92–95.)

Death in the Open

LEWIS THOMAS

Lewis Thomas was born in 1913 in New York and attended Princeton University and the Harvard Medical School. Thomas has had a distinguished career as a physician, administrator, researcher, teacher, and writer. Having been affiliated with the University of Minnesota Medical School, the New York University–Bellevue Medical Center, and the Yale University Medical School, Thomas is currently the president of the Memorial Sloan-Kettering Cancer Center. In 1971 he began writing a series of essays for The New England Journal of Medicine, *many of which were collected in* The Lives of a Cell: Notes of a Biology Watcher, *which won a National Book Award in 1974. A second collection of essays,* The Medusa and the Snail: More Notes of a Biology Watcher, *appeared in 1979.*

In the following selection taken from The Lives of a Cell, *Thomas contemplates death as part of a larger natural process.*

Most of the dead animals you see on highways near the cities   1
are dogs, a few cats. Out in the countryside, the forms and
coloring of the dead are strange; these are the wild creatures.
Seen from a car window they appear as fragments, evoking
memories of woodchucks, badgers, skunks, voles, snakes,
sometimes the mysterious wreckage of a deer.

It is always a queer shock, part a sudden upwelling of grief,   2
part unaccountable amazement. It is simply astounding to see
an animal dead on a highway. The outrage is more than just the
location; it is the impropriety of such visible death, anywhere.
You do not expect to see dead animals in the open. It is the

nature of animals to die alone, off somewhere, hidden. It is
wrong to see them lying out on the highway; it is wrong to see
them anywhere.

Everything in the world dies, but we only know about it as   3
a kind of abstraction. If you stand in a meadow, at the edge of
a hillside, and look around carefully, almost everything you can
catch sight of is in the process of dying, and most things will
be dead long before you are. If it were not for the constant
renewal and replacement going on before your eyes, the whole
place would turn to stone and sand under your feet.

There are some creatures that do not seem to die at all; they   4
simply vanish totally into their own progeny. Single cells do
this. The cell becomes two, then four, and so on, and after a
while the last trace is gone. It cannot be seen as death; barring
mutation, the descendants are simply the first cell, living all
over again. The cycles of the slime mold have episodes that
seem as conclusive as death, but the withered slug, with its
stalk and fruiting body, is plainly the transient tissue of a
developing animal; the free-swimming amebocytes use this
organ collectively in order to produce more of themselves.

There are said to be a billion billion insects on the earth at   5
any moment, most of them with very short life expectancies by
our standards. Someone has estimated that there are 25 million
assorted insects hanging in the air over every temperate square
mile, in a column extending upward for thousands of feet,
drifting through the layers of the atmosphere like plankton.
They are dying steadily, some by being eaten, some just
dropping in their tracks, tons of them around the earth,
disintegrating as they die, invisibly.

Who ever sees dead birds, in anything like the huge numbers   6
stipulated by the certainty of the death of all birds? A dead bird
is an incongruity, more startling than an unexpected live bird,
sure evidence to the human mind that something has gone
wrong. Birds do their dying off somewhere, behind things,
under things, never on the wing.

Animals seem to have an instinct for performing death alone,   7
hidden. Even the largest, most conspicuous ones find ways to
conceal themselves in time. If an elephant missteps and dies in
an open place, the herd will not leave him there; the others will

pick him up and carry the body from place to place, finally putting it down in some inexplicably suitable location. When elephants encounter the skeleton of an elephant out in the open, they methodically take up each of the bones and distribute them, in a ponderous ceremony, over neighboring acres.

It is a natural marvel. All of the life of the earth dies, all of the time, in the same volume as the new life that dazzles us each morning, each spring. All we see of this is the odd stump, the fly struggling on the porch floor of the summer house in October, the fragment on the highway. I have lived all my life with an embarrassment of squirrels in my backyard, they are all over the place, all year long, and I have never seen, anywhere, a dead squirrel. 8

I suppose it is just as well. If the earth were otherwise, and all the dying were done in the open, with the dead there to be looked at, we would never have it out of our minds. We can forget about it much of the time, or think of it as an accident to be avoided, somehow. But it does make the process of dying seem more exceptional than it really is, and harder to engage in at the times when we must ourselves engage. 9

In our way, we conform as best we can to the rest of nature. The obituary pages tell us of the news that we are dying away, while the birth announcements in finer print, off at the side of the page, inform us of our replacements, but we get no grasp from this of the enormity of scale. There are 3 billion of us on the earth, and all 3 billion must be dead, on a schedule, within this lifetime. The vast mortality, involving something over 50 million of us each year, takes place in relative secrecy. We can only really know of the deaths in our households, or among our friends. These, detached in our minds from all the rest, we take to be unnatural events, anomalies, outrages. We speak of our own dead in low voices: struck down, we say, as though visible death can only occur for cause, by disease or violence, avoidably. We send off for flowers, grieve, make ceremonies, scatter bones, unaware of the rest of the 3 billion on the same schedule. All of that immense mass of flesh and bone and consciousness will disappear by absorption into the earth, without recognition by the transient survivors. 10

Less than a half century from now, our replacements will have 11 more than doubled the numbers. It is hard to see how we can continue to keep the secret, with such multitudes doing the dying. We will have to give up the notion that death is catastrophe, or detestable, or avoidable, or even strange. We will need to learn more about the cycling of life in the rest of the system, and about our connection to the process. Everything that comes alive seems to be in trade for something that dies, cell for cell. There might be some comfort in the recognition of synchrony, in the information that we all go down together, in the best of company.

FOR STUDY AND DISCUSSION

Questions on Subject

1. Why, according to Thomas, is it "wrong" to see dead animals on the highway?
2. What does Thomas mean when he says that "everything in the world dies, but we only know about it as a kind of abstraction" (3)?
3. We generally think of death as an event. In what ways does Thomas see death as a process?
4. What implications for people are there in Thomas's view of death?

Questions on Strategy

1. How are paragraphs 4 through 7 related? Could paragraphs 4 through 7 be rearranged without loss to the essay? (Glossary: *Coherence*)
2. What is the relationship between paragraphs 4 through 7 and paragraph 8? (Glossary: *Induction/Deduction*)
3. Describe the tone of this essay. What specific evidence in the essay supports your assessment? (Glossary: *Tone*)
4. What is the literal meaning of Thomas's title? Are there other meanings as well? (Glossary: *Title*)

Questions on Diction and Vocabulary

1. Identify three clichés that Thomas uses in this essay. Do you find his use of these clichés annoying? Explain. (Glossary: *Clichés*)

2. Comment on the connotative value of the italicized words and phrases in each of the following excerpts from this essay:

   a. "the mysterious *wreckage* of a deer" (1)
   b. "an instinct for *performing* death" (7)
   c. "a *ponderous* ceremony" (7)
   d. "an *embarrassment* of squirrels" (8)
   e. "the *recognition of synchrony*" (11)

3. Refer to your desk dictionary to determine the meanings of the following words as they are used in this selection: *progeny* (4), *mutation* (4), *transient* (4), *temperate* (5), *incongruity* (6), *inexplicably* (7), *anomalies* (10).

For Classroom Discussion

Lewis Thomas believes that in the future we will find it increasingly difficult to deny the reality of death if only because there will be so many more deaths. Is death the "secret" that Thomas claims it to be? Are there any indications that American society is becoming more or less realistic in its attitudes toward death and dying?

(Note: Activities and Writing Suggestions for Process Analysis appear on pages 92–95.)

Activities and Writing Suggestions for Process Analysis

ACTIVITIES

1. In *The New York Times Complete Manual of Home Repair,* Bernard Gladstone gives the following directions for applying blacktop sealer to a driveway. We have rearranged the sentences in his directions. First, carefully read all of Gladstone's sentences. Next, place the sentences in what seems to you a meaningful sequence, paying particular attention to the process involved and to transitional devices. Finally, be prepared to explain the reasons for your placement of each sentence.

   a. A long-handled pushbroom or roofing brush is used to spread the coating evenly over the entire area.
   b. Care should be taken to make certain the entire surface is uniformly wet, though puddles should be swept away if water collects in low spots.
   c. Greasy areas and oil slicks should be scraped up, then scrubbed thoroughly with a detergent solution.
   d. With most brands there are just three steps to follow.
   e. In most cases one coat of sealer will be sufficient.
   f. The application of blacktop sealer is best done on a day when the weather is dry and warm, preferably while the sun is shining on the surface.
   g. This should not be applied until the first coat is completely dry.
   h. First sweep the surface absolutely clean to remove all dust, dirt and foreign material.
   i. To simplify spreading and to assure a good bond, the surface of the driveway should be wet down thoroughly by sprinkling with a hose.
   j. However, for surfaces in poor condition a second coat may be required.
   k. The blacktop sealer is next stirred thoroughly and poured on while the surface is still damp.
   l. The sealer should be allowed to dry overnight (or longer if recommended by the manufacturer) before normal traffic is resumed.

2. In order to give another person directions about how to do something, you yourself need a thorough understanding of the process. Analyze one of the following activities, listing (1) the materials you would need and (2) the steps you would follow in completing it:

   a. making your favorite sandwich
   b. making scrambled eggs
   c. writing a short essay
   d. studying for an examination
   e. painting your room

3. In preparing to write an informational process analysis that explains how something works, you first need to analyze your subject so as to be sure you understand its operation. Select one of the following items, and list the various steps involved in its operation.

   a. a bicycle
   b. the grading system at your school
   c. a particular diet plan
   d. zip codes
   e. the student health insurance plan at your school

4. The following is an exercise in writing directions for getting from one place to another. In this exercise students will work in teams of two or three. During the first half of the exercise, each team will write directions for getting from the front door of the classroom building, or some other agreed-upon starting place, to a mystery destination within five minutes walking distance. Each team should write their directions as they actually walk the route to the destination they have selected. The directions should be clear and accurate without the aid of maps, drawings, or place names. Of course, the destination, which could be a particular street corner, fire hydrant, water fountain, bicycle rack, or street lamp, should not be identified in the directions. During the second half of the exercise, the accuracy of the directions will be tested. Teams should exchange directions and follow them to the mystery destinations. Once all teams have returned to the classroom, destinations should be verified with the teams that chose them. The class should then discuss the principles involved in writing effective directions and the kinds of problems that can occur both in writing and in following directions.

WRITING SUGGESTIONS

1. Write a directional process analysis on one of the following topics:

    a. how to make chocolate chip cookies
    b. how to adjust brakes on a bicycle
    c. how to change a tire
    d. how to give a permanent
    e. how to use the memory function on a calculator
    f. how to add, drop, or change a course
    g. how to wax cross-country skis
    h. how to wash a sweater
    i. how to develop film
    j. how to make a pizza
    k. how to make a long distance call from a phone booth and charge it to your home phone
    l. how to do batik dyeing
    m. how to select a major
    n. how to winterize a car
    o. how to rent an apartment
    p. how to develop confidence
    q. how to operate a small business
    r. how to run for a student government office

2. Write an informational process analysis on one of the following topics:

    a. how your heart functions
    b. how a United States president is elected
    c. how ice cream is made
    d. how a hurricane forms
    e. how hailstones are formed
    f. how a volcano erupts
    g. how the circulatory system works
    h. how a camera works
    i. how photosynthesis takes place
    j. how an atomic bomb works
    k. how fertilizer is made
    l. how a refrigerator works
    m. how water evaporates
    n. how an eclipse of the sun takes place

o. how a recession occurs
p. how an automobile is made
q. how a bill becomes law in your state

4
DEFINITION

To communicate precisely what you want to say, you will frequently need to *define* key words, to explain their exact meanings. For example, your reader needs to know just what you mean when you use words that are unfamiliar, like *litigious;* or words that are open to various interpretations, like *democracy;* or words that, while generally familiar, are used in a particular sense. Failure to define important terms, or failure to define them accurately, will surely confuse your reader and lead to a breakdown in communication. In the essays in this section, the authors come to terms with important words and concepts.

There are three basic ways to define a word; each is useful in its own way. The first method is to give a *synonym,* a word that has nearly the same meaning as the word you wish to define: *dictionary* for *lexicon, nervousness* for *anxiety.* No two words ever have exactly the same meaning, but you can, nevertheless, pair a familiar word with an unfamiliar one and thereby clarify your meaning.

Another way to define quickly, often within the space of a single sentence, is to give a *formal definition;* that is, to place the term to be defined in a general class and then to distinguish it from other members of that class by describing its particular characteristics. For example:

WORD	CLASS	CHARACTERISTICS
A *canoe*	is a *small boat*	that has *curved sides* and *pointed ends* and is *narrow, made of lightweight materials,* and *propelled by paddles.*
A *rowboat*	is a *small boat*	that has a *shallow draft* and usually a *flat* or *rounded bottom,* a *squared-off* or *V-shaped stern,* and *oar locks* for the *oars with which it is propelled.*

The third method is known as *extended definition.* This type of definition requires a paragraph of an essay or even an entire essay. Occasionally, you will need to spend several paragraphs in an essay defining a new and difficult term, as Jan Harold Brunvand does with the term *urban legend* in his essay in this section. And sometimes you will need to devote an entire essay to a controversial word in order to rescue it from misconceptions and emotional associations that threaten to obscure its meaning. A controversial term that illustrates the importance of definition is *obscenity.* What is obscene? Books that are banned as obscene in one school system are considered perfectly acceptable in another. People go to jail for producing or selling obscene materials, and yet the members of the Supreme Court themselves cannot entirely agree on a definition of obscenity.

There is no prescription or set pattern of organization for an essay that is based upon or is itself an extended definition. You may begin with an illustrative anecdote, as Laurence Perrine does in "Paradox." You may also define by *negation,* that is, tell what a term does *not* mean, as Brunvand does in "Alligators in the Sewers and Other Urban Legends." Or you may list the most revealing characteristics of a term and then discuss them in detail as Judy Syfers does with *wife* in "I Want a Wife" and as Joan Didion does with *migraine* in "In Bed."

In addition to these suggestions for writing an essay of extended definition, any or all of the rhetorical strategies discussed in this text may be called upon. Let us imagine, for example, that you wish to define a *diabetic.* It might be useful in different parts of your essay *to describe the most important characteristics* of a diabetic, or *to present a narration* of what it is like to be a diabetic, or *to analyze* the causes of diabetes, or *to classify* the various types of diabetes and diabetics, or *to contrast* the diabetic with people suffering from similar disorders, or *to discuss the effects* of various medications available to the diabetic. Any or all of these strategies can be of use to you in writing an extended definition.

Paradox

LAURENCE PERRINE

Laurence Perrine is professor of English at Southern Meth-
odist University. Born in Toronto in 1915, Perrine received
his B.A. and M.A. degrees from Oberlin College and his
Ph.D. from Yale University. Author of numerous scholarly
articles, Perrine has also edited and written a number of
books, the best known of which is his engaging text Sound
and Sense: An Introduction to Poetry. *First published in*
1956, this textbook has introduced generations of high-
school and college students to the excitement and art of
poetry.

In "Paradox," an excerpt from Sound and Sense, *Perrine*
uses examples to establish his definition.

Aesop tells the tale of a traveler who sought refuge with a   1
Satyr on a bitter winter night. On entering the Satyr's lodging,
he blew on his fingers, and was asked by the Satyr what he
did it for. "To warm them up," he explained. Later, on being
served with a piping hot bowl of porridge, he blew also on
it, and again was asked what he did it for. "To cool it off,"
he explained. The Satyr thereupon thrust him out of doors, for
he would have nothing to do with a man who could blow hot
and cold with the same breath.

A *paradox* is an apparent contradiction that is nevertheless   2
somehow true. It may be either a situation or a statement.
Aesop's tale of the traveler illustrates a paradoxical situation.
As a figure of speech, paradox is a statement. When Alexander
Pope wrote that a literary critic of his time would "damn with

faint praise," he was using a verbal paradox, for how can a man damn by praising?

When we understand all the conditions and circumstances involved in a paradox, we find that what at first seemed impossible is actually entirely plausible and not strange at all. The paradox of the cold hands and hot porridge is not strange to a man who knows that a stream of air directed upon an object of different temperature will tend to bring that object closer to its own temperature. And Pope's paradox is not strange when we realize the *damn* is being used figuratively, and that Pope means only that a too reserved praise may damage an author with the public almost as much as adverse criticism. In a paradoxical statement the contradiction usually stems from one of the words being used figuratively or in more than one sense.

The value of paradox is its shock value. Its seeming impossibility startles the reader into attention and, thus, by the fact of its apparent absurdity, it underscores the truth of what is being said.

FOR STUDY AND DISCUSSION

Questions on Subject

1. What is a paradox? What two types of paradox does Perrine discuss? Discuss any examples of paradox that you have encountered. (Glossary: *Paradox*)
2. Who was Alexander Pope? What does it mean to "damn with faint praise" (2)?
3. What does Perrine mean when he says that "the value of paradox is its shock value"?

Questions on Strategy

1. Why does Perrine retell Aesop's tale before giving a definition of *paradox*? What is the relationship between this tale and the discussion of the shock value of paradox in the final paragraph? (Glossary: *Beginnings*)

2. How does Perrine use Aesop's tale and Pope's statement in defining the concept of paradox? What does Perrine achieve by using two historical rather than contemporary examples of paradox? (Glossary: *Examples*)

Questions on Diction and Vocabulary

1. What is a figure of speech? (Glossary: *Figures of Speech*)
2. Explain what Perrine means when he says that "*damn* is being used figuratively" (3).
3. What, literally, does *piping* mean? Does *piping* mean the same thing in "piping hot bowl of porridge" (1)?
4. Refer to your desk dictionary to determine the meanings of the following words as they are used in this selection: *Satyr* (1), *plausible* (3), *adverse* (3), *underscores* (4).

For Classroom Discussion

As figures of speech, paradox and irony are sometimes confused. What is irony? How does it differ from paradox? Provide several examples of each that illustrate the distinction that you have made. (Glossary: *Paradox* and *Irony*)

(Note: Activities and Writing Suggestions for Definition appear on pages 132–134.)

Alligators in the Sewers and Other Urban Legends

JAN HAROLD BRUNVAND

Jan Harold Brunvand, a professor of English at the University of Utah, teaches courses in folklore. He received his doctoral degree from Indiana University, where he studied with the distinguished folklorist Richard Dorson. Brunvand currently serves as editor of the Journal of American Folklore *and has written, among his other books, the standard introduction to folklore.*

"Alligators in the Sewers and Other Urban Legends" was first published in the June 1980 issue of Psychology Today. *In this essay, Brunvand defines urban legend, and to illustrate his definition he retells a number of the strange stories that are circulating around the country.*

"A man in California saw an ad for an 'almost new' Porsche, in excellent condition—price, $50. He was certain the printers had made a typographical error, but even at $5,000 it would be a bargain, so he hurried to the address to look at the car. A nice-looking woman appeared at the front door. Yes, she had placed the ad. The price was indeed $50. 'The car is in the garage,' she said. 'Come and look at it.' The fellow was overwhelmed. It was a beautiful Porsche and, as the ad promised, nearly new. He asked if he could drive the car around the block. The woman said, 'of course,' and went with him. The Porsche drove like a dream. The young man peeled off $50 and handed it over, somewhat sheepishly. The woman gave him the necessary papers, and the car was his. Finally, the new owner couldn't stand it any longer. He had to know why the woman was selling the Porsche at such a ridiculously low price. Her reply was simple: with a half-smile, she said, 'My husband ran off with his secretary and left a note instructing me to sell the car and send him the money.' "

This story, which has been in circulation for years, turned up 2 in a recent Ann Landers column. It was sent in by a reader who claimed to have seen it in the *Chicago Tribune*. Ann Landers accepted the story as true, and many of her readers probably did also. But when she checked with the *Chicago Tribune*, the paper could find no actual record of it.

The story seems believable at first, but when you stop to 3 think about it, wouldn't a man running off with his secretary do so in his own Porsche? And if not, would he really trust his abandoned wife to sell such a car to help finance his departure?

Many people have heard stories of this kind and accepted 4 them as true accounts of actual experiences. But scholars of contemporary American folklore recognize tales like "The Philanderer's Porsche" as characteristic examples of what they call "urban legends." ("Urban," as used by folklorists in this case, means "modern," and is not specifically related to cities.) Other widely known urban legends have titles such as "The Boyfriend's Death," "The Cat in the Oven," "The Runaway Grandmother," "The Snake in the K-Mart," and "The Solid Cement Cadillac."

Urban legends are realistic stories that are said to have 5 happened recently. Like old legends of lost mines, buried treasure, and ghosts, they usually have an ironic or supernatural twist. They belong to a subclass of folk narratives that (unlike fairy tales) are believed—or at least believable—and (unlike myths) are set in the recent past, involving ordinary human beings rather than extraordinary gods and demigods.

Unlike rumors, which are generally fragmentary or vague 6 reports, legends have a specific narrative quality and tend to attach themselves to different local settings. Although they may explain or incorporate current rumors, legends tend to have a longer life and wider acceptance; rumors flourish and then die out rather quickly. Urban legends circulate, by word of mouth, among the "folk" of modern society, but the mass media frequently help to disseminate and validate them. While they vary in particular details from one telling to another, they preserve a central core of traditional themes. In some instances, these seemingly fresh stories are merely updatings of classic folklore plots, while other urban legends spring directly from recent conditions and then develop their own traditional patterns in repeated retellings. For example, "The Vanishing Hitchhiker," which describes the disappearance of a rider picked up on a highway, has evolved from a 19th-century horse-and-buggy legend into modern variants incorporating freeway travel. A story called "Alligators in the Sewers," on the other hand, goes back no further than the 1930s and seems to be a New York City invention. Often, it begins with people who bring pet baby alligators back from Florida and eventually flush them down the drains.

What most interests the modern folklorist is *why* these stories recur. We suspect that the reasons will tell us something about the character of the society in which they circulate.

The Boyfriend's Death

One genre of urban legend is the horror story, which seems to appeal particularly to American adolescents. Consider the well-known legend that folklorists have named "The Boyfriend's Death." The version below might typically be told in a darkened college dormitory room with fellow students sprawled on the furniture and floor:

> "This happened just a few years ago out on the road that turns off Highway 59 by the Holiday Inn. This couple was parked under a tree out on this road. Well, it got to be time for the girl to be back at the dorm, so she told her boyfriend that they should start back. But the car wouldn't start, so he told her to lock herself in the car and he would go down to the Holiday Inn and call for help. Well, he didn't come back and he didn't come back, and pretty soon she started hearing a scratching noise on the roof of the car. Scratch, scratch . . . scratch, scratch. She got scareder and scareder, but he didn't come back. Finally, when it was almost daylight, some people

came along and stopped and helped her out of the car, and she looked up and there was her bodyfriend hanging from the tree, and his feet were scraping against the roof of the car."

Here is a story that has rapidly achieved nationwide oral 9 circulation, in the process becoming structured in the typical manner of folk narratives. The traditional and fairly stable elements in it are the parked couple, the abandoned girl, the mysterious scratching, the daybreak rescue, and the horrible climax. The precise location, the reason for her abandonment, the nature of the rescuers, and the murder details may vary. For example, the rescuers may be the police, who are either called by the missing teens' parents or simply appear on the scene in the morning to check the car. In a 1969 variant from Maryland, the police utter this warning: "Miss, please get out of the car and walk to the police car with us, but don't look back." Of course the standard rule of folk-narrative plot development now applies: the taboo must be broken. The girl *does* always look back, à la Orpheus in the Underworld, and her hair may turn white from the shock of what she sees.

The style in which such oral narratives are told deserves 10 attention, for a telling that is dramatic, fluid, and possibly quite gripping in actual performance before a sympathetic audience may seem stiff, repetitious, and awkward when simply read. The setting of the legend-telling also plays a vital role, along with the storyteller's vocal and facial expression, gestures, and the audience's reactions.

However, even the bare texts retain some earmarks of effective 11 oral performance. In "The Boyfriend's Death," notice the artful use of repetition (typical of folk-narrative style): "Well, he didn't come back and he didn't come back. . . ." The repeated use of "well" and the building of lengthy sentences with "and" are also hallmarks of oral style that give the narrator control over his performance and tend to squeeze out interruptions or lapses in attention among listeners. The scene that is set for the incident—lonely road, night, a tree looming over a car out of gas—and the sound effects—scratches or bumps on the car—all contribute to the style.

The Pet in the Oven

Probably the ghastliest of these believed horror stories is the one involving a living creature put into an oven, an old legend that recently merged in oral tradition with the cycle of babysitter stories. It appeals most to adolescents, though older people tell it, too.

Folklorists as much as any scholars love to report a new discovery, so it was with understandable pride that Keith Cunningham of Northern Arizona University headlined an article in a recent issue of *Southwest Folklore:* "Hot Dog! Another Urban Belief Tale." Here is how it went:

> "It seems there was an old lady who had been given a microwave oven by her children. After bathing her dog she put it in the microwave to dry it off. Naturally, when she opened the door the dog was cooked from the inside out."

Such tales, said Cunningham, show that "modern technology has a way of getting out of control and wreaking ill instead of good." The legend of the cooked pooch or pussycat has enjoyed a good deal of recent circulation, but it has been around for many years in the form of cautionary tales about the fates of unlucky pets that get themselves into untended gas ovens or clothes dryers.

Beginning in 1976, I began to hear microwave variants: for example, a child "accidentally sprinkles the cat with a hose and puts it into a microwave oven to dry out, whereupon the cat explodes." The idea in the Arizona text of the animal being "cooked from the inside out" is a more accurate description of the molecule-jiggling effect of microwaves on meat than is my description of the pet exploding. People's notions about what would happen if a living creature were caught in a microwave oven are doubtless influenced by a vague fear of the new devices and their mysterious invisible waves.

In spring of 1978, a student in my folklore class at the University of Utah collected a few samples of "scientific" versions of the story, in which technicians who ought to have known better bypassed built-in safety features and operated their laboratory microwave ovens with open doors, thereby cooking their own insides as they stood nearby. But the bulk of her findings were what she called "gross tales"—accounts of ordinary people foolishly putting pet cats, wet dogs, even their own damp heads of hair into home microwave ovens to be dried, but that ended up cooked or exploded. . . .

Many urban legends preserve the basic shock effect of classic 17 ghost stories or horror tales. They play on the fears of physical assault or of contamination. Another group concerns fear of the dead. Some of these deal with the tragic/comic adventures of a person with a corpse on his hands—either a pet cat's or a grandmother's—which is stolen by an innocent, or not so innocent, bystander. For example, in the urban legend of "The Runaway Grandmother," an American family—from Grandma down to toddler—are taking an automobile trip in Mexico when Grandma dies. To make more room in the car (or because of the smell, or because of fear of official inquiries in a foreign country), the family places her corpse on the car-top carrier, wrapped in a blanket or sleeping bag. But before the family makes it back across the border, someone steals either the blanket or the whole car. Neither ever shows up again.

The Solid Cement Cadillac

Another significant group of legends depends on soap-opera 18 plots rather than on scare stories. In these tales, the characters are merely threatened with the discovery of a supposed infidelity or with having their naked bodies exposed, both of which they fear will amount to public proof of their foolishness.

Sometimes the situation is clearly one of dalliance, with 19 someone getting caught in the act—or at least caught in preparing for the act. So realistic are the plots and so ordinary the characters that it seems completely possible not only that such adventures *could* have happened but also that they could in fact happen again to anyone.

I was taken in by one of these stories myself when I was still 20 wet behind my folklorist's ears: I eventually christened it "The Solid Cement Cadillac." One day in the early summer of 1961, proud of my freshly earned Ph.D. in folklore, I lounged on a beach along Lake Michigan with family and friends and day-dreamed about my first teaching job. A neighbor of my parents began to tell us about a funny incident that she said had happened recently to a cement-truck driver in Kalamazoo. Her story soon had my full attention:

> "It seems that the truck driver was delivering a load of wet mix to an address near his own neighborhood one day when he decided to detour slightly and say hello to his wife. When he came in sight of his home, he saw a shiny new Cadillac in the driveway, and so he parked the ready-mix truck and walked around the house to check things out. Voices were heard coming from the kitchen; when he peeped in through the window, there was his wife talking to a strange man. Without checking any further, and certainly without alerting the couple inside, the truck driver proceeded to lower a window of the new Cadillac, and he emptied the entire load of wet cement into it, filling the car completely. But when he got off work that evening and returned home, his tearful wife informed him that the new (now solid cement) car was for him—bought with her own hardearned savings—and that the stranger was merely the local Cadillac dealer who had just delivered the car and was arranging the papers on it with her."

I made a mental note of the story, for even though it seemed to have some details that could be corroborated (police had been called, a wrecking company towed the car away, the name of the cement company had been mentioned), it surely had the ring of other urban legends I had heard and studied. For example, I wondered how one of those big, noisy, ready-mix trucks could have parked right outside a house—let alone unloaded—without attracting attention from the two people who were chatting quietly inside.

Later that summer, I received the first issue of the *Oregon Folklore Bulletin* and read this notice: "An interesting story is presently circulating in all parts of the United States. It is told as if it were right out of last week's newspaper, and concerns a cement-truck driver who stops by his own house for a midmorning cup of coffee while on the way to deliver a load.

But when he drives down his street he notices that there is a flashy car parked in front of his house, and. . . ."

The only variation in the story as reported from Oregon   23 turned out to be that the driver "finds his wife and a strange man in a compromising situation and sees that he is a bit too late to intervene successfully." In the next two issues of the *Oregon Folklore Bulletin*, the editor reported on his findings about the cement-truck driver story. He described "a plethora of versions mailed from all over the country," and in the third issue of the *Bulletin* provided a summary of 43 versions then on file. The majority of the accounts contained supposed authenticating details about police, tow trucks, or newspaper reports, but no really solid documentation was ever offered. The make and model of the car varied, of course, but only two other significant changes were reported: a Utah version had it that the car belonged to the company boss who had come around to set up a surprise party for the driver for faithful service to the company; in Massachusetts the car was said to be one that the wife had just won in a raffle.

American folklorists did not pay much further attention to   24 the story, except to record it regularly from their students and acquaintances. Like many urban legends, it tends to run in unpredictable cycles of popularity. Its continued appeal clearly derives from the belief that philandering spouses should "get what they deserve," a viewpoint tempered with the warning that a person ought to be absolutely sure of the evidence before doing something drastic. Thus, the truck driver, who looks like a decisive, aggressive, he-man hero at first, is shown up finally as an impulsive dummy who jumped to an incomplete conclusion before making his move.

Lady Godiva and the Bare Hiker

Moving from dalliance to simple nudity, let us consider the   25 legend I call "The Nude in the Camper." A man—and it's always a man—is napping in the nude, or nearly so, riding in the back of his own truck camper or trailer.

The Associated Press news wire carried a "true" version of   26 this incident datelined Prince Albert, Saskatchewan, on August 3, 1962; doubtless, many newspapers picked it up. The *Salt Lake Tribune*, for instance, placed it on page one the next day under the headline "Bare Hiker—Bear Alibi":

> "It was really quite simple, an American tourist explained to Royal Canadian Mounted Police who found him wandering along a highway near here clad in his undershorts. His story: His wife was driving the family car while he relaxed in the trailer. She stopped to let some bears cross the road and the husband stepped out to see what the trouble was. His wife drove on. The police drove 70 miles before catching up with the wife and reuniting the couple."

In the many versions of this story, as in "The Runaway Grandmother," tourists suffer an inconvenience while abroad and on the road. The nudity theme takes several further twists and turns in urban legendry. One example that has had re-markable persistence and credibility is "The Nude Housewife." As described in a letter to Ann Landers, the story is about an Ohio woman who was doing her laundry in the basement when . . . 27

> "She impulsively decided to take off her soiled housedress and put it in the machine. Her hair was in rollers, and the pipes overhead were leaking. She spotted her son's football helmet and put it on her head. There she was, stark naked (except for the football helmet), when she heard a cough. The woman turned around and found herself staring into the face of the meter reader. As he headed for the door his comment was, 'I hope your team wins, lady.' "

Some oral versions of this story provide better reasons for the situation: the dress is put into the machine because there are not enough other dirty clothes for a full load, and the surprised intruder is the plumber who was called by the husband to fix those leaking pipes. The characters in such stories, the build-up situations, and the punchlines may change, but never, apparently, does the solid human appeal of being caught with your pants down, a theme as old as Lady Godiva. 28

Tracking Down the Story

A great mystery of folklore research is where oral traditions 29 originate and who invents them. One might expect that, at least in modern folklore, we could come up with answers to such questions, but that is seldom, if ever, the case. Most leads pointing to possible authors or original events lying behind urban legends simply fizzle out.

Whatever their origins, the dissemination process is no 30 mystery. Groups of age-mates, especially adolescents, form one important legend channel; other paths of transmission include gatherings of office workers and club members, or religious, recreational, and regional groups, like the Ozark hill folk or the Pennsylvania Dutch. Some people seem to specialize in knowing every recent rumor or tale and can enliven any coffee break, party, or trip with the latest supposed news. The telling of one episode inspires other people to share what they have read or heard, and in a short time, a lively exchange of details occurs, with new variants often created.

The difficulties in tracing a story can be illustrated by "The 31 Snake at K-Mart," an urban legend involving a modern sub-urban discount store. A dangerous creature is discovered in an unexpected place; this time it's a poisonous snake which supposedly strikes an unaware shopper who is looking at some imported rugs, blankets, or sweaters in the store.

Although there are dozens of oral versions of "The Snake at 32 K-Mart," a news story in the *Dallas Morning News* (1970) illustrates the hopeless circular quest for origins that anyone hoping to track down such an urban legend as this is likely to undergo:

" 'I'd like some information,' a male caller told the *Dallas News* City Desk some weeks ago. It seems he'd heard about a woman who had gone to a local discount store to look at some fur coats imported from Mexico. When the woman put her hand in the coat pocket, she felt a sudden, sharp pain. A few minutes later her arm supposedly had started turning black and blue.

" 'Well,' the man continued, 'they rushed her to the hospital. It seems that pain was a snake in the coat pocket. The woman's arm had to be amputated.'

"The reporter said he'd check the story. About that time a woman called with the same story, only she'd heard the woman had died right in Presbyterian Hospital's emergency ward. Presbyterian Hospital said it had no such case on record.

" 'My brother is a doctor,' another caller explained. 'He's on the staff at Baylor Hospital, and he was present when they brought the woman in.'

"Baylor Hospital said it had no such case on record. Nor did the police or the health department. When the doctor was questioned, he said it wasn't actually he who was present but a friend. The friend explained that he had not been present either, but that he had just overheard two nurses talking about it.

"After about 10 calls from other interested' persons the fur coat turned into some material that had come in from India.

"One man gave the name of the insurance company that was handling the case. The insurance man said it wasn't actually his company, but his next door neighbor's cousin's company.

"Finally, a caller came up with the victim's name. The *News* called and the supposed victim answered the phone. She said she had never been in better health. Someone must have had confused her with someone else, but she had heard the rumor. Only she had heard the snake was found in a basket of fruit."

For a folklorist—unlike a journalist—the purpose of trying to trace an urban legend is not merely to validate or debunk a good story. For us, collecting a story's variations and tracing its disseminations and change through time and across space are only the beginning of an analysis. The larger theme in "The Snake at K-Mart" is the fear of danger or contamination of commercial products, as with "The Mouse in the Coke Bottle" or "The Rat in the Fried Chicken." This theme seems to grow out of the widespread anxiety about a multitude of health risks in our environment, many of them possibly caused by individual or corporate negligence. The legend sounds plausible and serves effectively as a warning against the dangers that may be lurking in terrific bargains, fast-food restaurants, and cheap goods from underdeveloped countries.

Interpreting Urban Legends

Along with the best-known urban legends, which circulate over   34
a wide territory (including other countries) in various well-
wrought versions, there are numerous other fragmentary rumors
and stories going around—sometimes only within a specific
folk group. Some of these are takeoffs on older traditional
themes that come alive again suddenly after years of inactivity.
Others may have intense local or regional life for a time, but
fail to catch on with the general public, usually because they
are too much the esoteric possession of a particular ethnic or
occupational group.

For example, in 1978, several students in my class began   35
reporting the kidnapping of a small child during a family outing
in a large amusement park called Lagoon located just north of
Salt Lake City. It seemed quite believable that an infant or child
could be snatched from the popular and usually crowded park
and whisked away via the nearby freeway.

There were a few variations on the story: some said the child   36
was sold into a black-market adoption ring, while others said
she (never he) had been recognized later as an actor in a kiddy-
porn film. Such a story may have served to explain by what
means there could be such horrible things as kiddy-porn and
black-market adoption rings.

It is tempting to take one or two of the most typical examples   37
of urban legends as inclusive symbols of distinctive aspects of
our recent history. "The Snake in the K-Mart," some have
suggested, draws on our guilt stemming from the war in
Vietnam and implies that the venomous intentions we fear
Asian peoples may feel toward us take the form of revenge via
imported goods. Personally, I see the story simply as a new
twist on the old theme of xenophobia. . . .

Without denying that such themes may be implied, I believe   38
that a great deal of the legends' continuing popularity might be
explained much more simply. Goods *are* imported in quantity
from some countries that have tropical climates: what if a snake
or snake eggs got into them (as insects sometimes stow away
in fruit shipments)? . . . From a literal view, a legend such as
"The Nude in the Camper" may be quite simply about a

common nightmare that could come true. What the nightmare means is another question.

In any age or with any subject, when a skilled oral storyteller 39 begins to play around with such ideas and when members of the audience respond, repeat the stories, and begin to add their own flourishes, such legends will begin to be formed and to circulate. I expect to hear many more examples of the old favorite urban legends in the coming years and to hear many more new ones as well. And I expect that these stories will continue to suggest how people believe things have happened, or how they either hope—or fear—that things *could* happen.

FOR STUDY AND DISCUSSION

Questions on Subject

1. What is an urban legend? How do urban legends differ from rumors?
2. How do urban legends spread through the population?
3. Why are folklorists interested in urban legends?
4. What, according to Brunvand, do urban legends tell us about our national character?

Questions on Strategy

1. How does Brunvand go about defining the term *urban legend*? Review paragraphs 4 through 6, and identify the various techniques he uses.
2. How has Brunvand organized the examples of urban legends in his essay? (Glossary: *Unity*)
3. Brunvand begins his essay with an extended example of an urban legend. What are the advantages or disadvantages of beginning an essay with an extended example? Is Brunvand's beginning effective? (Glossary: *Beginnings*)
4. How specifically does Brunvand make the transition from his introductory example to his definition of *urban legend*? (Glossary: *Transitions*)

Questions on Diction and Vocabulary

1. Explain the allusions that Brunvand makes to "Orpheus in the Underworld" (9) and to "Lady Godiva" (28). (Glossary: *Allusion*)
2. Choose one of the urban legends that Brunvand retells in his essay, and explain what, if anything, is distinctive about its diction and narrative style. (Glossary: *Diction* and *Style*)
3. Refer to your desk dictionary to determine the meanings of the following words as they are used in this selection: *disseminate* (6), *variants* (6), *genre* (8), *dalliance* (19), *plethora* (23), *xenophobia* (37).

For Classroom Discussion

Had you heard of any of the legends Brunvand discusses before reading his essay? Did you believe them? Have you heard any urban legends that Brunvand does not discuss? Are they variations of Brunvand's examples, or are they totally new legends? What makes us so willing to believe these stories?

(Note: Activities and Writing Suggestions for Definition appear on pages 132–134.)

The Barrio

ROBERT RAMIREZ

Born in 1949 in Edinburg, Texas, Robert Ramirez attended the University of Texas in Austin and later took his degree in English and Spanish from Pan American University in Edinburg. Ramirez has worked as a cameraman, reporter, anchorman, and producer for the news team at KGBT-TV in Texas. Presently he is working in the Latin American Division of the Northern Trust Bank in Chicago, Illinois.

In the following essay, Robert Ramirez discusses those characteristics that for him define a Chicano barrio.

The train, its metal wheels squealing as they spin along the silvery tracks, rolls slower now. Through the gaps between the cars blinks a streetlamp, and this pulsing light on a barrio streetcorner beats slower, like a weary heartbeat, until the train shudders to a halt, the light goes out, and the barrio is deep asleep.

Throughout Aztlán (the Nahuatl term meaning "land to the north"), trains grumble along the edges of a sleeping people. From Lower California, through the blistering Southwest, down the Rio Grande to the muddy Gulf, the darkness and mystery of dreams engulf communities fenced off by railroads, canals, and expressways. Paradoxical communities, isolated from the rest of the town by concrete columned monuments of progress, and yet stranded in the past. They are surrounded by change. It eludes their reach, in their own backyards, and the people, unable and unwilling to see the future, or even touch the present, perpetuate the past.

Leaning from the expressway or jolting across the tracks, one enters a different physical world permeated by a different

116

attitude. The physical dimensions are impressive. It is a large section of town which extends for fifteen blocks north and south along the tracks, and then advances eastward, thinning into nothingness beyond the city limits. Within the invisible (yet sensible) walls of the barrio, are many, many people living in too few houses. The homes, however, are much more numerous than on the outside.

Members of the barrio describe the entire area as their home. It is a home, but it is more than this. The barrio is a refuge from the harshness and the coldness of the Anglo world. It is a forced refuge. The leprous people are isolated from the rest of the community and contained in their section of town. The stoical pariahs of the barrio accept their fate, and from the angry seeds of rejection grow the flowers of closeness between outcasts, not the thorns of bitterness and the mad desire to flee. There is no want to escape, for the feeling of the barrio is known only to its inhabitants, and the material needs of life can also be found here.

The *tortillería* fires up its machinery three times a day, producing steaming, round, flat slices of barrio bread. In the winter, the warmth of the tortilla factory is a wool *sarape* in the chilly morning hours, but in the summer, it unbearably toasts every noontime customer.

The *panadería* sends its sweet messenger aroma down the dimly lit street, announcing the arrival of fresh, hot sugary *pan dulce*.

The small corner grocery serves the meal-to-meal needs of customers, and the owner, a part of the neighborhood, willingly gives credit to people unable to pay cash for foodstuffs.

The barbershop is a living room with hydraulic chairs, radio, and television, where old friends meet and speak of life as their salted hair falls aimlessly about them.

The pool hall is a junior level country club where 'chucos, strangers in their own land, get together to shoot pool and rap, while veterans, unaware of the cracking, popping balls on the green felt, complacently play dominoes beneath rudely hung *Playboy* foldouts.

The *cantina* is the night spot of the barrio. It is the country club and the den where the rites of puberty are enacted. Here the young become men. It is in the taverns that a young dude shows his *machismo* through the quantity of beer he can hold, the stories of *rucas* he has had, and his willingness and ability to defend his image against hardened and scarred old lions.

No, there is no frantic wish to flee. It would be absurd to leave the familiar and nervously step into the strange and cold Anglo community when the needs of the Chicano can be met in the barrio.

The barrio is closeness. From the family living unit, familial relationships stretch out to immediate neighbors, down the block, around the corner, and to all parts of the barrio. The feeling of family, a rare and treasurable sentiment, pervades and accounts for the inability of the people to leave. The barrio is this attitude manifested on the countenances of the people, on the faces of their homes, and in the gaiety of their gardens.

The color-splashed homes arrest your eyes, arouse your curiosity, and make you wonder what life scenes are being played out in them. The flimsy, brightly colored, wood-frame houses ignore no neon-brilliant color. Houses trimmed in orange, chartreuse, lime-green, yellow, and mixtures of these and other hues beckon the beholder to reflect on the peculiarity of each home. Passing through this land is refreshing like Brubeck, not narcoticizing like revolting rows of similar houses, which neither offend nor please.

In the evenings, the porches and front yards are occupied with men calmly talking over the noise of children playing baseball in the unpaved extension of the living room, while the women cook supper or gossip with female neighbors as they water the *jardines*. The gardens mutely echo the expressive verses of the colorful houses. The denseness of multicolored plants and trees gives the house the appearance of an oasis or a tropical island hideaway, sheltered from the rest of the world.

Fences are common in the barrio, but they are fences and not the walls of the Anglo community. On the western side of town, the high wooden fences between houses are thick, impenetrable walls, built to keep the neighbors at bay. In the barrio, the fences may be rusty, wire contraptions or thick green shrubs. In either case you can see through them and feel no sense of intrusion when you cross them.

Many lower-income families of the barrio manage to maintain 16
a comfortable standard of living through the communal action
of family members who contribute their wages to the head of
the family. Economic need creates interdependence and closeness. Small barefooted boys sell papers on cool, dark Sunday
mornings, deny themselves pleasantries, and give their earnings
to *mamá*. The older the child, the greater the responsibility to
help the head of the household provide for the rest of the
family.

There are those, too, who for a number of reasons have not 17
achieved a relative sense of financial security. Perhaps it results
from too many children too soon, but it is the homes of these
people and their situation that numbs rather than charms. Their
houses, aged and bent, oozing children, are fissures in the horn
of plenty. Their wooden homes may have brick-pattern asbestos
tile on the outer walls, but the tile is not convincing.

Unable to pay city taxes or incapable of influencing the city 18
to live up to its duty to serve all the citizens, the poorer barrio
families remain trapped in the nineteenth century and survive
as best they can. The backyards have well-worn paths to the
outhouses, which sit near the alley. Running water is considered
a luxury in some parts of the barrio. Decent drainage is usually
unknown, and when it rains, the water stands for days, an
incubator of health hazards and an avoidable nuisance. Streets,
costly to pave, remain rough, rocky trails. Tires do not last long,
and the constant rattling and shaking grind away a car's life
and spread dust through screen windows.

The houses and their *jardines*, the jollity of the people in an 19
adverse world, the brightly feathered alarm clock pecking away
at supper and cautiously eyeing the children playing nearby,
produce a mystifying sensation at finding the noble savage
alive in the twentieth century. It is easy to look at the positive
qualities of life in the barrio, and look at them with a distantly
envious feeling. One wishes to experience the feelings of the
barrio and not the hardships. Remembering the illness, the
hunger, the feeling of time running out on you, the walls, both
real and imagined, reflecting on living in the past, one finds
his envy becoming more elusive, until it has vanished altogether.

Back now beyond the tracks, the train creaks and groans, the 20
cars jostle each other down the track, and as the light begins
its pulsing, the barrio, with all its meanings, greets a new dawn
with yawns and restless stretchings.

FOR STUDY AND DISCUSSION

Questions on Subject

1. What is a barrio? How does it provide for the needs of its Chicano
   inhabitants?
2. Ramirez says, "The feeling of family, a rare and treasurable
   sentiment, pervades and accounts for the inability of the people
   to leave" (12). What evidence does Ramirez give to indicate that
   people might want to leave?
3. What is Ramirez's attitude toward the barrio? In what paragraph
   is his attitude most clearly revealed? Why does he refer to barrios
   as "paradoxical communities" (2)? (Glossary: *Attitude*)

Questions on Strategy

1. In defining the word *barrio*, Ramirez relies heavily on description.
   He describes the physical appearance of the barrio as well as the
   emotions and feelings that the inhabitants have for the barrio.
   Briefly summarize the important physical details and emotional
   associations he provides, and comment on their contribution to
   his definition. (Glossary: *Description*)
2. Ramirez briefly catalogues the commercial and social centers of
   the barrio in paragraphs 5 through 10. How does he make the
   transitions between this section and paragraphs 4 and 11? (Glossary: *Transitions*)
3. Explain Ramirez's use of walls and fences to develop his theme
   of cultural isolation. (Glossary: *Symbol*)
4. For what audience is Ramirez writing? What evidence do you
   find within the essay to support your answer? (Glossary: *Audience*)

Questions on Diction and Vocabulary

1. Identify three of the similes or metaphors that Ramirez uses in
   this essay, and comment on the appropriateness and the effectiveness of each. (Glossary: *Figures of Speech*)

2. In defining barrio, Ramirez uses the words *home, refuge, family, closeness,* and *neighborhood.* What connotations do these words have, and how do the words help to further Ramirez's purposes in the essay? (Glossary: *Connotation*)
3. Refer to your desk dictionary to determine the meanings of the following words as they are used in this selection: *permeated* (3), *stoical* (4), *pariahs* (4), *countenances* (12), *fissures* (17), *elusive* (19).

For Classroom Discussion

It can be argued that the very virtues of the Chicano culture work to keep it isolated from the larger Anglo community in this country. To what extent has this also been true of other minority groups when they have come into contact with the dominant culture? What has been done or is being done in this country to relieve the tensions between cultures? Is it possible for minority groups to enter the dominant society and still retain their ethnic identities?

(Note: Activities and Writing Suggestions for Definition appear on pages 132–134.)

I Want a Wife

JUDY SYFERS

*Born in San Francisco in 1937, Judy Syfers studied painting
at the University of Iowa, where she received her B.F.A.
in 1960. Now a free-lance writer interested in a number
of humanitarian causes, Syfers lives in San Francisco with
her husband and two daughters.*

*In the following essay, which first appeared in the
December 1971 issue of* Ms., *Syfers tells us why she wants
a wife and, in the process, defines a wife.*

I belong to that classification of people known as wives. I am   1
A Wife. And, not altogether incidentally, I am a mother.

Not too long ago a male friend of mine appeared on the   2
scene fresh from a recent divorce. He had one child, who is,
of course, with his ex-wife. He is obviously looking for another
wife. As I thought about him while I was ironing one evening,
it suddenly occurred to me that I, too, would like to have a
wife. Why do I want a wife?

I would like to go back to school so that I can become   3
economically independent, support myself, and, if need be,
support those dependent upon me. I want a wife who will
work and send me to school. And while I am going to school
I want a wife to take care of my children. I want a wife to
keep track of the children's doctor and dentist appointments.
And to keep track of mine, too. I want a wife to make sure
my children eat properly and are kept clean. I want a wife
who will wash the children's clothes and keep them mended.
I want a wife who is a good nurturant attendant to my children,
who arranges for their schooling, makes sure that they have
an adequate social life with their peers, takes them to the park,

the zoo, etc. I want a wife who takes care of the children when they are sick, a wife who arranges to be around when the children need special care, because, of course, I cannot miss classes at school. My wife must arrange to lose time at work and not lose the job. It may mean a small cut in my wife's income from time to time, but I guess I can tolerate that. Needless to say, my wife will arrange and pay for the care of the children while my wife is working.

I want a wife who will take care of *my* physical needs. I 4
want a wife who will keep my house clean. A wife who will pick up after me. I want a wife who will keep my clothes clean, ironed, mended, replaced when need be, and who will see to it that my personal things are kept in their proper place so that I can find what I need the minute I need it. I want a wife who cooks the meals, a wife who is a *good* cook. I want a wife who will plan the menus, do the necessary grocery shopping, prepare the meals, serve them pleasantly, and then do the cleaning up while I do my studying. I want a wife who will care for me when I am sick and sympathize with my pain and loss of time from school. I want a wife to go along when our family takes a vacation so that someone can continue to care for me and my children when I need a rest and change of scene.

I want a wife who will not bother me with rambling com- 5
plaints about a wife's duties. But I want a wife who will listen to me when I feel the need to explain a rather difficult point I have come across in my course of studies. And I want a wife who will type my papers for me when I have written them.

I want a wife who will take care of the details of my social 6
life. When my wife and I are invited out by my friends, I want a wife who will take care of the babysitting arrangements. When I meet people at school that I like and want to entertain, I want a wife who will have the house clean, will prepare a special meal, serve it to me and my friends, and not interrupt when I talk about the things that interest me and my friends. I want a wife who will have arranged that the children are fed and ready for bed before my guests arrive so that the children do not bother us. I want a wife who takes care of the needs of my guests so that they feel comfortable, who makes

sure that they have an ashtray, that they are passed the hors d'oeuvres, that they are offered a second helping of the food, that their wine glasses are replenished when necessary, that their coffee is served to them as they like it. And I want a wife who knows that sometimes I need a night out by myself.

I want a wife who is sensitive to my sexual needs, a wife who makes love passionately and eagerly when I feel like it, a wife who makes sure that I am satisfied. And, of course, I want a wife who will not demand sexual attention when I am not in the mood for it. I want a wife who assumes the complete responsibility for birth control, because I do not want more children. I want a wife who will remain sexually faithful to me so that I do not have to clutter up my intellectual life with jealousies. And I want a wife who understands that *my* sexual needs may entail more than strict adherence to monogamy. I must, after all, be able to relate to people as fully as possible. 7

If, by chance, I find another person more suitable as a wife than the wife I already have, I want the liberty to replace my present wife with another one. Naturally, I will expect a fresh, new life; my wife will take the children and be solely responsible for them so that I am left free. 8

When I am through with school and have a job, I want my wife to quit working and remain at home so that my wife can more fully and completely take care of a wife's duties. 9

My God, who *wouldn't* want a wife? 10

FOR STUDY AND DISCUSSION

Questions on Subject

1. What is Syfers's purpose in defining *wife*? Explain. (Glossary: *Purpose*)

2. What tasks does Syfers assign to a wife? What is her attitude toward these tasks? (Glossary: *Attitude*) In your opinion, is her description of a wife's tasks and responsibilities realistic? Explain.

3. What are the implications of Syfers's definition?

Questions on Strategy

1. What is the function of the short narrative about the author's friend? (Glossary: *Beginnings*)
2. What is the function of the question that ends paragraph 2? the question that concludes the essay? (Glossary: *Endings*)
3. How does the author develop her definition? Do you see any pattern in the way she arranges the list of services she expects from a wife?

Questions on Diction and Vocabulary

1. Syfers carefully avoids using the pronoun *he* or *she* when referring to the wife. Why?
2. What do the phrases "not altogether incidentally" (1) and "of course" (2) tell you about the author's attitude?
3. Refer to your desk dictionary to determine the meanings of the following words as they are used in this selection: *nurturant* (3), *peers* (3), *replenished* (6), *entail* (7), *monogamy* (7).

For Classroom Discussion

As a class, gather the specific information that you might need to write a companion piece to Syfers's essay entitled "I Want a Husband."

(Note: Activities and Writing Suggestions for Definition appear on pages 132–134.)

In Bed

JOAN DIDION

Joan Didion, born in the Sacramento Valley region of California in 1935, was an associate editor at Vogue *and contributing editor to the* National Review *and* The Saturday Evening Post. *Her articles, columns, and essays have appeared in* Mademoiselle, Holiday, The American Scholar, *and* Life. *She has written three novels,* Run River, Play It as It Lays, *and* A Book of Common Prayer, *and two collections of essays,* Slouching Towards Bethlehem *and* The White Album.

In the following selection from The White Album, *Didion reflects on her own experiences with migraine headaches in order to define what migraine is.*

Three, four, sometimes five times a month, I spend the day in bed with a migraine headache, insensible to the world around me. Almost every day of every month, between these attacks, I feel the sudden irrational irritation and the flush of blood into the cerebral arteries which tell me that migraine is on its way, and I take certain drugs to avert its arrival. If I did not take the drugs, I would be able to function perhaps one day in four. The physiological error called migraine is, in brief, central to the given of my life. When I was 15, 16, even 25, I used to think that I could rid myself of this error by simply denying it, character over chemistry. "Do you have headaches *sometimes? frequently? never?*" the application forms would demand. "Check one." Wary of the trap, wanting whatever it was that the successful circumnavigation of that particular form could bring (a job, a scholarship, the respect of mankind and the grace of God), I would check one. *"Sometimes,"* I would lie. That in fact I spent one or two days a week almost unconscious with pain seemed a shameful secret, evidence not merely of some chemical inferiority but of all my bad attitudes, unpleasant tempers, wrongthink.

For I had no brain tumor, no eyestrain, no high blood 2 pressure, nothing wrong with me at all: I simply had migraine headaches, and migraine headaches were, as everyone who did not have them knew, imaginary. I fought migraine then, ignored the warnings it sent, went to school and later to work in spite of it, sat through lectures in Middle English and presentations to advertisers with involuntary tears running down the right side of my face, threw up in washrooms, stumbled home by instinct, emptied ice trays onto my bed and tried to freeze the pain in my right temple, wished only for a neurosurgeon who would do a lobotomy on house call, and cursed my imagination.

It was a long time before I began thinking mechanistically 3 enough to accept migraine for what it was: something with which I would be living, the way some people live with diabetes. Migraine is something more than the fancy of a neurotic imagination. It is an essentially hereditary complex of symptoms, the most frequently noted but by no means the most unpleasant of which is a vascular headache of blinding severity, suffered by a surprising number of women, a fair number of men (Thomas Jefferson had migraine, and so did Ulysses S. Grant, the day he accepted Lee's surrender), and by some unfortunate children as young as two years old. (I had my first when I was eight. It came on during a fire drill at the Columbia School in Colorado Springs, Colorado. I was taken first home and then to the infirmary at Peterson Field, where my father was stationed. The Air Corps doctor prescribed an enema.) Almost anything can trigger a specific attack of migraine: stress, allergy, fatigue, an abrupt change in barometric pressure, a contretemps over a parking ticket. A flashing light. A fire drill. One inherits, of course, only the predisposition. In other words I spent yesterday in bed with a headache not merely because of my bad attitudes, unpleasant tempers and wrongthink, but because both my grandmothers had migraine, my father has migraine and my mother has migraine.

No one knows precisely what it is that is inherited. The chemistry of migraine, however, seems to have some connection with the nerve hormone named serotonin, which is naturally present in the brain. The amount of serotonin in the blood falls sharply at the onset of migraine, and one migraine drug, methysergide, or Sansert, seems to have some effect on serotonin. Methysergide is a derivative of lysergic acid (in fact Sandoz Pharmaceuticals first synthesized LSD-25 while looking for a migraine cure), and its use is hemmed about with so many contraindications and side effects that most doctors prescribe it only in the most incapacitating cases. Methysergide, when it is prescribed, is taken daily, as a preventive; another preventive which works for some people is old-fashioned ergotamine tartrate, which helps to constrict the swelling blood vessels during the "aura," the period which in most cases precedes the actual headache.

Once an attack is under way, however, no drug touches it. Migraine gives some people mild hallucinations, temporarily blinds others, shows up not only as a headache but as a gastrointestinal disturbance, a painful sensitivity to all sensory stimuli, an abrupt overpowering fatigue, a strokelike aphasia, and a crippling inability to make even the most routine connections. When I am in a migraine aura (for some people the aura lasts fifteen minutes, for others several hours), I will drive through red lights, lose the house keys, spill whatever I am holding, lose the ability to focus my eyes or frame coherent sentences, and generally give the appearance of being on drugs, or drunk. The actual headache, when it comes, brings with it chills, sweating, nausea, a debility that seems to stretch the very limits of endurance. That no one dies of migraine seems, to someone deep into an attack, an ambiguous blessing.

My husband also has migraine, which is unfortunate for him but fortunate for me: perhaps nothing so tends to prolong an attack as the accusing eye of someone who has never had a headache. "Why not take a couple of aspirin," the unafflicted will say from the doorway, or "I'd have a headache, too, spending a beautiful day like this inside with all the shades drawn." All of us who have migraine suffer not only from the attacks themselves but from this common conviction that we are perversely refusing to cure ourselves by taking a couple of aspirin, that we are making ourselves sick, that we "bring it on ourselves." And in the most immediate sense, the sense of why we have a headache this Tuesday and not last Thursday, of course we often do. There certainly is what doctors call a "migraine personality," and that personality tends to be ambitious, inward, intolerant of error, rather rigidly organized, perfectionist. "You don't look like a migraine personality," a doctor once said to me. "Your hair's messy. But I suppose you're a compulsive housekeeper." Actually my house is kept even more negligently than my hair, but the doctor was right nonetheless: perfectionism can also take the form of spending most of a week writing and rewriting and not writing a single paragraph.

But not all perfectionists have migraine, and not all migrain-   7
ous people have migraine personalities. We do not escape heredity. I have tried in most of the available ways to escape my own migrainous heredity (at one point I learned to give myself two daily injections of histamine with a hypodermic needle, even though the needle so frightened me that I had to close my eyes when I did it), but I still have migraine. And I have learned now to live with it, learned when to expect it, how to outwit it, even how to regard it, when it does come, as more friend than lodger. We have reached a certain understanding, my migraine and I. It never comes when I am in real trouble. Tell me that my house is burned down, my husband has left me, that there is gunfighting in the streets and panic in the banks, and I will not respond by getting a headache. It comes instead when I am fighting not an open but a guerrilla war with my own life, during weeks of small household confusions, lost laundry, unhappy help, canceled appointments, on days when the telephone rings too much and I get no work done and the wind is coming up. On days like that my friend comes uninvited.

And once it comes, now that I am wise in its ways, I no   8
longer fight it. I lie down and let it happen. At first every small apprehension is magnified, every anxiety a pounding terror. Then the pain comes, and I concentrate only on that. Right there is the usefulness of migraine, there in that imposed yoga,

the concentration on the pain. For when the pain recedes, ten or twelve hours later, everything goes with it, all the hidden resentments, all the vain anxieties. The migraine has acted as a circuit breaker, and the fuses have emerged intact. There is a pleasant convalescent euphoria. I open the windows and feel the air, eat gratefully, sleep well. I notice the particular nature of a flower in a glass on the stair landing. I count my blessings.

FOR STUDY AND DISCUSSION

Questions on Subject

1. What is migraine? Why, according to Didion, do people get migraine?
2. What is a "migraine personality" (6)?
3. Why do people who suffer from migraine feel guilty about their affliction? How did Didion overcome her feelings of guilt?
4. In what ways has Didion attempted to deal with the pain of migraine? How effective have these various methods been?
5. Now that she has come to an understanding of migraine, what value does Didion see in it?

Questions on Strategy

1. Explain the techniques that Didion uses to define migraine.
2. What is Didion's tone in this essay? (Glossary: *Tone*)
3. How would you characterize Didion's attitude toward her subject? (Glossary: *Attitude*)
4. What does Didion, a migraine sufferer herself, bring to our understanding of the affliction that a dictionary or a medical textbook would not?
5. Didion could have titled her essay differently, using, for example, any one of the following: "Migraine," "The Migraine Headache," "Coping," "Coping with Migraines." Explain what would have been gained or lost with each alternate title. (Glossary: *Title*)

Questions on Diction and Vocabulary

1. What is an "aura" (4)? Does Didion adhere to the strict dictionary definition of the term? If not, how does her use of the term differ? (Glossary: *Connotation/Denotation*)

2. Where does Didion use personification to indicate her familiarity with migraine? (Glossary: *Personification*)

3. In the context of this essay, comment on the appropriateness of each of the following possible substitutions for Didion's diction. Which word is better in each case? Why? (Glossary: *Appropriateness*)

   a. *oblivious* for *insensible* (1)
   b. *unreasonable* for *irrational* (1)
   c. *sick* for *neurotic* (3)
   d. *tendency* for *predisposition* (3)
   e. *belief* for *conviction* (6)
   f. *joy* for *euphoria* (8)

4. Didion says, "The migraine has acted as a circuit breaker, and the fuses have emerged intact" (8). Identify the two figures of speech in this sentence, and explain how they work. (Glossary: *Figures of Speech*)

5. Refer to your desk dictionary to determine the meanings of the following words as they are used in this selection: *cerebral* (1), *physiological* (1), *circumnavigation* (1), *vascular* (3), *contretemps* (3), *derivative* (4), *aphasia* (5), *guerrilla* (7).

For Classroom Discussion

In writing about migraine Didion says that "nothing so tends to prolong an attack as the accusing eye of someone who has never had a headache" (6). Sufferers of other afflictions have experienced similar feelings. What is there about human nature that causes nonsufferers so often to feel that the sick have brought their troubles on themselves?

(Note: Activities and Writing Suggestions for Definition appear on pages 132–134.)

Activities and Writing Suggestions for Definition

ACTIVITIES

1. One way of defining a term is to place it in a class of similar terms and then show how it differs from the other items in that class; for example:

WORD	CLASS	CHARACTERISTICS
A *watch*	is a *small timepiece*	*designed to be carried in the pocket or worn.*
Semantics	is an *area of linguistics*	*concerned with the study of the meanings of words.*

Certainly such definitions are not complete, and one could write an entire paragraph, essay, or book to define these terms more fully. Nonetheless, this process is useful both for thinking and for writing.

Place each of the following terms in a class, and then write a brief statement differentiating each term from other items in its class.

   a. a paper clip
   b. a pamphlet
   c. anxiety
   d. a bicycle

2. Dictionary makers often have to write definitions for new words based on the ways those words are used. After examining the following six sentences, write a brief (fewer than twenty-five words) definition of a *lasto.*

   a. A *lasto* is sometimes difficult to clean.
   b. Mary put too much food into her *lasto,* and it overflowed.
   c. A knife will do many of the jobs that a *lasto* will do but cannot do them as efficiently.
   d. The blades of a *lasto* must be bent for it to work well.
   e. Some *lastos* have only three speeds, whereas others have as many as ten speeds.
   f. A *lasto* can be purchased at any hardware or housewares store.

3. Without referring to a dictionary, define a common object such as

an apple or an orange. Once you have completed your definition, compare it with a dictionary definition. What conclusions can you draw? Explain.

4. Every generation develops its own slang, which enlivens the speech and writing of those who use it. Ironically, however, no generation can arrive at a consensus definition of even its most popular slang terms (for example, *cool, dude, groovy,* and the like). Select a slang term that you use frequently, and write a one- or two-paragraph essay in which you define the term. Read your definition aloud in class. Do the other members of your class agree with your definition?

WRITING SUGGESTIONS

1. Some of the most pressing social issues in American life today are further complicated by imprecise definition of critical terms. Various medical cases, for example, have brought worldwide attention to the legal and medical definitions of the word *death.* Debates continue about the meanings of other controversial words such as:

a. morality	g. drug
b. minority (ethnic)	h. censorship
c. alcoholism	i. remedial
d. cheating	j. insanity
e. pornography	k. monopoly (business)
f. kidnapping	l. literacy

Select one of these words, and write an essay in which you discuss not only the definition of the term but also the problems associated with defining it.

2. Write an essay in which you define one of the words listed below by telling not only what it *is* but also what it *is not.* (For example, it has been said that "poetry is that which cannot be expressed in any other way.") Remember, however, that defining by negation does not relieve you of the responsibility of defining the term in other ways as well.

a. poetry	d. happiness
b. harmony	e. democracy
c. fear	f. poverty

3. In his book *The Second Sin,* psychiatrist Thomas Szasz makes the following observations about contemporary American life:
   a. The prevention of parenthood is called "planned parenthood."
   b. Policemen receive "bribes"; politicians receive "campaign contributions."

c. Homicide by physicians is called "euthanasia."
d. Marijuana and heroin are sold by "pushers"; cigarettes and alcohol are sold by "businessmen."
e. Imprisonment by psychiatrists is called "mental hospitalization."

Select one of Szasz's comments, and write a multiparagraph essay in which you discuss ways in which people manipulate words and meanings to suit their particular needs.

4. In the process of defining a particular term or concept, several of the writers in this section use illustrative and engaging narration. Write a narrative in which you recount an experience you have had that has given you new insight into or understanding of a common human feeling. You may find the following suggestions useful:

a. disappointment
b. boredom
c. surprise
d. tension
e. guilt
f. success

Be sure that your narrative leads the reader to a clarification of the term.

5

CLASSIFICATION

To *classify* is to arrange things, to sort them into categories according to their differing characteristics so as to make them more manageable and understandable for the writer and the reader. Every classification has a practical purpose, and often that purpose involves the decision-making process. For example, in selecting a book to buy, you could classify books into the categories hardcover and paperback. Similarly, you could classify television programs into the categories children's programs, family programs, and adult programs and, based on your classification, determine which network is more interested in airing children's programs.

In establishing a classification, you first analyze your subject, then divide it into categories, and finally classify individual items according to those categories. For example, a student wished to determine whether the socioeconomic status of a group of people was related to their voting behavior. She decided to focus her study on the fifteen families living on Maple Street. First, she established three subclasses or categories based on socioeconomic status (low income, middle income, high income) and after confidential interviews classified each family according to its income. Next she talked with each of the families to determine if at least one member of each household had voted in at least one state or federal election during the previous four years. She then classified each of the families in the three socioeconomic groups as either voting or nonvoting.

During the process of classifying the information from her study, the student found it helpful to construct the following classification diagram:

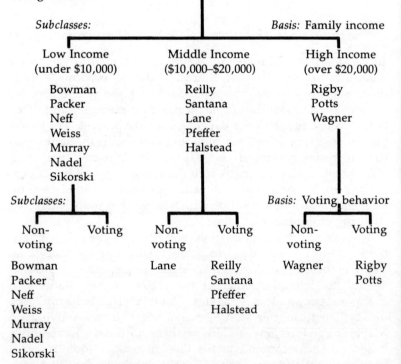

Class: The 15 families on Maple Street

Purpose: To group the families according to socioeconomic status in order to study the relationship between socioeconomic status and voting behavior.

Subclasses: *Basis:* Family income

Low Income (under $10,000)	Middle Income ($10,000–$20,000)	High Income (over $20,000)
Bowman	Reilly	Rigby
Packer	Santana	Potts
Neff	Lane	Wagner
Weiss	Pfeffer	
Murray	Halstead	
Nadel		
Sikorski		

Subclasses: *Basis:* Voting behavior

Non-voting	Voting	Non-voting	Voting	Non-voting	Voting
Bowman		Lane	Reilly	Wagner	Rigby
Packer			Santana		Potts
Neff			Pfeffer		
Weiss			Halstead		
Murray					
Nadel					
Sikorski					

Conclusion: On Maple Street there seems to be a relationship between socioeconomic status and voting behavior: the low-income families are nonvoters.

You, too, may find such a diagram helpful both as you work out your classification system and as you write your essay. The classification diagram allows you to visualize the classification system and its essential components: *class, purpose, basis, subclasses,* and *conclusion*.

Depending on your particular purpose, different bases of classification may be used to classify the same group of items. To determine the makeup of the student body, you might classify students according to college or program, major, class level, or sex. The Director of Admissions interested in the geographical distribution of the student body might classify students according to state or country of origin. The Director of Financial Aid might classify students on the basis of family income or economic resources. And the basketball coach might be interested in classifying prospective players by height or speed.

Whatever your purpose in writing a classification essay, you should be guided by the following rules:

1. *Divide your subject into categories that are mutually exclusive.* An item can belong to only *one* category. For example, it would be unsatisfactory to classify students as men, women, and athletes.
2. *Make your classification complete.* Your categories should account for *all* items in a subject class. In classifying students on the basis of geographical origin, it would be inappropriate to consider only home states. Such a classification would be incomplete because it would not account for foreign students.
3. *Be sure that you have a purpose and that your basis of classification is appropriate.* It would not be helpful to classify students on the basis of what toothpaste they use unless your purpose gave you a clear reason for doing so.
4. *Be sure to state clearly the conclusion that your classification leads you to draw.*

In the essays in this section, the authors use classification to make their topics more understandable and meaningful for readers. For example, Peter Farb discusses the various types of abusive names children commonly call one another, Paul Stevens analyzes and classifies successful advertising slogans, and Eric Berne establishes a classification system for people according to body shapes and personality types.

Name-Calling

PETER FARB

Since his undergraduate years at Vanderbilt University, Peter Farb (1929–1980) had an intense interest in language and the role it plays in human behavior. His fascination with the languages of North American Indians is reflected in his book Man's Rise to Civilization as Shown by the Indians of North America. *Farb was a consultant to the Smithsonian Institution, a curator of the Riverside Museum in New York City, and a visiting lecturer in English at Yale University. With George Armelagos, Farb wrote* Consuming Passions: The Anthropology of Eating, *which was published posthumously in 1980.*

In this essay, taken from Word Play: What Happens When People Talk *(1973), Farb classifies the names children commonly call one another.*

The insults spoken by adults are usually more subtle than the simple name-calling used by children, but children's insults make obvious some of the verbal strategies people carry into adult life. Most parents engage in wishful thinking when they regard name-calling as good-natured fun which their children will soon grow out of. Name-calling is not good-natured and children do not grow out of it; as adults they merely become more expert in its use. Nor is it true that "sticks and stones may break my bones, but names will never hurt me." Names can hurt very much because children seek out the victim's true weakness, then jab exactly where the skin is thinnest. Name-calling can have a major impact on a child's feelings about his identity, and it can sometimes be devastating to his psychological development.

1

Almost all examples of name-calling by children fall into four categories:

1. Names based on physical peculiarities, such as deformities, use of eyeglasses, racial characteristics, and so forth. A child may be called *Flattop* because he was born with a misshapen skull—or, for obvious reasons, *Fat Lips, Gimpy, Four Eyes, Peanuts, Fatso, Kinky,* and so on.
2. Names based on a pun or parody of the child's own name. Children with last names like Fitts, McClure, and Farb usually find them converted to *Shits, Manure,* and *Fart.*
3. Names based on social relationships. Examples are *Baby* used by a sibling rival or *Chicken Shit* for someone whose courage is questioned by his social group.
4. Names based on mental traits—such as *Clunkhead, Dummy, Jerk,* and *Smartass.*

These four categories were listed in order of decreasing offensiveness to the victims. Children regard names based on physical peculiarities as the most cutting, whereas names based on mental traits are, surprisingly, not usually regarded as very offensive. Most children are very vulnerable to names that play upon the child's rightful name—no doubt because one's name is a precious possession, the mark of a unique identity and one's masculinity or femininity. Those American Indian tribes that had the custom of never revealing true names undoubtedly avoided considerable psychological damage.

FOR STUDY AND DISCUSSION

Questions on Subject

1. Why does Farb feel that name-calling should not be dismissed lightly?
2. Farb states that "children regard names based on physical peculiarities as the most cutting" (2). Why do you suppose this is true?

Questions on Strategy

1. On what basis does Farb establish his four categories of children's insults? On what basis does he rank them?
2. What is Farb's major contention in this selection, and where is it revealed? Why does Farb choose to classify children's insults? (Glossary: *Thesis* and *Purpose*)
3. List examples of name-calling that you recall from your own childhood. Classify the items on your list according to Farb's system. Are there any items on your list that do not fit into one of his four categories? Explain.

Questions on Diction and Vocabulary

1. Why does Farb refer to insults as "verbal strategies" (1)?
2. Refer to your desk dictionary to determine the meanings of the following words as they are used in this selection: *subtle* (1), *peculiarities* (2), *deformities* (2), *sibling* (2), *unique* (2).

For Classroom Discussion

Discuss the validity of Farb's assertion that "name-calling is not good-natured and children do not grow out of it; as adults they merely become more expert in its use" (1).

(Note: Activities and Writing Suggestions for Classification appear on pages 172–175.)

Weasel Words: God's Little Helpers

PAUL STEVENS

Paul Stevens is the pen name of Carl Wrighter, an advertising copywriter who works for a major advertising firm in New York City. Stevens, a graduate of Syracuse University, was a teacher of English and music before pursuing a career in advertising.

In 1972 Stevens wrote I Can Sell You Anything, *a bristling exposé of questionable advertising language and techniques. In this selection from his book, Stevens classifies successful advertising slogans.*

First of all, you know what a weasel is, right? It's a small, slimy animal that eats small birds and other animals, and is especially fond of devouring vermin. Now, consider for a moment the kind of winning personality he must have. I mean, what kind of a guy would get his jollies eating rats and mice? Would you invite him to a party? Take him home to meet your mother? This is one of the slyest and most cunning of all creatures; sneaky, slippery, and thoroughly obnoxious. And so it is with great and warm personal regard for these attributes that we humbly award this King of All Devious the honor of bestowing his name upon our golden sword: the weasel word.

A weasel word is "a word used in order to evade or retreat from a direct or forthright statement or position" (Webster). In other words, if we can't say it, we'll weasel it. And, in fact, a weasel word has become more than just an evasion or retreat. We've trained our weasels. They can do anything. They can make you hear things that aren't being said, accept as truths things that have only been implied, and believe things that have only been suggested. Come to think of it, not only do we have our weasels trained, but they, in turn, have got you trained. When *you* hear a weasel word, you automatically hear the implication. Not the real meaning, but the meaning *it* wants *you* to hear. So if you're ready for a little re-education, let's take a good look under a strong light at the two kinds of weasel words.

Words That Mean Things They Really Don't Mean

Help

That's it. "Help." It means "aid" or "assist." Nothing more.   3
Yet, "help" is the one single word which, in all the annals of advertising, has done the most to say something that couldn't be said. Because "help" is the great qualifier; once you say it, you can say almost anything after it. In short, "help" has helped help us the most.

> *Helps keep you young*
> *Helps prevent cavities*
> *Helps keep your house germ-free*

"Help" qualifies everything. You've never heard anyone say,   4
"This product will keep you young," or "This toothpaste will positively prevent cavities for all time." Obviously, we can't say anything like that, because there aren't any products like that made. But by adding that one little word, "help," in front, we can use the strongest language possible afterward. And the most fascinating part of it is, you are immune to the word. You literally don't hear the word "help." You only hear what comes after it. And why not? That's strong language, and likely to be much more important to you than the silly little word at the front end.

I would guess that 75 percent of all advertising uses the   5
word "help." Think, for a minute, about how many times each day you hear these phrases:

> *Helps stop . . .*
> *Helps prevent . . .*

Helps fight . . .
Helps overcome . . .
Helps you feel . . .
Helps you look . . .

I could go on and on, but so could you. Just as a simple exercise, call it homework if you wish, tonight when you plop down in front of the boob tube for your customary three and a half hours of violence and/or situation comedies, take a pad and pencil, and keep score. See if you can count how many times the word "help" comes up during the commercials. Instead of going to the bathroom during the pause before Marcus Welby operates, or raiding the refrigerator prior to witnessing the Mod Squad wipe out a nest of dope pushers, stick with it. Count the "helps," and discover just how dirty a four-letter word can be.

Like

Coming in second, but only losing by a nose, is the word "like," used in comparison. Watch:

It's like getting one bar free
Cleans like a white tornado
It's like taking a trip to Portugal

Okay. "Like" is a qualifier, and is used in much the same way as "help." But "like" is also a comparative element, with a very specific purpose; we use "like" to get you to stop thinking about the product per se, and to get you thinking about something that is bigger or better or different from the product we're selling. In other words, we can make you believe that the product is more than it is by likening it to something else.

Take a look at that first phrase, straight out of recent Ivory Soap advertising. On the surface of it, they tell you that four bars of Ivory cost about the same as three bars of most other soaps. So, if you're going to spend a certain amount of money on soap, you can buy four bars instead of three. Therefore, it's like getting one bar free. Now, the question you have to ask yourself is, "Why the weasel? Why do they say 'like'? Why don't they just come out and say, 'You get one bar free'?" The answer is, of course, that for one reason or another, you really don't. Here are two possible reasons. One: sure, you get four bars, but in terms of the actual amount of soap that you get, it may very well be the same as in three bars of another brand. Remember, Ivory has a lot of air in it—that's what makes it float. And air takes up room. Room that could otherwise be occupied by more soap. So, in terms of pure product, the amount of actual soap in four bars of Ivory may be only as much as the actual amount of soap in three bars of most others. That's why we can't—or won't—come out with a straightforward declaration such as, "You get 25 percent more soap," or "Buy three bars, and get the fourth one free."

Reason number two: the actual cost and value of the product.   9
Did it ever occur to you that Ivory may simply be a cheaper soap to make and, therefore, a cheaper soap to sell? After all, it doesn't have any perfume or hexachlorophene, or other additives that can raise the cost of manufacturing. It's plain, simple, cheap soap, and so it can be sold for less money while still maintaining a profit margin as great as more expensive soaps. By way of illustrating this, suppose you were trying to decide whether to buy a Mercedes-Benz or a Ford. Let's say the Mercedes cost $7,000, and the Ford $3,500. Now the Ford salesman comes up to you with this deal: as long as you're considering spending $7,000 on a car, buy my Ford for $7,000 and I'll give you a second Ford, free! Well, the same principle can apply to Ivory: as long as you're considering spending 35 cents on soap, buy my cheaper soap, and I'll give you more of it.

I'm sure there are other reasons why Ivory uses the weasel   10
"like." Perhaps you've thought of one or two yourself. That's good. You're starting to think.

Now, what about that wonderful white tornado? Ajax pulled   11
that one out of the hat some eight years ago, and you're still buying it. It's a classic example of the use of the word "like" in which we can force you to think, not about the product itself, but about something bigger, more exciting, certainly more powerful than a bottle of fancy ammonia. The word

"like" is used here as a transfer word, which gets you away from the obvious—the odious job of getting down on your hands and knees and scrubbing your kitchen floor—and into the world of fantasy, where we can imply that this little bottle of miracles will supply all the elbow grease you need. Isn't that the name of the game? The whirlwind activity of the tornado replacing the whirlwind motion of your arm? Think about the swirling of the tornado, and all the work it will save you. Think about the power of that devastating windstorm; able to lift houses, overturn cars, and now, pick the dirt up off your floor. And we get the license to do it simply by using the word "like."

It's a copywriter's dream, because we don't have to substantiate anything. When we compare our product to "another leading brand," we'd better be able to prove what we say. But how can you compare ammonia to a windstorm? It's ludicrous. It can't be done. The whole statement is so ridiculous it couldn't be challenged by the government or the networks. So it went on the air, and it worked. Because the little word "like" let us take you out of the world of reality, and into your own fantasies.

Speaking of fantasies, how about that trip to Portugal? Mateus Rosé is actually trying to tell you that you will be transported clear across the Atlantic Ocean merely by sipping their wine. "Oh, come on," you say. "You don't expect me to believe that." Actually, we don't expect you to believe it. But we do expect you to get our meaning. This is called "romancing the product," and it is made possible by the dear little "like." In this case, we deliberately bring attention to the word, and we ask you to join us in setting reality aside for a moment. We take your hand and gently lead you down the path of moonlit nights, graceful dancers, and mysterious women. Are we saying that these things are all contained inside our wine? Of course not. But what we mean is, our wine is part of all this, and with a little help from "like," we'll get you to feel that way, too. So don't think of us as a bunch of peasants squashing a bunch of grapes. As a matter of fact, don't think of us at all. Feel with us.

"Like" is a virus that kills. You'd better get immune to it.

Other Weasels

"Help" and "like" are the two weasels so powerful that they can stand on their own. There are countless other words, not quite so potent, but equally effective when used in conjunction with our two basic weasels, or with each other. Let me show you a few.

VIRTUAL *or* VIRTUALLY.   How many times have you responded to an ad that said:

> *Virtually trouble-free . . .*
> *Virtually foolproof . . .*
> *Virtually never needs service . . .*

Ever remember what "virtual" means? It means "in essence or effect, but not in fact." Important—"but not in fact." Yet today the word "virtually" is interpreted by you as meaning "almost or just about the same as. . . ." Well, gang, it just isn't true. "Not," in fact, means not, in fact. I was scanning, rather longingly I must confess, through the brochure Chevrolet publishes for its Corvette, and I came to this phrase: "The seats in the 1972 Corvette are virtually handmade." They had me, for a minute. I almost took the bait of that lovely little weasel. I almost decided that those seats were just about completely handmade. And then I remembered. Those seats were not, *in fact*, handmade. Remember, "virtually" means "not, in fact," or you will, in fact, get sold down the river.

ACTS *or* WORKS.   These two action words are rarely used alone, and are generally accompanied by "like." They need help to work, mostly because they are verbs, but their implied meaning is deadly, nonetheless. Here are the key phrases:

> *Acts like . . .*
> *Acts against . . .*
> *Works like . . .*
> *Works against . . .*
> *Works to prevent* (or *help prevent*) *. . .*

You see what happens? "Acts" or "works" brings an action to the product that might not otherwise be there. When we say that a certain cough syrup "acts on the cough control center," the implication is that the syrup goes to this mysterious organ and immediately makes it better. But the implication here far exceeds what the truthful promise should be. An act is simply a deed. So the claim "acts on" simply means it performs a deed on. What that deed is, we may never know.

The rule of thumb is this: if we can't say "cures" or "fixes" or use any other positive word, we'll nail you with "acts like" or "works against," and get you thinking about something else. Don't.

Miscellaneous Weasels

CAN BE. This is for comparison, and what we do is to find an announcer who can really make it sound positive. But keep your ears open. "Crest can be of significant value when used in . . . ," etc., is indicative of an ideal situation, and most of us don't live in ideal situations.

UP TO. Here's another way of expressing an ideal situation. Remember the cigarette that said it was aged, or "cured for up to eight long, lazy weeks"? Well, that could, and should, be interpreted as meaning that the tobaccos used were cured anywhere from one hour to eight weeks. We like to glamorize the ideal situation; it's up to you to bring it back to reality.

AS MUCH AS. More of the same. "As much as 20 percent greater mileage" with our gasoline again promises the ideal, but qualifies it.

REFRESHES, COMFORTS, TACKLES, FIGHTS, COMES ON. Just a handful of the same action weasels, in the same category as "acts" and "works," though not as frequently used. The way to complete the thought here is to ask the simple question, "How?" Usually, you won't get an answer. That's because, usually, the weasel will run and hide.

FEEL *or* THE FEEL OF. This is the first of our subjective weasels.

When we deal with a subjective word, it is simply a matter of opinion. In our opinion, Naugehyde has the feel of real leather. So we can say it. And, indeed, if you were to touch leather, and then touch Naugehyde, you may very well agree with us. But that doesn't mean it is real leather, only that it feels the same. The best way to handle subjective weasels is to complete the thought yourself, by simply saying, "But it isn't." At least that way you can remain grounded in reality.

THE LOOK OF *or* LOOKS LIKE. "Look" is the same as "feel," 24 our subjective opinion. Did you ever walk into a Woolworth's and see those $29.95 masterpieces hanging in their "Art Gallery"? "The look of a real oil painting," it will say. "But it isn't," you will now reply. And probably be $29.95 richer for it.

Words That Have No Specific Meaning

If you have kids, then you have all kinds of breakfast cereals 25 in the house. When I was a kid, it was Rice Krispies, the breakfast cereal that went snap, crackle, and pop. (One hell of a claim for a product that is supposed to offer nutritional benefits.) Or Wheaties, the breakfast of champions, whatever that means. Nowadays, we're forced to a confrontation with Quisp, Quake, Lucky Stars, Cocoa-Puffs, Clunkers, Blooies, Snarkles and Razzmatazz. And they all have one thing in common: they're all "fortified." Some are simply "fortified with vitamins," while others are specifically "fortified with vitamin D," or some other letter. But what does it all mean?

"Fortified" means "added on to." But "fortified," like so 26 many other weasel words of indefinite meaning, simply doesn't tell us enough. If, for instance, a cereal were to contain one unit of vitamin D, and the manufacturers added some chemical which would produce two units of vitamin D, they could then claim that the cereal was "fortified with twice as much vitamin D." So what? It would still be about as nutritional as sawdust.

The point is, weasel words with no specific meaning don't tell us enough, but we have come to accept them as factual 27 statements closely associated with something good that has been done to the product. Here's another example.

Enriched

We use this one when we have a product that starts out with nothing. You mostly find it in bread, where the bleaching process combined with the chemicals used as preservatives renders the loaves totally void of anything but filler. So the manufacturer puts a couple of drops of vitamins into the batter, and presto! It's enriched. Sounds great when you say it. Looks great when you read it. But what you have to determine is, is it really great? Figure out what information is missing, and then try to supply that information. The odds are, you won't. Even the breakfast cereals that are playing it straight, like Kellogg's Special K, leave something to be desired. They tell you what vitamins you get, and how much of each in one serving. The catch is, what constitutes a serving? They say, one ounce. So now you have to whip out your baby scale and weigh one serving. Do you have any idea how much that is? Maybe you do. Maybe you don't care. Okay, so you polish off this mound of dried stuff, and now what? You have ostensibly received the minimum, repeat, minimum dosage of certain vitamins for the day. One day. And you still have to go find the vitamins you didn't get. Try looking it up on a box of frozen peas. Bet you won't find it. But do be alert to "fortified" and "enriched." Asking the right questions will prove beneficial.

Did you buy that last sentence? Too bad, because I weaseled you, with the word "beneficial." Think about it.

Flavor and Taste

These are two totally subjective words that allow us to claim marvelous things about products that are edible. Every cigarette in the world has claimed the best taste. Every supermarket has advertised the most flavorful meat. And let's not forget "aroma," a subdivision of this category. Wouldn't you like to have a nickel for every time a room freshener (a weasel in itself) told you it would make your home "smell fresh as all outdoors"? Well, they can say it, because smell, like taste and flavor, is a subjective thing. And, incidentally, there are no less than three weasels in that phrase. "Smell" is the first. Then, there's "as" (a substitute for the ever-popular "like"), and, finally, "fresh," which, in context, is a subjective comparison, rather than the primary definition of "new."

Now we can use an unlimited number of combinations of these weasels for added impact. "Fresher-smelling clothes." "Fresher-tasting tobacco." "Tastes like grandma used to make." Unfortunately, there's no sure way of bringing these weasels down to size, simply because you can't define them accurately. Trying to ascertain the meaning of "taste" in any context is like trying to push a rope up a hill. All you can do is be aware that these words are subjective, and represent only one opinion—usually that of the manufacturer.

Style and Good Looks
Anyone for buying a new car? Okay, which is the one with the good looks? The smart new styling? What's that you say? All of them? Well, you're right. Because this is another group of subjective opinions. And it is the subjective and collective opinion of both Detroit and Madison Avenue that the following cars have "bold new styling": Buick Riviera, Plymouth Satellite, Dodge Monaco, Mercury Brougham, and you can fill in the spaces for the rest. Subjectively, you have to decide on which bold new styling is, indeed, bold new styling. Then, you might spend a minute or two trying to determine what's going on under that styling. The rest I leave to Ralph Nader.

Different, Special, and Exclusive
To be different, you have to be not the same as. Here, you must rely on your own good judgment and common sense. Exclusive formulas and special combinations of ingredients are coming at you every day, in every way. You must constantly assure yourself that, basically, all products in any given category are the same. So when you hear "special," "exclusive," or "different," you have to establish two things: on what basis are they different, and is that difference an important one? Let me give you a hypothetical example.

All so-called "permanent" antifreeze is basically the same.

It is made from a liquid known as ethylene glycol, which has two amazing properties: It has a lower freezing point than water, and a higher boiling point than water. It does not break down (lose its properties), nor will it boil away. And every permanent antifreeze starts with it as a base. Also, just about every antifreeze has now got antileak ingredients, as well as antirust and anticorrosion ingredients. Now, let's suppose that, in formulating the product, one of the companies comes up with a solution that is pink in color, as opposed to all the others, which are blue. Presto—an exclusivity claim. "Nothing else looks like it, nothing else performs like it." Or how about, "Look at ours, and look at anyone else's. You can see the difference our exclusive formula makes." Granted, I'm exaggerating. But did I prove a point?

FOR STUDY AND DISCUSSION

Questions on Subject

1. What are *weasel words*? Why do advertisers find them useful? Why is it important for the average American to know about weasel words?
2. Why has Stevens chosen the weasel to describe certain types of advertising language; that is, what characteristics of the weasel make this association appropriate? Explain.

Questions on Strategy

1. What is the function of paragraph 1? What effect do Stevens's questions have on you? (Glossary: *Beginnings*)
2. In paragraph 2 Stevens presents the definition of a *weasel word*. What is the relationship between paragraph 2 and the rest of the essay?
3. How does Stevens organize his classification of weasel words? What technical devices does he use to guide his readers through the various subdivisions of weasel words?
4. When advertisers use the word *like*, they often create similes: "Ajax cleans *like* a white tornado." What, according to Stevens, is the advertisers' intent in using the simile? What value do similes have for you as a student of composition? (Glossary: *Figures of Speech*)

Questions on Diction and Vocabulary

1. Stevens has consciously employed an informal tone in this essay; he wishes to create the impression that he is talking directly to you, his reader. What technical and structural devices does Stevens use to establish this informal tone? How does his diction reinforce this informality? (Glossary: *Tone* and *Diction*)
2. Refer to your desk dictionary to determine the meanings of the following words as they are used in this selection: *obnoxious* (1), *attributes* (1), *implication* (2), *ludicrous* (12), *subjective* (23), *renders* (28), *ostensibly* (28), *assure* (33).

For Classroom Discussion

As Stevens suggests, "tonight when you plop down in front of the boob tube for your customary three and a half hours of violence and/or situation comedies, take a pad and pencil, and keep score" (5). Count the number of weasels that come up during the commercials. Make a list of ten or twelve of these, and compare it with the lists made by others in your class.

(Note: Activities and Writing Suggestions for Classification appear on pages 172–175.)

Can People Be Judged by Their Appearance?

ERIC BERNE

Eric Berne (1910–1970) was born in Montreal and was a graduate of the McGill University Medical School. A well-known psychiatrist, Berne was a member of the psychiatric staff at Mt. Sinai Hospital in New York City and frequently lectured at colleges and universities both here and abroad. A prolific author, Berne came to national attention with the publication of his best-selling Games People Play, *a provocative analysis of human behavior.*

The following selection originally appeared in Berne's Mind in Action *and was later reprinted in his* A Layman's Guide to Psychiatry and Psychoanalysis. *In this essay Berne establishes a classification system for behavior and human body types in an effort to answer the question "Can people be judged by their appearance?"*

Everyone knows that a human being, like a chicken, comes from an egg. At a very early stage, the human embryo forms a three-layered tube, the inside layer of which grows into the stomach and lungs, the middle layer into bones, muscles, joints, and blood vessels, and the outside layer into the skin and nervous system.

Usually these three grow about equally, so that the average human being is a fair mixture of brains, muscles, and inward organs. In some eggs, however, one layer grows more than the others, and when the angels have finished putting the child together, he may have more gut than brain, or more brain than muscle. When this happens, the individual's activities will often be mostly with the overgrown layer.

We can thus say that while the average human being is a 3 mixture, some people are mainly "digestion-minded," some "muscle-minded," and some "brain-minded," and correspondingly digestion-bodied, muscle-bodied, or brain-bodied. The digestion-bodied people look thick; the muscle-bodied people look wide; and the brain-bodied people look long. This does not mean the taller a man is the brainier he will be. It means that if a man, even a short man, looks long rather than wide or thick, he will often be more concerned about what goes on in his mind than about what he does or what he eats; but the key factor is slenderness and not height. On the other hand, a man who gives the impression of being thick rather than long or wide will usually be more interested in a good steak than in a good idea or a good long walk.

Medical men use Greek words to describe these types of 4 bodybuild. For the man whose body shape mostly depends on the inside layer of the egg, they use the word *endomorph*. If it depends mostly upon the middle layer, they call him a *mesomorph*. If it depends upon the outside layer, they call him an *ectomorph*. We can see the same roots in our English words "enter," "medium," and "exit," which might just as easily have been spelled "ender," "mesium," and "ectit."

Since the inside skin of the human egg, or endoderm, forms 5 the inner organs of the belly, the viscera, the endomorph is usually belly-minded; since the middle skin forms the body tissues, or soma, the mesomorph is usually muscle-minded; and since the outside skin forms the brain, or cerebrum, the ectomorph is usually brain-minded. Translating this into Greek, we have the viscerotonic endomorph, the somatotonic mesomorph, and the cerebrotonic ectomorph.

Words are beautiful things to a cerebrotonic, but a viscerotonic 6 knows you cannot eat a menu no matter what language it is printed in, and a somatotonic knows you cannot increase your chest expansion by reading a dictionary. So it is advisable to leave these words and see what kinds of people they actually apply to, remembering again that most individuals are fairly equal mixtures and that what we have to say concerns only the extremes. Up to the present, these types have been thoroughly studied only in the male sex.

VISCEROTONIC ENDOMORPH.   If a man is definitely a thick type   7
rather than a broad or long type, he is likely to be round and soft, with a big chest but a bigger belly. He would rather eat than breathe comfortably. He is likely to have a wide face, short, thick neck, big thighs and upper arms, and small hands and feet. He has overdeveloped breasts and looks as though he were blown up a little like a balloon. His skin is soft and smooth, and when he gets bald, as he does usually quite early, he loses the hair in the middle of his head first.

The short, jolly, thickset, red-faced politician with a cigar in   8
his mouth, who always looks as though he were about to have a stroke, is the best example of this type. The reason he often makes a good politician is that he likes people, banquets, baths, and sleep; he is easygoing, soothing, and his feelings are easy to understand.

His abdomen is big because he has lots of intestines. He   9
likes to take in things. He likes to take in food, and affection and approval as well. Going to a banquet with people who like him is his idea of a fine time. It is important for a psychiatrist to understand the natures of such men when they come to him for advice.

SOMATOTONIC MESOMORPH.   If a man is definitely a broad type   10
rather than a thick or long type, he is likely to be rugged and have lots of muscle. He is apt to have big forearms and legs, and his chest and belly are well formed and firm, with the chest bigger than the belly. He would rather breathe than eat. He has a bony head, big shoulders, and a square jaw. His skin is thick, coarse, and elastic, and tans easily. If he gets bald, it usually starts on the front of the head.

Dick Tracy, Li'l Abner, and other men of action belong to this   11
type. Such people make good lifeguards and construction workers. They like to put out energy. They have lots of muscles and they like to use them. They go in for adventure, exercise, fighting, and getting the upper hand. They are bold and

unrestrained, and love to master the people and things around them. If the psychiatrist knows the things which give such people satisfaction, he is able to understand why they may be unhappy in certain situations.

CEREBROTONIC ECTOMORPH. The man who is definitely a long 12
type is likely to have thin bones and muscles. His shoulders are apt to sag and he has a flat belly with a dropped stomach, and long, weak legs. His neck and fingers are long, and his face is shaped like a long egg. His skin is thin, dry, and pale, and he rarely gets bald. He looks like an absent-minded professor and often is one.

Though such people are jumpy, they like to keep their energy 13
and don't fancy moving around much. They would rather sit quietly by themselves and keep out of difficulties. Trouble upsets them, and they run away from it. Their friends don't understand them very well. They move jerkily and feel jerkily. The psychiatrist who understands how easily they become anxious is often able to help them get along better in the sociable and aggressive world of endomorphs and mesomorphs.

In the special cases where people definitely belong to one 14
type or another, then, one can tell a good deal about their personalities from their appearance. When the human mind is engaged in one of its struggles with itself or with the world outside, the individual's way of handling the struggle will be partly determined by his type. If he is a viscerotonic he will often want to go to a party where he can eat and drink and be in good company at a time when he might be better off attending to business; the somatotonic will want to go out and do something about it, master the situation, even if what he does is foolish and not properly figured out, while the cerebrotonic will go off by himself and think it over, when perhaps he would be better off doing something about it or seeking good company to try to forget it.

Since these personality characteristics depend on the growth 15
of the layers of the little egg from which the person developed, they are very difficult to change. Nevertheless, it is important for the individual to know about these types, so that he can

have at least an inkling of what to expect from those around him, and can make allowances for the different kinds of human nature, and so that he can become aware of and learn to control his own natural tendencies, which may sometimes guide him into making the same mistakes over and over again in handling his difficulties.

FOR STUDY AND DISCUSSION

Questions on Subject

1. Carefully review each of Berne's main categories of personality-body type. What characteristics are generally associated with each of the three groups?
2. Into which of Berne's categories would you place yourself? Do you feel that his description accurately describes you? In what ways, if any, do you differ from his description?
3. Why, according to Berne, is it important for an individual to know about the basic human types?

Questions on Strategy

1. A good classification system must be complete and useful. Its categories should be mutually exclusive. Evaluate Berne's classification according to these criteria.
2. Berne's essay is primarily one of classification. He does, however, use other rhetorical strategies. Identify these strategies, and point out an example of each.
3. How would you characterize the tone of this essay? (Glossary: *Tone*) How appropriate is Berne's tone for his topic and audience?

Questions on Diction and Vocabulary

1. How does Berne ensure that the technical terms for the body and personality types are easy to understand and remember? (Glossary: *Technical Language*)
2. Identify Berne's intended audience, and explain in what ways his diction is appropriate for this audience? (Glossary: *Diction*)
3. Refer to your desk dictionary to determine the meanings of the following words as they are used in this selection: *embryo* (1), *viscera* (5), *thickset* (8), *inkling* (15).

For Classroom Discussion

The title of Berne's essay raises an important question. Now that you have read the essay and discussed it with others in the class, how would you answer Berne's question?

(Note: Activities and Writing Suggestions for Classification appear on pages 172–175.)

Sexism in English:
A Feminist View

ALLEEN PACE NILSEN

Alleen Pace Nilsen of Arizona State University is actively involved in efforts to improve the accuracy of the presentation of both males and females in books for children and adolescents. Her doctoral dissertation is a study of one aspect of linguistic sexism in children's books. With Haig Bosmajian, H. Lee Gershuny, and Julie P. Stanley, she has written Sexism and Language. *In 1978 she and Don L. F. Nilsen published* Language Play: An Introduction to Linguistics.

"Sexism in English: A Feminist View" first appeared in Female Studies VI *(1972). In it Nilsen classifies dictionary entries that she feels are sexist.*

Does culture shape language? Or does language shape culture? This is as difficult a question as the old puzzler of which came first, the chicken or the egg, because there's no clear separation between language and culture.

A well-accepted linguistic principle is that as culture changes so will the language. The reverse of this—as a language changes so will the culture—is not so readily accepted. This is why some linguists smile (or even scoff) at feminist attempts to replace *Mrs.* and *Miss* with *Ms.* and to find replacements for those all-inclusive words which specify masculinity, e.g., *chairman, mankind, brotherhood, freshman,* etc.

Perhaps they are amused for the same reason that it is the doctor at a cocktail party who laughs the loudest at the joke about the man who couldn't afford an operation so he offered the doctor a little something to touch up the X-ray. A person working constantly with language is likely to be more aware of how really deep-seated sexism is in our communication system.

Last winter I took a standard desk dictionary and gave it a place of honor on my night table. Every night that I didn't have anything more interesting to do, I read myself to sleep making a card for each entry that seemed to tell something about male and female. By spring I had a rather dog-eared dictionary, but I also had a collection of note cards filling two shoe boxes. The cards tell some rather interesting things about American English.

First, in our culture it is a woman's body which is considered important while it is a man's mind or his activities which are valued. A woman is sexy. A man is successful.

I made a card for all the words which came into modern English from somebody's name. I have a two-and-one-half inch stack of cards which are men's names now used as everyday words. The women's stack is less than a half inch high and most of them came from Greek mythology. Words coming from the names of famous American men include *lynch*, *sousaphone, sideburns, Pullman, rickettsia, Schick test, Winchester rifle, Franklin stove, Bartlett pear, teddy bear,* and *boysenberry.* The only really common words coming from the names of American women are *bloomers* (after Amelia Jenks Bloomer) and *Mae West jacket.* Both of these words are related in some way to a woman's physical anatomy, while the male words (except for *sideburns* after General Burnsides) have nothing to do with the namesake's body.

This reminded me of an earlier observation that my husband and I made about geographical names. A few years ago we became interested in what we called "Topless Topography" when we learned that the Grand Tetons used to be simply called *The Tetons* by French explorers and *The Teats* by American frontiersmen. We wrote letters to several map makers and found the following listings: *Nippletop* and *Little Nipple Top* near Mt. Marcy in the Adirondacks, *Nipple Mountain* in Archuleta County, Colorado, *Nipple Peak* in Coke County, Texas, *Nipple Butte* in Pennington, South Dakota, *Squaw Peak* in Placer

County, California (and many other places), *Maiden's Peak* and *Squaw Tit* (they're the same mountain) in the Cascade Range in Oregon, *Jane Russell Peaks* near Stark, New Hampshire, and *Mary's Nipple* near Salt Lake City, Utah.

We might compare these names to Jackson Hole, Wyoming, or Pikes Peak, Colorado. I'm sure we would get all kinds of protests from the Jackson and Pike descendants if we tried to say that these topographical features were named because they in some way resembled the bodies of Jackson and Pike, respectively.

This preoccupation with women's breasts is neither new nor strictly American. I was amused to read the derivation of the word *Amazon*. According to Greek folk etymology, the *a* means "without" as in *atypical* or *amoral* while *mazon* comes from *mazōs* meaning "breast." According to the legend, these women cut off one breast so that they could better shoot their bows. Perhaps the feeling was that the women had to trade in part of their femininity in exchange for their active or masculine role.

There are certain pairs of words which illustrate the way in which sexual connotations are given to feminine words while the masculine words retain a serious, businesslike aura. For example, being a *callboy* is perfectly respectable. It simply refers to a person who calls actors when it is time for them to go on stage, but being a *call girl* is being a prostitute.

Also we might compare *sir* and *madam*. *Sir* is a term of respect while *madam* has acquired the meaning of a brothel manager. The same thing has happened to the formerly cognate terms, *master* and *mistress*. Because of its acquired sexual connotations, *mistress* is now carefully avoided in certain contexts. For example, the Boy Scouts have *scoutmasters* but certainly not *scoutmistresses*. And in a dog show the female owner of a dog is never referred to as the *dog's mistress*, but rather as the *dog's master*.

Master appears in such terms as *master plan*, *concert master*, *schoolmaster*, *mixmaster*, *master charge*, *master craftsman*, etc. But *mistress* appears in very few compounds. This is the way it is with dozens of words which have male and female counterparts. I found two hundred such terms, e.g., *usher–usherette, heir–heiress, hero–heroine*, etc. In nearly all cases it is the masculine word which is the base with a feminine suffix being added for the alternate version. The masculine word also travels into compounds while the feminine word is a dead end; e.g., from *king–queen* comes *kingdom* but not *queendom*, from *sportsman–sportslady* comes *sportsmanship* but not *sportsladyship*, etc. There is one—and only one—semantic area in which the masculine word is not the base or more powerful word. This is in the area dealing with sex and marriage. Here it is the feminine word which is dominant. *Prostitute* is the base word with *male prostitute* being the derived term. *Bride* appears in *bridal shower, bridal gown, bridal attendant, bridesmaid,* and even in *bridegroom,* while *groom* in the sense of *bridegroom* does not appear in any compounds, not even to name the groom's attendants or his prenuptial party.

At the end of a marriage, this same emphasis is on the female. If it ends in divorce, the woman gets the title of *divorcée* while the man is usually described with a statement, such as, "He's divorced." When the marriage ends in death, the woman is a *widow* and the -*er* suffix which seems to connote masculine (probably because it is an agentive or actor type suffix) is added to make *widower*. *Widower* doesn't appear in any compounds (except for *grass widower*, which is another companion term), but *widow* appears in several compounds and in addition has some acquired meanings, such as the extra hand dealt to the table in certain card games and an undesirable leftover line of type in printing. 13

If I were an anthropological linguist making observations about a strange and primitive tribe, I would duly note on my tape recorder that I had found linguistic evidence to show that in the area of sex and marriage the female appears to be more important than the male, but in all other areas of the culture, it seems that the reverse is true. 14

But since I am not an anthropological linguist, I will simply go on to my second observation, which is that women are expected to play a passive role while men play an active one. 15

One indication of women's passive role is the fact that they are often identified as something to eat. What's more passive than a plate of food? Last spring I saw an announcement advertising the Indiana University English Department picnic. 16

It read "Good Food! Delicious Women!" The publicity committee was probably jumped on by local feminists, but it's nothing new to look on women as "delectable morsels." Even women compliment each other with "You look good enough to eat," or "You have a peaches and cream complexion." Modern slang constantly comes up with new terms, but some of the old standbys for women are: *cute tomato, dish, peach, sharp cookie, cheese cake, honey, sugar,* and *sweetie-pie.* A man may occasionally be addressed as *honey* or described as a *hunk of meat,* but certainly men are not laid out on a buffet and labeled as women are.

Women's passivity is also shown in the comparisons made to plants. For example, to *deflower* a woman is to take away her virginity. A girl can be described as a *clinging vine,* a *shrinking violet,* or a *wall flower.* On the other hand, men are too active to be thought of as plants. The only time we make the comparison is when insulting a man we say he is like a woman by calling him a *pansy.*

We also see the active-passive contrast in the animal terms used with males and females. Men are referred to as *studs, bucks,* and *wolves,* and they go *tomcatting around.* These are all aggressive roles, but women have such pet names as *kitten, bunny, beaver, bird, chick, lamb,* and *fox.* The idea of being a pet seems much more closely related to females than to males. For instance, little girls grow up wearing *pigtails* and *ponytails* and they dress in *halters* and *dog collars.*

The active-passive contrast is also seen in the proper names given to boy babies and girl babies. Girls are much more likely to be given names like *Ivy, Rose, Ruby, Jewel, Pearl, Flora, Joy,* etc., while boys are given names describing active roles such as *Martin* (warlike), *Leo* (lion), *William* (protector), *Ernest* (resolute fighter), and so on.

Another way that women play a passive role is that they are defined in relationship to someone else. This is what feminists are protesting when they ask to be identified as *Ms.* rather than as *Mrs.* or *Miss.* It is a constant source of irritation to women's organizations that when they turn in items to newspapers under their own names, that is, Susan Glascoe, Jeanette Jones, and so forth, the editors consistently rewrite the item so that the names read Mrs. John Glascoe, Mrs. Robert E. Jones.

In the dictionary I found what appears to be an attitude on the part of editors that it is almost indecent to let a respectable woman's name march unaccompanied across the pages of a dictionary. A woman's name must somehow be escorted by a male's name regardless of whether or not the male contributed to the woman's reason for being in the dictionary, or in his own right was as famous as the woman. For example, Charlotte Brontë is identified as Mrs. Arthur B. Nicholls, Amelia Earhart is identified as Mrs. George Palmer Putnam, Helen Hayes is identified as Mrs. Charles MacArthur, Zona Gale is identified as Mrs. William Llwelyn Breese, and Jenny Lind is identified as Mme. Otto Goldschmidt. [21]

Although most of the women are identified as Mrs. ——— or as the wife of ———, other women are listed with brothers, fathers, or lovers. Cornelia Otis Skinner is identified as the daughter of Otis, Harriet Beecher Stowe is identified as the sister of Henry Ward Beecher, Edith Sitwell is identified as the sister of Osbert and Sacheverell, Nell Gwyn is identified as the mistress of Charles II, and Madame Pompadour is identified as the mistress of Louis XV. [22]

The women who did get into the dictionary without the benefit of a masculine escort are a group sort of on the fringes of respectability. They are the rebels and the crusaders: temperance leaders Frances Elizabeth Caroline Willard and Carry Nation, women's rights leaders Carrie Chapman Catt and Elizabeth Cady Stanton, birth control educator Margaret Sanger, religious leader Mary Baker Eddy, and slaves Harriet Tubman and Phillis Wheatley. [23]

I would estimate that far more than fifty percent of the women listed in the dictionary were identified as someone's wife. But of all the men—and there are probably ten times as many men as women—only one was identified as "the husband of. . . ." This was the unusual case of Frederic Joliot who took the last name of Joliot-Curie and was identified as "husband of Irene." Apparently Irene, the daughter of Pierre and Marie Curie, did not want to give up her maiden name when she married and so the couple took the hyphenated last name. [24]

There are several pairs of words which also illustrate the more powerful role of the male and the relational role of the female. For example, a *count* is a high political officer with a *countess* being simply the wife of a count. The same is true for a *duke* and a *duchess* and a *king* and a *queen*. The fact that a king is usually more powerful than a queen might be the reason that Queen Elizabeth's husband is given the title of *prince* rather than *king*. Since *king* is a stronger word than *queen*, it is reserved for a true heir to the throne because if it were given to someone coming into the royal family by marriage, then the subjects might forget where the true power lies. With the weaker word of *queen*, this would not be a problem; so a woman marrying a ruling monarch is given the title without question.

My third observation is that there are many positive connotations connected with the concept of masculine, while there are either trivial or negative connotations connected with the corresponding feminine concept.

Conditioning toward the superiority of the masculine role starts very early in life. Child psychologists point out that the only area in which a girl has more freedom than a boy is in experimenting with an appropriate sex role. She is much freer to be a *tomboy* than is her brother to be a *sissy*. The proper names given to children reflect this same attitude. It's perfectly all right for a girl to have a boy's name, but not the other way around. As girls are given more and more of the boys' names, parents shy away from using boy names that might be mistaken for girl names, so the number of available masculine names is constantly shrinking. Fifty years ago *Hazel, Beverley, Marion, Frances*, and *Shirley* were all perfectly acceptable boys' names. Today few parents give these names to baby boys and adult men who are stuck with them self-consciously go by their initials or by abbreviated forms such as *Haze* or *Shirl*. But parents of little girls keep crowding the masculine set and currently popular girls' names include *Jo, Kelly, Teri, Cris, Pat, Shawn, Toni*, and *Sam*.

When the mother of one of these little girls tells her to *be a lady*, she means for her to sit with her knees together. But when the father of a little boy tells him to *be a man*, he means for him to be noble, strong, and virtuous. The whole concept of manliness has such positive connotations that it is a compliment to call a male a *he-man*, a *manly man*, or a *virile man* (*virile* comes from the Indo-European *vir*, meaning "man"). In each of these three terms, we are implying that someone is doubly good because he is doubly a man.

Compare *chef* with *cook, tailor* and *seamstress*, and *poet* with *poetess*. In each case, the masculine form carries with it an added degree of excellence. In comparing the masculine *governor* with the feminine *governess* and the masculine *major* with the feminine *majorette*, the added feature is power.   29

The difference between positive male and negative female connotations can be seen in several pairs of words which differ denotatively only in the matter of sex. For instance compare *bachelor* with the terms *spinster* and *old maid*. *Bachelor* has such positive connotations that modern girls have tried to borrow the feeling in the term *bachelor-girl*. *Bachelor* appears in glamorous terms such as *bachelor pad, bachelor party*, and *bachelor button*. But *old maid* has such strong negative feelings that it has been adopted into other areas, taking with it the feeling of undesirability. It has the metaphorical meaning of shriveled and unwanted kernels of pop corn, and it's the name of the last unwanted card in a popular game for children.   30

Patron and *matron* (Middle English for *father* and *mother*) are another set where women have tried to borrow the positive masculine connotations, this time through the word *patroness*, which literally means "female father." Such a peculiar term came about because of the high prestige attached to the word *patron* in such phrases as *"a patron of the arts"* or *"a patron saint."* *Matron* is more apt to be used in talking about a woman who is in charge of a jail or a public restroom.   31

Even *lord* and *lady* have different levels of connotations. *Our Lord* is used as a title for deity, while the corresponding *Our Lady* is a relational title for Mary, the mortal mother of Jesus. *Landlord* has more dignity than *landlady* probably because the landlord is more likely to be thought of as the owner while the landlady is the person who collects the rent and enforces   32 the rules. *Lady* is used in many insignificant places where the corresponding *lord* would never be used, for example, *ladies room, ladies sizes, ladies aid society, ladybug,* etc.

This overuse of *lady* might be compared to the overuse of *queen* which is rapidly losing its prestige as compared to *king.* Hundreds of beauty queens are crowned each year and nearly every community in the United States has its *Dairy Queen* or its *Freezer Queen,* etc. Male homosexuals have adopted the term to identify the "feminine" partner. And advertisers who are constantly on the lookout for euphemisms to make unpleasant sounding products salable have recently dealt what might be a death blow to the prestige of the word *queen.* They have begun to use it as an indication of size. For example, *queen-size* panty hose are panty hose for fat women. The meaning comes through a comparison with *king-size,* meaning big. However, there's a subtle difference in that our culture considers it desirable for males to be big because size is an indication of power, but we prefer that females be small and petite. So using *king-size* as a term to indicate bigness partially enhances the prestige of *king,* but using *queen-size* to indicate bigness brings unpleasant associations to the word *queen.*

Another set that might be compared are *brave* and *squaw.* The word *brave* carries with it the connotations of youth, vigor, and courage, while *squaw* implies almost opposite characteristics. With the set *wizard* and *witch,* the main difference is that *wizard* implies skill and wisdom combined with magic, while *witch* implies evil intentions combined with magic. Part of the unattractiveness of both *squaw* and *witch* is that they suggest old age, which in women is particularly undesirable. When I lived in Afghanistan (1967–1969), I was horrified to hear a proverb stating that when you see an old man you should sit down and take a lesson, but when you see an old woman you should throw a stone. I was equally startled when I went to compare the connotations of our two phrases *grandfatherly advice* and *old wives' tales.* Certainly it isn't expressed with the same force as in the Afghan proverb, but the implication is similar.

In some of the animal terms used for women the extreme undesirability of female old age is also seen. For instance consider the unattractiveness of *old nag* as compared to *filly*, of *old crow* or *old bat* as compared to *bird*, and of being *catty* as compared to being *kittenish*. The chicken metaphor tells the whole story of a girl's life. In her youth she is a *chick*, then she marries and begins feeling *cooped up*, so she goes to *hen parties* where she *cackles* with her friends. Then she has her *brood* and begins to *henpeck* her husband. Finally she turns into *an old biddy*.

FOR STUDY AND DISCUSSION

Questions on Subject

1. What is sexism? After reading Nilsen's essay, do you feel that the English language is inherently sexist? Explain.
2. Whereas Nilsen notes that "a well-accepted linguistic principle is that as culture changes so will the language" (2), she admits that the reverse is not a widely held belief. Why is this so? What are the implications of this principle and its reverse for feminist attempts to change the English language?
3. Nilsen's examination of her standard desk dictionary revealed to her several important cultural attitudes that are reinforced by our language. What are these cultural attitudes?
4. How does Nilsen use the word *queen* to support two of her observations about sexism in the language?

Questions on Strategy

1. Nilsen, when confronted with her "collection of note cards filling two shoe boxes" (4), determined that classification would be the best method for organizing her materials. When presenting her analysis of the dictionary in essay form, she was careful to mark the various divisions of her classification clearly so as to guide her readers and to make her material easier to understand. Examine Nilsen's essay for structural cues that signal her pattern of organization. (Glossary: *Transitions*)
2. Nilsen makes three statements about cultural attitudes inherent in our language. How does she classify the examples she uses to document each statement?
3. Nilsen concludes her essay by citing various animal metaphors that are used in association with women. Why is the "chicken

metaphor" (35) appropriate for her argument? (Glossary: *Figures of Speech* and *Appropriateness*) How, precisely, does it serve to summarize the essay? (Glossary: *Endings*)

Questions on Diction and Vocabulary

1. In paragraph 6, Nilsen cites a number of words that came into modern English from people's names. Such words are called *eponyms*. Identify each of the following words and phrases and the individuals whose names are associated with them:

   a. *lynch*   g. *Winchester rifle*
   b. *sousaphone*   h. *Franklin stove*
   c. *sideburns*   i. *Bartlett pear*
   d. *Pullman*   j. *teddy bear*
   e. *rickettsia*   k. *boysenberry*
   f. *Schick test*

2. Why does Nilsen refer to "American English" in paragraph 4?

3. Nilsen's essay originally appeared in the feminist publication *Female Studies VI*. Remembering that her audience might not be linguistically trained, Nilsen sought to minimize the linguistic jargon without sacrificing precision and clarity of meaning. She has, nevertheless, found it necessary to use some technical terminology. (Glossary: *Technical Language*) Consult your desk dictionary to determine the meanings of the following language-related terms: *derivation* (9), *folk etymology* (9), *connotations* (11), *compounds* (12), *feminine suffix* (12), *agentive* (13), *slang* (16), *denotatively* (30), *euphemisms* (33).

For Classroom Discussion

Listed below are some substitutes that have been proposed to eliminate sexist language. While no one knows which of these substitutions will take hold, it is nonetheless interesting to speculate about their chances for surviving in the language. Classify these items into the following categories: (1) likely to survive, (2) not likely to survive, (3) cannot determine chances of survival at this time. Tell why you feel that certain terms are likely to survive and others are not. As a result of your classification, what can you conclude about efforts to eliminate sexist language?

a. *genkind* for *mankind*
b. *Ms.* for *Mrs.* or *Miss*

c. *herstory* for *history*
d. *salesworker* for *salesman*
e. *himicanes* for *hurricanes*
f. *flight attendant* for *airline stewardess*
g. *otto-it* for *ottoman*
h. *gentlepeople* for *gentlemen*
i. *mailperson* for *mailman*
j. *spokesperson* for *spokesman*
k. *chairone* for *chairman*
l. *personfinger* for *ladyfinger*
m. *he/she* for *he*
n. *personkind* for *mankind*
o. *mail carrier* for *mailman*
p. *chairperson* for *chairman*
q. *freshperson* for *freshman*

(Note: Activities and Writing Suggestions for Classification appear on pages 172–175.)

Activities and Writing Suggestions for Classification

ACTIVITIES

1. The following is a basic exercise in classification. By determining the features that the figures on page 173 have in common, establish the general class to which they all belong. Next, establish subclasses by determining the distinctive features that distinguish one subclass from another. Finally, place each figure in an appropriate subclass within your classification system. You may wish to compare your classification system with those developed by other members of your class and to discuss any differences that exist.

2. Examine the following lists of hobbies, books, and buildings. Determine at least six criteria that could be used to classify the items listed in each group. Finally, classify the items in each group according to three of the criteria you have established.

   HOBBIES
   stamp collecting
   woodworking
   drawing
   needlepoint
   model airplane building
   flower arranging
   scuba diving
   jewelry making
   sewing
   pottery making

   BOOKS
   The Adventures of Huckleberry Finn
   The American Heritage Dictionary (College Edition)
   Guinness Book of World Records
   Gone with the Wind
   The Joy of Cooking
   The Making of the President 1972
   Moby-Dick
   Catch-22
   Encyclopaedia Britannica
   World Atlas

BUILDINGS
Empire State Building
White House
Buckingham Palace
Library of Congress
Museum of Modern Art
The Alamo
Macy's Department Store
Parthenon
Taj Mahal
Mount Vernon

3. Visit a local supermarket, department store, or drugstore, and select one of the many departments or product areas (such as frozen foods, dairy products, cereals, soft drinks, meats, produce) for an exercise in classification. First, in the area you have selected, establish the general class of the products by determining their common features. Next, establish subclasses by determining the features that distinguish one subclass from another. Finally, place the products from your selected area in their appropriate subclasses.

WRITING SUGGESTION

To write a meaningful paper of classification, you must analyze a body of unorganized material, arranging it for a particular purpose. For example, for the purpose of identifying for a buyer the most economical cars currently on the market, you might initially determine which cars can be purchased for under $6,000, which cost between $6,000 and $8,000, and which cost more than $8,000. Then, using a second basis of selection—fuel economy—you could determine which cars have the best gas mileage within each price range. A different purpose would result in a different classification. For example, you might initially wish to determine which cars on the market comfortably accommodate a family of six. Next, using a second principle of selection—price—you could determine which vehicles might be purchased for under $7,000. Such a classification would identify for a buyer all six-passenger cars available for under $7,000.

Select one of the following subjects, and write a paper of classification. Be sure that your purpose is clearly explained and that your bases of selection are chosen and ordered in accordance with your purpose.

a. attitudes toward physical fitness
b. contemporary American music
c. reading materials
d. reasons for going to college
e. attitudes toward the religious or spiritual side of life
f. choosing a hobby
g. television comedies
h. college professors
i. local restaurants
j. choosing a career
k. college courses
l. recreational activities
m. ways of financing a college education
n. parties or other social events

6

COMPARISON
AND CONTRAST

A *comparison* points out the similarities between two or more subjects in the same class or general category; a *contrast* points out the differences. The process of comparing and contrasting is so much a part of your daily life that you probably tend to overlook it. When you decide what to eat, where to eat, what to wear, what to watch on TV, where to go to college, what courses to take, or what career to pursue, you most likely use comparison and contrast to arrive at your decision. And often such decisions are made almost instantaneously, seemingly without method. In all written uses of comparison and contrast, however, the method or system of your thinking must be made evident to the reader. You have to make clear not only what you are comparing and contrasting but also why and on what basis you are doing so. Moreover, your comparison and contrast should be meaningful—that is, it should be more than an exercise in pointing out the obvious or the obscure. As a rule, therefore, you should focus primarily on the differences between things that are perceived as being similar or on the likenesses between things perceived as different.

The function of any comparison and contrast is to clarify—to reach some conclusion about the things being compared and contrasted. The writer's purpose may be simply to inform, to point out similarities or differences that are interesting and significant in themselves, as Bruce Catton does in "Grant and Lee: A Study in Contrasts" or as Michael J. Arlen does in "Good Morning." On other occasions, the writer may analyze and explain the unfamiliar by comparing it with the familiar, perhaps explaining rugby by comparing it with football or describing an avocado by comparing it with a pear. Finally, the writer can point out the superiority of one subject by contrasting it with another; in "The Death of Silence," for example, Robert Paul Dye argues that current radio broadcasting is inferior to old-time broadcasting.

Organization is often the key to a clear and effective comparison and contrast. Suppose you want to analyze four significant differences between solar energy and wind energy, two items in the class *energy*. In your introductory paragraph you explain what you are contrasting and why and mention some of the similarities between solar and wind energy. Then you have two basic ways of presenting your materials in the body of your essay: these are known as the *block-by-block* and *point-by-point* patterns. Each of these organizational patterns lets you move back and forth between the items being compared or, in this case, contrasted:

BLOCK-BY-BLOCK	POINT-BY-POINT
I. Solar energy	I. Cost
A. Cost	A. Solar
B. Efficiency	B. Wind
C. Convenience	II. Efficiency
D. Maintenance	A. Solar
II. Wind energy	B. Wind
A. Cost	III. Convenience
B. Efficiency	A. Solar
C. Convenience	B. Wind
D. Maintenance	IV. Maintenance
	A. Solar
	B. Wind

Each organizational pattern has its advantages and disadvantages. Block-by-block encourages a fuller, more unified discussion of each subject, whereas point-by-point encourages more precise and focused treatments of the similarities or differences between the subjects. The first pattern can be effective when the subjects are relatively simple and the points to be compared or contrasted are rather general and few in number; here the reader is able to remember important relationships between widely separated points. The second pattern, however, is more suitable when the two subjects are relatively complex and the points of comparison or contrast are highly specific and numerous; in this case, the reader is able to follow precise distinctions because both subjects are treated close together.

Analogy, a special form of comparison, is an effective and useful technique for explaining or illustrating a point. In an analogy, the writer employs a subject that is familiar to the reader to explain a subject that is unfamiliar. Unlike comparison, however, analogy points to similarities between things in different classes. Robert Paul Dye uses analogy to explain the complex role of silence in old-time radio:

> Silence, like the white space between magazine articles, signalled conclusions and promised beginnings. Silence served as comma, period and paragraph, just as those marks served to signal silence.

Note that Dye's analogy establishes no direct relationship between silence and the white space or the marks of punctuation on a printed page. The analogy is effective precisely because it enables the reader to "visualize" something that is abstract and hard to grasp—silence—by comparing it to things quite different from it but familiar and concrete.

Comparison and contrast is used primarily to explain and clarify. It heightens our awareness of significant similarities and differences between two things. As with each of the other rhetorical strategies, comparison and contrast frequently is combined with other expository techniques. For example, it can clarify a description or delineate different positions in an argument. Remember that you should have a purpose in using comparison and contrast and that the organizational pattern you choose should suit that purpose.

In the essays in this section, each author uses comparison

and contrast to develop his subject more fully. For example, Russell Baker comments upon Bing Crosby and Elvis Presley and the eras that produced them; Robert Paul Dye contrasts old-time radio broadcasting with the contemporary "screamers"; and Bruce Catton studies the differences between the two great Civil War generals, Grant and Lee.

From Song to Sound: Bing and Elvis

RUSSELL BAKER

*Russell Baker was born in Virginia in 1925. After graduating
from Johns Hopkins University in 1947, he joined the staff
of the* Baltimore Sun *and later worked in the Washington
bureau of* The New York Times. *Since 1962 he has written
a syndicated column for* The New York Times *for which
he was awarded a Pulitzer Prize in 1979. His books include*
An American in Washington, No Cause for Panic, All
Things Considered, *and* Poor Russell's Almanac.

In the following selection, which first appeared in The
New York Times *shortly after Bing Crosby's death in 1977,
Baker compares and contrasts two of our most popular
entertainers as well as the generations they reflected.*

The grieving for Elvis Presley and the commercial exploitation   1
of his death were still not ended when we heard of Bing
Crosby's death the other day. Here is a generational puzzle.
Those of an age to mourn Elvis must marvel that their elders
could really have cared about Bing, just as the Crosby generation
a few weeks ago wondered what all the to-do was about when
Elvis died.

Each man was a mass culture hero to his generation, but it   2
tells us something of the difference between generations that
each man's admirers would be hard-pressed to understand why
the other could mean very much to his devotees.

There were similarities that ought to tell us something. Both   3
came from obscurity to national recognition while quite young
and became very rich. Both lacked formal music education and

180

went on to movie careers despite lack of acting skills. Both developed distinctive musical styles which were originally scorned by critics and subsequently studied as pioneer developments in the art of popular song.

In short, each man's career followed the mythic rags-to-triumph pattern in which adversity is conquered, detractors are given their comeuppance and estates, fancy cars and world tours become the reward of perseverance. Traditionally this was supposed to be the history of the American business striver, but in our era of committee capitalism it occurs most often in the mass entertainment field, and so we look less and less to the board room for our heroes and more and more to the microphone.

Both Crosby and Presley were creations of the microphone. It made it possible for people with frail voices not only to be heard beyond the third row but also to caress millions. Crosby was among the first to understand that the microphone made it possible to sing to multitudes by singing to a single person in a small room.

Presley cuddled his microphone like a lover. With Crosby the microphone was usually concealed, but Presley brought it out on stage, detached it from its fitting, stroked it, pressed it to his mouth. It was a surrogate for his listener, and he made love to it unashamedly.

The difference between Presley and Crosby, however, reflected generational differences which spoke of changing values in American life. Crosby's music was soothing; Presley's was disturbing. It is too easy to be glib about this, to say that Crosby was singing to, first, Depression America and, then, to wartime America, and that his audiences had all the disturbance they could handle in their daily lives without buying more at the record shop and movie theater.

Crosby's fans talk about how "relaxed" he was, how "natural," how "casual and easy going." By the time Presley began causing sensations, the entire country had become relaxed, casual and easy going, and its younger people seemed to be tired of it, for Elvis's act was anything but soothing and scarcely what a parent of that placid age would have called "natural" for a young man.

Elvis was unseemly, loud, gaudy, sexual—that gyrating pel- 9
vis!—in short, disturbing. He not only disturbed parents who
thought music by Crosby was soothing but also reminded their
young that they were full of the turmoil of youth and an appetite
for excitement. At a time when the country had a population
coming of age with no memory of troubled times, Presley spoke
to a yearning for disturbance.

It probably helped that Elvis's music made Mom and Dad 10
climb the wall. In any case, people who admired Elvis never
talk about how relaxed and easy going he made them feel. They
are more likely to tell you he introduced them to something
new and exciting.

To explain each man in terms of changes in economic and 11
political life probably oversimplifies the matter. Something in
the culture was also changing. Crosby's music, for example,
paid great attention to the importance of lyrics. The "message"
of the song was as essential to the audience as the tune. The
words were usually inane and witless, but Crosby—like Sinatra
a little later—made them vital. People remembered them, sang
them. Words still had meaning.

Although many of Presley's songs were highly lyrical, in 12
most it wasn't the words that moved audiences; it was the
"sound." Rock 'n' roll, of which he was the great popularizer,
was a "sound" event. Song stopped being song and turned
into "sound," at least until the Beatles came along and solved
the problem of making words sing to the new beat.

Thus a group like the Rolling Stones, whose lyrics are often 13
elaborate, seems to the Crosby-tuned ear to be shouting only
gibberish, a sort of accompanying background noise in a
"sound" experience. The Crosby generation has trouble hearing
rock because it makes the mistake of trying to understand the
words. The Presley generation has trouble with Crosby because
it finds the sound unstimulating and cannot be touched by the
inanity of the words. The mutual deafness may be a measure
of how far we have come from really troubled times and of how
deeply we have come to mistrust the value of words.

FOR STUDY AND DISCUSSION

Questions on Subject

1. What similarities between Crosby and Presley does Russell Baker see? What differences does he see?
2. Does Baker see the similarities or the differences between these two singers to be more important? What in the essay leads you to this conclusion?
3. What conclusion does Baker draw from his comparison and contrast of Bing Crosby and Elvis Presley?

Questions on Strategy

1. What is Baker's thesis in this essay? Where is the thesis stated? (Glossary: *Thesis*)
2. Does Baker use a point-by-point or a block-by-block pattern of organization in his essay? Why do you suppose he chose the pattern that he did?
3. Why does Baker consider the similarities between these two singers before considering their differences?
4. Identify several examples of Baker's use of parallelism in this essay. What does Baker achieve by its use? (Glossary: *Parallelism*)

Questions on Diction and Vocabulary

1. How would you describe the tone of Baker's essay? (Glossary: *Tone*)
2. In paragraphs 12 and 13 Baker uses *song* and *sound* to label Crosby and Presley respectively. What does Baker gain by using these labels? What different qualities do these two labels convey?
3. Refer to your desk dictionary to determine the meanings of the following words as they are used in this selection: *mythic* (4), *surrogate* (6), *glib* (7), *inane* (11).

For Classroom Discussion

Russell Baker suggests that we are living at a time when words have become meaningless. In your opinion, is this an accurate assessment? Why, or why not?

(Note: Activities and Writing Suggestions for Comparison and Contrast appear on pages 203–205.)

Grant and Lee: A Study in Contrasts

BRUCE CATTON

Bruce Catton (1899–1978) was born in Petoskey, Michigan, and attended Oberlin College. Early in his career, Catton worked as a reporter for various newspapers, among them the Cleveland Plain Dealer. *Having an interest in history, Catton became a leading authority on the Civil War and published a number of books on this subject. These include* Mr. Lincoln's Army, Glory Road, A Stillness at Appomattox, The Hallowed Ground, The Coming Fury, Never Call Retreat, *and* Gettysburg: The Final Fury. *Catton was awarded both the Pulitzer Prize and the National Book Award in 1954.*

The following selection was included in The American Story, *a collection of historical essays edited by Earl Schenk Miers. In this essay Catton considers "two great Americans, Grant and Lee—very different, yet under everything very much alike."*

When Ulysses S. Grant and Robert E. Lee met in the parlor of a modest house at Appomattox Court House, Virginia, on April 9, 1865, to work out the terms for the surrender of Lee's Army of Northern Virginia, a great chapter in American life came to a close, and a great new chapter began.

These men were bringing the Civil War to its virtual finish. To be sure, other armies had yet to surrender, and for a few days the fugitive Confederate government would struggle desperately and vainly, trying to find some way to go on living now that its chief support was gone. But in effect it was all over when Grant and Lee signed the papers. And the little room where they wrote out the terms was the scene of one of the poignant, dramatic contrasts in American history.

They were two strong men, these oddly different generals, 3 and they represented the strengths of two conflicting currents that, through them, had come into final collision.

Back of Robert E. Lee was the notion that the old aristocratic 4 concept might somehow survive and be dominant in American life.

Lee was tidewater Virginia, and in his background were 5 family, culture, and tradition . . . the age of chivalry transplanted to a New World which was making its own legends and its own myths. He embodied a way of life that had come down through the age of knighthood and the English country squire. America was a land that was beginning all over again, dedicated to nothing much more complicated than the rather hazy belief that all men had equal rights and should have an equal chance in the world. In such a land Lee stood for the feeling that it was somehow of advantage to human society to have a pronounced inequality in the social structure. There should be a leisure class, backed by ownership of land; in turn, society itself should be keyed to the land as the chief source of wealth and influence. It would bring forth (according to this ideal) a class of men with a strong sense of obligation to the community; men who lived not to gain advantage for themselves, but to meet the solemn obligations which had been laid on them by the very fact that they were privileged. From them the country would get its leadership; to them it could look for the higher values—of thought, of conduct, of personal deportment—to give it strength and virtue.

Lee embodied the noblest elements of this aristocratic ideal. 6 Through him, the landed nobility justified itself. For four years, the Southern states had fought a desperate war to uphold the ideals for which Lee stood. In the end, it almost seemed as if the Confederacy fought for Lee; as if he himself was the Confederacy . . . the best thing that the way of life for which the Confederacy stood could ever have to offer. He had passed into legend before Appomattox. Thousands of tired, underfed, poorly clothed Confederate soldiers, long since past the simple enthusiasm of the early days of the struggle, somehow considered Lee the symbol of everything for which they had been willing to die. But they could not quite put this feeling into words. If the Lost Cause, sanctified by so much heroism and so many deaths, had a living justification, its justification was General Lee.

Grant, the son of a tanner on the Western frontier, was everything Lee was not. He had come up the hard way and embodied nothing in particular except the eternal toughness and sinewy fiber of the men who grew up beyond the mountains. He was one of a body of men who owed reverence and obeisance to no one, who were self-reliant to a fault, who cared hardly anything for the past but who had a sharp eye for the future.

These frontier men were the precise opposite of the tidewater aristocrats. Back of them, in the great surge that had taken people over the Alleghenies and into the opening Western country, there was a deep, implicit dissatisfaction with a past that had settled into grooves. They stood for democracy, not from any reasoned conclusion about the proper ordering of human society, but simply because they had grown up in the middle of democracy and knew how it worked. Their society might have privileges, but they would be privileges each man had won for himself. Forms and patterns meant nothing. No man was born to anything, except perhaps to a chance to show how far he could rise. Life was competition.

Yet along with this feeling had come a deep sense of belonging to a national community. The Westerner who developed a farm, opened a shop, or set up in business as a trader, could hope to prosper only as his own community prospered—and his community ran from the Atlantic to the Pacific and from Canada down to Mexico. If the land was settled, with towns and highways and accessible markets, he could better himself. He saw his fate in terms of the nation's own destiny. As its horizons expanded, so did his. He had, in other words, an acute dollars-and-cents stake in the continued growth and development of his country.

And that, perhaps, is where the contrast between Grant and Lee becomes most striking. The Virginia aristocrat, inevitably, saw himself in relation to his own region. He lived in a static society which could endure almost anything except change. Instinctively, his first loyalty would go to the locality in which that society existed. He would fight to the limit of endurance to defend it, because in defending it he was defending everything that gave his own life its deepest meaning.

The Westerner, on the other hand, would fight with an equal   11
tenacity for the broader concept of society. He fought so because everything he lived by was tied to growth, expansion, and a constantly widening horizon. What he lived by would survive or fall with the nation itself. He could not possibly stand by unmoved in the face of an attempt to destroy the Union. He would combat it with everything he had, because he could only see it as an effort to cut the ground out from under his feet.

So Grant and Lee were in complete contrast, representing   12
two diametrically opposed elements in American life. Grant was the modern man emerging; beyond him, ready to come on the stage, was the great age of steel and machinery, of crowded cities and a restless burgeoning vitality. Lee might have ridden down from the old age of chivalry, lance in hand, silken banner fluttering over his head. Each man was the perfect champion of his cause, drawing both his strengths and his weaknesses from the people he led.

Yet it was not all contrast, after all. Different as they were—   13
in background, in personality, in underlying aspiration—these two great soldiers had much in common. Under everything else, they were marvelous fighters. Furthermore, their fighting qualities were really very much alike.

Each man had, to begin with, the great virtue of utter tenacity   14
and fidelity. Grant fought his way down the Mississippi Valley in spite of acute personal discouragement and profound military handicaps. Lee hung on in the trenches at Petersburg after hope itself had died. In each man there was an indomitable quality . . . the born fighter's refusal to give up as long as he can still remain on his feet and lift his two fists.

Daring and resourcefulness they had, too; the ability to think   15
faster and move faster than the enemy. These were the qualities which gave Lee the dazzling campaigns of Second Manassas and Chancellorsville and won Vicksburg for Grant.

Lastly, and perhaps greatest of all, there was the ability, at the end, to turn quickly from war to peace once the fighting was over. Out of the way these two men behaved at Appomattox came the possibility of a peace of reconciliation. It was a possibility not wholly realized, in the years to come, but which did, in the end, help the two sections to become one nation again . . . after a war whose bitterness might have seemed to make such a reunion wholly impossible. No part of either man's life became him more than the part he played in their brief meeting in the McLean house at Appomattox. Their behavior there put all succeeding generations of Americans in their debt. Two great Americans, Grant and Lee—very different, yet under everything very much alike. Their encounter at Appomattox was one of the great moments of American history.

FOR STUDY AND DISCUSSION

Questions on Subject

1. According to Catton, Grant and Lee "represented the strengths of two conflicting currents" (3). What were those currents, and what are the most striking characteristics of each?
2. In paragraphs 9, 10, and 11 Catton discusses what he considers to be the most striking contrast between Grant and Lee. What is that difference?
3. List the similarities that Catton sees between Grant and Lee. Which similarity does Catton feel is most important? Why?

Questions on Strategy

1. What would have been gained or lost had Catton discussed the similarities between Grant and Lee before he discussed the differences between them?
2. How does Catton organize the body of his essay (3 through 16)? You may find it helpful in answering this question to label each paragraph as being concerned with Lee, Grant, or both.
3. Catton has very carefully made clear transitions between paragraphs. Identify the various transitional devices he uses, and explain how each works. (Glossary: *Transitions*)

Questions on Diction and Vocabulary

1. Identify at least two metaphors that Catton uses, and explain how each works. (Glossary: *Figures of Speech*)
2. Refer to your desk dictionary to determine the meanings of the following words as they are used in this selection: *poignant* (2), *chivalry* (5), *sanctified* (6), *sinewy* (7), *obeisance* (7), *tidewater* (8), *tenacity* (11), *aspiration* (13).

For Classroom Discussion

Catton says that Grant and Lee represented two conflicting views of American life and its future that clashed in the Civil War. Did the Civil War resolve the conflict, or are these cultural differences still with us today?

(Note: Activities and Writing Suggestions for Comparison and Contrast appear on pages 203–205.)

The Death of Silence

ROBERT PAUL DYE

In the following essay, Robert Paul Dye of the University of Hawaii contrasts the way radio broadcasting used to be and the way it is now. Dye believes that a major change that has occurred in radio broadcasting is the elimination of the artistic use of silence. "The Death of Silence" was first published in the Journal of Broadcasting *in 1968.*

Radio's funniest moment occurred on the *Jack Benny* program when a thief demanded from the great tightwad, "Your money or your life." The long silence that followed was more violently hysterical than any of the quick retorts that are the stock in trade of most comedians. Benny's use of silence, his great sense of timing, made him one of the most popular comics of this century. Benny, of course, was not the only radio artist who recognized that silence could be more effective than sound: silence followed the crash of Fibber McGee's closet, preceded McCarthy's responses to Bergen. The chillers became more chilling when there were moments of silence. Silence was used to make the romances erotic and the quiz shows suspenseful.

Radio has changed. The cacophony of today's radio has been dignified as "The Poetica of 'Top 40' " by University of Oklahoma professor Sherman P. Lawton. Dr. Lawton tells us to "Face up to the fact that, like it or not, from the bowels of radio has come a new art form." The practitioners of the new art are the managers of the "screamer" stations, ". . . stations with an extreme foreground treatment, playing only the top tunes, with breathless and witless striplings making like carnival barkers."

The bible of the practitioners, Lawton tells us, is *The Nuts and Bolts of Radio,* authored by George Skinner and published by the Katz Agency. One of Mr. Skinner's prescriptions is that there should be no silence longer than a fifth of a second; from sign-on to sign-off *there shalt be continuous sound*. Lawton writes,

> On two stations, which I consider the prototypes of the new art, news headlines are proclaimed in a style which can best be described as one well suited to be the second Annunciation. Then, quick segue music, overlapping with the headline that follows. And then, Bam, we might get a roll of drums.

It is curious that the elimination of silence, so long in symbiosis with sound, should be the major difference between the "new art" and old time radio. It was silence which made radio visual; it gave the listener time to imagine the faces, places and action suggested by sound. Silence, like the white space between magazine articles, signalled conclusions and promised beginnings. Silence served as comma, period and paragraph, just as those marks served to signal silence.

Not all radio is continuous sound. Competing with the screamers for popularity are the phone-in programs, an adaptation of two rural America pastimes—listening in on the party line and speaking at the town meeting. This is reactionary programming, an attempt to again involve people in radio by providing a means for do-it-yourself programming. For the most part, the telephone programs are not planned; they happen. They appear to serve as an antidote and as an alternative to the screamers. However, on many stations the antidote and the alternative are more appearance than reality and Mr. Skinner's prescription that there shalt be continuous sound is obeyed.

The death of silence limits some types of aural communication, in some cases eliminates them. The meaningful reporting of Ed Murrow, the stirring rhetoric of Winston Churchill and the fireside chats of Franklin Roosevelt would not have been possible if radio had screamed in the Forties. When silence is prohibited so is drama and poetry. Men like Orson Welles and Archibald MacLeish are forever barred from using the "new art" for their art. Dialogue is also impossible: people just don't speak to each other without so much as a second of silence to signal meaning. Formerly, only stereotyped, fictional creations spoke without pause.

The talkers Ring Lardner satirized would have envied the screamers:

> Well girlie you see how busy I have been and am liable to keep right on being busy as we are not going to let the grass grow under our feet but as soon as we have got this number placed we will get busy on another one as a couple like that will put me on Easy st. even if they don't go as big as we expect but even 25 grand is a big bunch of money and if a man could only turn out one hit a year and make that much out of it I would be on Easy st. and no more hammering on the old music box in some cabaret . . . [2]

But even Lardner's characters eventually had to breathe and lose the floor. The screamers, armed with years' worth of recorded sounds, instantly available and always repeatable, can chatter incessantly.

But unlike Ring Lardner, the screamers do not satirize monologue—they spoof it. They even spoof the commercials. Screamer stations have no sacred cows; at least they give that illusion. The screamers take nothing seriously, except themselves. What at first hearing appears to be pure play turns out to be pseudo-play and devoid of fun. What appears to be a playathon is really instant and constant spoof. Spoof is both the strength and the weakness of the screamers. It is a strength because spoofing is "in"—James Bond and his imitators. It is a weakness because spoofing is hypocritical.

Spoof is described by David Sonstroem as "surgery with a rubber knife," as "a new kind of playful, ironic attitude toward the old conflict between good and evil." He says,

> Spoof is not true to itself. It cheats at its own game. It only pretends to take life as a game, but then inadvertently lets earnest break in and govern it. Although pretending to be above and beyond it all, spoof cares, and cares very much. This unconscious hypocrisy lies at the root of all that I find objectionable in spoof, with its enchanting trick of protecting foolish fantasy by pretending to expose it.

The screamers are spoofers. They lack the courage to be 10 moral and at the same time cannot deny the desire to be moral. The result is that the audience is cheated and deceived. It is neither shocked into moral consciousness, nor freed, for the moment, from moral considerations. It is mired in ambivalence, and the result is malaise.

Old time radio was not ambivalent, nor were its listeners. 11 The residents of Allen's Alley did not spoof American society; they satirized it. The rise of Senator Claghorn hurried the demise of Senator Bilbo. And there was fun on old time radio, the kind of fun that comes from playing and results in laughter. The laughter from old time radio was in the home, not merely the studio. There were belly laughs from the listeners, not merely self-conscious giggles from Lawton's "witless strip-lings."

Radio developed an art that quickened all the senses. The 12 screamers have developed a technique of monopolizing a single sense. Radio once allowed the listener to participate. The screamers force him into the role of observer. Radio once took life seriously. The screamers take only themselves seriously. Spoof is a degenerate form. It is not true to itself; it prohibits participation. Art is true to itself; it causes participation. The screams from the bowels of today's radio are not the birth cries of a new art form, but the death rattle of an old art medium. The death of silence is the death of sound broadcast-ing.

FOR STUDY AND DISCUSSION

Questions on Subject

1. What, according to Dye, is the main difference between radio as it used to be and radio as it is today?
2. What is Dye's attitude toward today's radio?
3. How have radio stations attempted to combat the "screamers"?
4. What is *spoof*? Why does Dye consider contemporary radio to be spoof? Explain the difference between *spoof* and *satire*.

Questions on Strategy

1. What is Dye's thesis, and where is it stated? (Glossary: *Thesis*)
2. Carefully review paragraphs 1 and 4. Explain how Dye has attempted to make the use and meaning of silence in radio broadcasting understandable to the reader?
3. How, specifically, does Dye's last paragraph emphasize the major differences between old-time and contemporary radio broadcasting? (Glossary: *Endings*)

Questions on Diction and Vocabulary

1. Dye has labeled contemporary radio stations as "screamer" stations (2). How effective is this label?
2. Refer to your desk dictionary to determine the meaning of the following words as they are used in this selection: *retorts* (1), *antidote* (5), *hypocritical* (8), *ironic* (9), *inadvertently* (9), *ambivalence* (10).

For Classroom Discussion

In his essay, Dye discusses radio broadcasting as it once was and as it is today. His discussion, however, concerns only AM radio. Some interesting comparisons and contrasts can be made between AM and FM radio broadcasting. What significant differences and similarities do you find between AM and FM radio?

(Note: Activities and Writing Suggestions for Comparison and Contrast appear on pages 203–205.)

Good Morning

MICHAEL J. ARLEN

Michael J. Arlen was born in England in 1930 and moved to New York in 1940. The son of Michael Arlen, a well-known writer of the 1920s, he has worked on the staffs of Life *and the* Reporter, *and is currently a regular contributor to* The New Yorker. *His book* The Living-Room War, *published in 1969, was described by* The New York Times *as "the only good book ever written about television." His other works include* Exiles; An American Verdict; Passage to Ararat, *Arlen's search for his Armenian roots;* The View from Highway 1, *his second collection of television criticism; and* Thirty Seconds, *a study of television commercials.*

In "Good Morning," first published in the February 24, 1975, issue of The New Yorker, *Arlen juxtaposes the real world with the world of television.*

The television screen showed an orange sun rising slowly   1
above an expanse of serene and empty farmland. There was a
scene of horses frisking about a dewy paddock. A freight train
rushed silently across a desert.

"I can't find my shirt anywhere," said Father.   2

"Here's your orange juice," said Mother.   3

"Good morning, I'm Bill Beutel," said Bill Beutel, his jacket   4
flickering in alternating shades of green and yellow. "The
Westminster Kennel Club Show is opening in New York, and
in a few moments we're going to be talking to you about
that."

"Don't you want your orange juice?" Mother said.   5

Father took the glass of orange juice and held it in his hand,   6
and then put it down on the kitchen counter.

"I saw it in the closet only last night," he said. "Joey, you leave the set alone. The color's automatic."

"Joey, go get your juice," said Mother.

Stephanie Edwards said, "I'm really looking forward to hearing about that dog show, Bill, but right now we're going to have a report on the unemployment picture that's been causing such widespread distress across the nation."

"Mom, did you see my homework anywhere?" said Clarice. "Hi, Dad. That looks real cool without a shirt."

Peter Jennings, in Washington, said, "President Ford's top economist, Alan Greenspan, testified yesterday on Capitol Hill that the country will just have to reconcile itself to 8 percent unemployment through 1976." Alan Greenspan said, "As I evaluate the current trade-off between stimulus and unemployment, I do not give great credence to the idea that a significant reduction will be caused by a stimulus greater than that proposed by the President."

"It was the white shirt," Father said. "The one with the shoe polish on the cuff. Is that coffee ready?"

"I'll get the coffee, Dad," said Clarice.

"Clarice, you do the toast," said Mother.

"Mother, I have all this *homework*. I have a quiz in social studies."

Bill Beutel said, "Johnny Miller's 69 keeps him out front in the Bob Hope Desert Classic. As of this moment, it looks as if the women are going to boycott Wimbledon."

Father switched channels. Frank Blair said, "Yesterday, in Cambodia, a direct hit was scored upon this school in Phnom Penh."

Father said, "I guess I'll go look for it myself."

Frank Blair said, "Repercussions from yesterday's rioting in Lima, Peru, are still being felt today in that strife-torn capital." There were scenes of tanks driving down a city street.

"Clarice, remember the left side of the toaster doesn't work," said Mother.

"Mother, I *know*," said Clarice.

Frank Blair said, "North Dakota has an advisory for snow. Pacific Ocean storms are moving toward the Pacific Coast."

The telephone rang. Father reappeared, holding his shoes

and a towel. He picked up the phone. "No, there isn't any Lisa here," he said, and started to put the phone back. "Oh, Dad, is that *Lisa*?" Clarice screamed. Father handed her the phone.

On the television screen, soldiers were now walking slowly 24 down a country road. "Patrols fan out from the city, looking for insurgents," said a voice.

Mother said, "Joey, you finish the toast." 25

Joey said, "How come I have to do the toast when I don't 26 eat toast?"

"Do you think it might be in the laundry?" Father said. "It 27 might have fallen to the floor of the closet, and somebody might have put it in the laundry." Father passed by Clarice on his way out of the kitchen. "Don't talk all day on the phone, Clarice," he said. Clarice rolled her eyes at the ceiling.

Frank Blair said, "Scattered fighting continued until well 28 toward evening." There were scenes of more tanks speeding three abreast down a road.

"Here's your coffee," Mother said. "Now, where did he 29 go?"

Frank Blair said, "Armored cars and Russian-made tanks 30 broke up the disorder. A curfew and a state of national emergency have been proclaimed."

There was the sound of a crash from the back of the house. 31

"Eggs are ready, everyone!" Mother said. On the television 32 screen, two tanks were firing into a brick wall. "Fix the set. That's too loud, Joey," she said. "Everyone! The eggs are getting cold."

Father came back into the kitchen, with a blue shirt hanging 33 partly out of his trousers, and clutching one of his fingers, from which a small drop of blood appeared. "Goddamn towel rack," he said.

"Here are your eggs," Mother said. "I thought you were 34 going to get it fixed."

"I think I may have hurt myself," Father said. 35

On the television set, Fred Flintstone was rolling a stone 36 wheel down a long hill. Father looked at the stone as it sped down the hill. At the bottom of the hill, there was a dinosaur sleeping. Father watched as the wheel rolled down the hill and then along the back of the dinosaur until it hit him on the head. "Who turned this on?" Father asked.

"Mom asked me to," said Joey.

"I did no such thing, Joey," said Mother. "Eat your eggs before they're cold. Clarice, come eat your eggs!"

Father switched channels. Stephanie Edwards said, "Nearly the entire central part of the country is in the grip of a cold-air mass. In Oklahoma City, the high today will be thirty-seven, the low around twenty."

"Did you know that thirty-two degrees is freezing, Mom?" said Joey.

"I don't like it when it gets that cold," said Mother.

"That was Oklahoma City," Father said. "Oklahoma City, Oklahoma."

"Clarice, you get off the phone this instant," Mother said.

Bill Beutel said, "In a little while, we're going to be talking about that Westminster Kennel Club Show, but right now we're going to Washington to visit with sociologist Donald Warren, who has been in the nation's capital all week examining the way that unemployed workers handle stress." Peter Jennings, in Washington, said, "Professor Warren, I understand that you're here in the nation's capital trying to find out more about how the unemployed react in times of stress. Is that correct?" Professor Warren said, "Yes, that's fundamentally correct, Peter. We've been following people through a series of crises, and these have been difficult times."

Mother said, "I ought to check at Garfields and see if they got in any of those new bird feeders yet. How come you're eating with your hand all bent like that?"

"Can't you see my finger is bleeding?" said Father.

"You're supposed to hold it above your head, Dad," said Joey. "If you hold it above your head, then gravity stops the blood from spurting up through your arm and sloshing all over everything."

"That's the most *disgusting* thing I ever heard," said Clarice, sitting down at the table. Clarice spread butter over a piece of toast and began to eat it.

"The fact is our formal institutions lie to us. They do not and are not able to give us the true picture of the crime rates and issues which confront people," said Professor Warren.

Clarice got to her feet. "Mom, I have to run." 50

"Eat your eggs, Clarice," said Joey. 51

"Where do you have to run to, young lady?" said Father. 52
He reached forward and changed the channel again. Jim Hartz
said, "In a moment, we'll be talking to a United Nations official
who says that five hundred million people in the world aren't
getting enough to eat. Here is Mr. Eric Ojala, head of the
United Nations food program. Mr. Ojala, I understand that
the United Nations has been developing an early-warning
system for the world food situation."

The telephone rang. Father answered it. "Lisa?" he said. "I 53
thought you just called."

"Oh, *Dad*," Clarice said, taking the phone. 54

The doorbell rang. Mr. Ojala said, "We receive reports 55
nowadays from all member countries."

A door slammed, and a boy's voice bellowed, "Joey!" 56

"Why, good morning, Gordon," Mother said. 57

Mr. Ojala said, "Although this system is still in its early 58
stages, nonetheless it gives us time to anticipate where certain
crops may fail." Jim Hartz said, "Mr. Ojala, do these reports
have to do with crops as well as weather?"

Father suddenly got to his feet. "Have you seen the car- 59
insurance papers?" he said.

"I can't imagine where," said Mother. "I thought you always 60
kept them in the envelope with the stereo warranty."

Mr. Ojala said, "It's true that fertilizer has been in short 61
supply all during the year, but I don't believe it is fair to
blame this shortage on the petroleum industry."

Father came back in. "I can't find the stereo warranty, either," 62
he said.

"Are we getting a new stereo?" asked Clarice, still on the 63
phone.

"Don't bother your father," said Mother. 64

Joey changed the channel. 65

"You'll be late for the bus," said Mother. Clarice hung up 66
the phone. "Who put this *disgusting* sticker on my notebook?"
she screamed.

Bill Beutel said, "Now we're going to see three very unusual 67 species of the canine family. This aristocratic pooch, I think, is called a Pharaoh hound, and I gather they're supposed to smile when they're happy, and they're supposed to blush."

Clarice said, "Joey, someday I'm going to kill you. Honestly, I am going to *kill* you. Mother, I'm going to Modern Dance this afternoon with Lisa."

Father reappeared, wearing an overcoat and holding a white shirt. "I found the white shirt," he said.

"Dad, you've got shaving cream on your ear," said Clarice.

Bill Beutel said, "Miss Laventhall, would you say he is blushing now?" Miss Laventhall said, "Oh, definitely. He is definitely blushing."

"I wouldn't feel safe with a dog like that," said Mother.

"I'll call you from the office," said Father.

"Can Lisa come overnight Thursday?" asked Clarice.

"Now, this is an extremely rare breed of Chinese dog. Two thousand years ago in China, it was the pet of the aristocratic set," said Bill Beutel.

"Don't forget to stop by Windsor Supply on your way home," said Mother.

"How come Clarice always has overnights?" said Joey.

"Can I have some ice cream?" asked Gordon.

"You run along now, boys," said Mother.

There was the sound of the storm door slamming, then reopening, then slamming. Mother changed the channel on the television set and started collecting the dishes. The door opened again. "Somebody left roller skates in the car," Father said. The door closed again. A car engine started, missed, started, missed, then started. Mother stood before the sink, rinsing dishes. On the set behind her, Barbara Walters said to Charles Colson, "Tell us about that prison experience, will you. Tell us about the first night." Charles Colson said, "Well, I think, Barbara, from my standpoint, it was just one of the most revealing experiences of my life." Mother put the dishes one by one into the dishwasher and turned the switch. Outside the window, two robins padded on the snow. The rumble of the dishwasher filled the room. Mother sprayed the skillet with a jet of hot water. Charles Colson said, "There was certain information of that nature which was passed to us in the White

House in 1972." The refrigerator clicked on. The dishwasher churned. The telephone began to ring. "Hi, Beth," Mother said. "Wait a minute while I turn the TV down. We were just listening to the morning news."

FOR STUDY AND DISCUSSION

Questions on Subject

1. In this story, Arlen juxtaposes a number of events that are reported on the morning news with the activities of a family about to begin a new day. For example, the worldwide food shortage is presented in contrast to Clarice's failure to finish breakfast. Make a list of other juxtapositions you find in the story. What is their overall effect?
2. What significance, if any, is there in the passage in which Father watches Fred Flintstone roll a stone wheel down a hill?
3. Many attempts at communication are made in this story. For example, the newscasters attempt to speak to the family while at the same time the family members speak to one another. How much actual communication takes place?
4. Comment on the significance of the mother's final comment: "Wait a minute while I turn the TV down. We were just listening to the morning news" (80).

Questions on Strategy

1. In what way is this essay one of comparison and contrast?
2. What is Arlen's point in this story, and why is comparison and contrast an effective strategy for making that point?
3. How has Arlen used italics to help characterize Clarice?
4. Examine the speeches of the television newscasters and the members of the family. How do they differ, and how do the differences help Arlen make his point?

Questions on Diction and Vocabulary

1. Examine the diction of the television newscasters. How does their word choice reveal them to be newscasters? Are any of their phrases clichés? (Glossary: *Clichés*)
2. In paragraph 11 Alan Greenspan is quoted. What in his diction indicates that he is an economist?

3. Refer to your desk dictionary to determine the meanings of the following words as they are used in this selection: *frisking* (1), *reconcile* (11), *credence* (11), *boycott* (16), *curfew* (30), *warranty* (60).

For Classroom Discussion

Arlen's essay contrasts reality as we experience it with reality as it is conveyed by television. To what extent can news programs accurately and convincingly capture reality? What about other types of television programs?

(Note: Activities and Writing Suggestions for Comparison and Contrast appear on pages 203–205.)

Activities and Writing Suggestions for Comparison and Contrast

ACTIVITIES

1. For each of the following topics for comparison and contrast, consider (1) whether you would emphasize similarities or differences, (2) what points you would discuss, and (3) what organizational pattern—point-by-point or block-by-block—you would use.

   a. two close friends
   b. two of your teachers
   c. two professional baseball teams
   d. two professional tennis players
   e. *Time* and *Newsweek*
   f. two cities you have visited

2. Prepare both block-by-block and point-by-point outlines for a comparison and contrast of each of the following topics:

   a. your local newspaper and *The New York Times*
   b. dogs and cats as pets
   c. print media and electronic media
   d. rock music and country blues
   e. economy cars and luxury cars

   Explain any advantages of one organizational method over the other.

WRITING SUGGESTIONS

1. Write an essay in which you compare and/or contrast two things to show at least one of the following:

   a. their important differences
   b. their significant similarities
   c. their relative value
   d. their distinctive qualities

   You may wish to use one of the subjects that you outlined in the second activity above.

2. Select a topic from the list below, and write an essay using comparison and/or contrast as your primary means of development.

Be sure that your essay has a definite purpose and a clear direction.

a. two methods of dieting
b. two TV situation comedies
c. two types of summer employment
d. two people who display different attitudes toward responsibility
e. two restaurants
f. two courses in the same subject area
g. two friends who exemplify different life styles
h. two TV network or local news programs
i. two professional quarterbacks
j. two ways of studying for an exam
k. two rooms in which you have classes
l. two of your favorite magazines
m. two attitudes toward death
n. two ways to heat a home

3. The following poems attempt to capture the essence of a moment of poetic truth in baseball and basketball, respectively. After reading the two poems, write an essay in which you compare and contrast the subjects and/or the way the poets have treated them.

THE BASE STEALER

Poised between going on and back, pulled
Both ways taut like a tightrope-walker,
Fingertips pointing the opposites,
Now bouncing tiptoe like a dropped ball
Or a kid skipping rope, come on, come on,
Running a scattering of steps sidewise,
How he teeters, skitters, tingles, teases,
Taunts them, hovers like an ecstatic bird,
He's only flirting, crowd him, crowd him,
Delicate, delicate, delicate, delicate—now!

Robert Francis

FOUL SHOT

With two 60's stuck on the scoreboard
And two seconds hanging on the clock,
The solemn boy in the center of eyes,
Squeezed by silence,
Seeks out the line with his feet,
Soothes his hands along his uniform,
Gently drums the ball against the floor,
Then measures the waiting net,

Raises the ball on his right hand,
Balances it with his left,
Calms it with fingertips,
Breathes,
Crouches,
Waits,
And then through a stretching of stillness,
Nudges it upward.

The ball
Slides up and out,
Lands,
Leans,
Wobbles,
Wavers,
Hesitates,
Exasperates,
Plays it coy
Until every face begs with unsounding screams—
And then

      And then

            And then,
Right before ROAR-UP,
Dives down and through.

                          Edwin A. Hoey

7

CAUSE AND EFFECT

Every time you try to answer a question that asks *why*, you engage in the process of *causal analysis*—you attempt to determine a *cause* or series of causes for an *effect*. Causal analysis is a natural process, one that you are very familiar with. From the time you were a child, your natural curiosity has prompted you to ask why. Why does water freeze? Why do we have wars? Why do people go to church? The process of causal analysis is not, however, just a matter of determining causes. It is, as well, the process of determining effects. That is to say, you can write an essay explaining the causes of white-collar crime (the effect), or you can write an essay explaining the effects of white-collar crime (the cause).

While the purpose of causal analysis is simple—to know—determining causes and effects is usually thought-provoking and quite complex. One reason for this is that there are two types of causes: (1) *immediate causes*, which are readily apparent because they are closest to the effect, and (2) *ultimate causes*, which are somewhat removed, not so apparent, or perhaps even obscure. Furthermore, ultimate causes may bring about effects which themselves become causes, thus creating what is called a *causal chain*. For example, the immediate cause of a flood may be the collapse of a dam. The ultimate cause might be an engineering error. An intermediate cause, however, might be faulty construction of the dam owing to corruption in the building trades.

A second reason for the complexity of causal analysis is that an effect may have any number of causes and a cause may have any number of effects. An upset stomach may be caused by what you have eaten, but it may also be caused by overeating, flu, nervousness, pregnancy, or any combination of influences. Similarly, the high cost of electricity may have multiple effects: higher profits for utility companies, fewer appliance sales, and the use of alternative sources of energy. In dealing with each of these complexities of causal analysis—deciding where on a causal chain to focus your analysis and how to handle multiple causes and/or effects—you must plan your writing thoroughly and present your ideas persuasively.

Sound reasoning and logic, while present in all good writing, should be central and readily apparent in any causal analysis. If your analysis is to be believable and convincing, you must not give your reader the slightest reason to question either the soundness of your thinking or the presentation of your ideas. What follows are suggestions for writing logical and convincing causal analyses.

1. *Write honestly and objectively.* If you examine your material objectively and develop your causal analysis carefully, you will of necessity write honestly. If, however, you are unconvinced by your own examination of the material or if you fail to admit other possible causes and effects, your reader is likely to become skeptical of your analysis.

2. *Be sure that your evidence is sufficient and that it is logically presented.* Readers are convinced by both the quality and the quantity of the evidence you present. The thoughtful and selective use of verifiable facts and statistics is always advisable. Above all, keep your own prejudices and opinions from detracting from the logic of your analysis and presentation.

3. *Be sure that you neither overstate nor understate your position.* It is always wise to let your evidence convince your reader. When you overstate, or become dogmatic, you not only annoy your reader but, more importantly, raise serious doubts about your own confidence in the power of the material to convince. At the same time, no analytical writer convinces by excessively

understating or qualifying information with words such as *perhaps, maybe, I think, sometimes, most often, nearly always*, or *in my opinion*. While you may intend to sound rational and sensible, you may appear to be indecisive and fuzzy-headed.

4. *Avoid a common fault in logical thinking: the "after this, therefore because of this"* (post hoc, ergo propter hoc) *fallacy.* It is essential that you consider all possible causes before you assign the single cause or combination of causes that leads to an effect. For example, it is erroneous to believe that whenever you take aspirin and then feel dizzy, your dizziness is caused by taking aspirin. There could be any number of other causes for this effect, and you are obliged to consider them all, singly and in combination.

In the essays in this section, the authors use causal analysis to understand better some of the social and technological problems confronting us. For example, Marya Mannes examines changing attitudes toward the law; Victor Cline analyzes the effect of television violence on children; and Barry Commoner discusses the causes of the near disaster in the nuclear facility at Three Mile Island.

The Thin Grey Line

MARYA MANNES

Marya Mannes, born in New York City in 1904, is a journalist, novelist, and social critic. She has served as feature editor of Vogue *and* Glamour *magazines and has published in such national publications as* New Republic *and* Esquire. *Her books include* Message from a Stranger, But Will It Sell, Out of My Time, *and* Uncoupling.

"The Thin Grey Line" is a shorter version of an article which first appeared in McCall's *in 1964. In it Mannes examines the reasons for our changing attitudes toward the law.*

"Aw, they all do it," growled the cabdriver. He was talking about cops who took payoffs for winking at double parking, but his cynicism could as well have been directed at any of a dozen other instances of corruption, big-time and small-time. Moreover, the disgust in his voice was overlaid by an unspoken "So what?": the implication that since this was the way things were, there was nothing anybody could do.

Like millions of his fellow Americans, the cabdriver was probably a decent human being who had never stolen anything, broken any law or willfully injured another; somewhere, a knowledge of what was probably right had kept him from committing what was clearly wrong. But that knowledge had not kept a thin grey line that separates the two conditions from being daily greyer and thinner—to the point that it was hardly noticeable.

On one side of this line are They: the bribers, the cheaters, the chiselers, the swindlers, the extortioners. On the other

209

side are We—both partners and victims. They and We are now so perilously close that the only mark distinguishing us is that They get caught and We don't.

The same citizen who voices his outrage at police corruption will slip the traffic cop on his block a handsome Christmas present in the belief that his car, nestled under a "No Parking" sign, will not be ticketed. The son of that nice woman next door has a habit of stealing cash from her purse because his allowance is smaller than his buddies'. Your son's friend admitted cheating at exams because "everybody does it."

Bit by bit, the resistance to and immunity against wrong that a healthy social body builds up by law and ethics and the dictation of conscience have broken down. And instead of the fighting indignation of a people outraged by those who prey on them, we have the admission of impotence: "They all do it."

Now, failure to uphold the law is no less corrupt than violation of the law. And the continuing shame of this country now is the growing number of Americans who fail to uphold and assist enforcement of the law, simply—and ignominiously —out of fear. Fear of "involvement," fear of reprisal, fear of "trouble." A man is beaten by hoodlums in plain daylight and in view of bystanders. These people not only fail to help the victim, but, like the hoodlums, flee before the police can question them. A city official knows of a colleague's bribe but does not report it. A pedestrian watches a car hit a woman but leaves the scene, to avoid giving testimony. It happens every day. And if the police get cynical at this irresponsibility, they are hardly to blame. Morale is a matter of giving support and having faith in one another; where both are lacking, "law" has become a worthless word.

How did we get this way? What started this blurring of what was once a thick black line between the lawful and the lawless? What makes a "regular guy," a decent fellow, accept a bribe? What makes a nice kid from a middle-class family take money for doing something he must know is not only illegal but wrong?

When you look into the background of an erring "kid" you

will often find a comfortable home and a mother who will tell you, with tears in her eyes, that she "gave him everything." She probably did, to his everlasting damage. Fearing her son's disapproval, the indulgent mother denies him nothing except responsibility. Instead of growing up, he grows to believe that the world owes him everything.

The nice kid's father crosses the thin grey line himself in a dozen ways, day in and day out. He pads his expenses on his income-tax returns as a matter of course. As a landlord, he pays the local inspectors of the city housing authority to overlook violations in the houses he rents. When his son flunked his driving test, he gave him ten dollars to slip to the inspector on his second test. "They all do it," he said. 9

The nice kid is brought up with boys and girls who have no heroes except people not much older than themselves who have made the Big Time, usually in show business or in sports. Publicity and money are the halos of their stars, who range from pop singers who can't sing to ballplayers who can't read: from teen-age starlets who can't act to television performers who can't think. They may be excited by the exploits of spacemen, but the work's too tough and dangerous. 10

The nice kids have no heroes because they don't believe in heroes. Heroes are suckers and squares. To be a hero you have to stand out, to excel, to take risks, and above all, not only choose between right and wrong, but defend the right and fight the wrong. This means responsibility—and who needs it? 11

Today, no one has to take any responsibility. The psychiatrists, the sociologists, the novelists, the playwrights have gone a long way to help promote irresponsibility. Nobody really is to blame for what he does. It's Society. It's Environment. It's a Broken Home. It's an Underprivileged Area. But it's hardly ever You. 12

Now we find a truckload of excuses to absolve the individual from responsibility for his actions. A fellow commits a crime because he's basically insecure, because he hated his stepmother at nine, or because his sister needs an operation. A policeman loots a store because his salary is too low. A city official accepts 13 a payoff because it's offered to him. Members of minority groups, racial or otherwise, commit crimes because they can't get a job, or are unacceptable to the people living around them. The words "right" and "wrong" are foreign to these people.

But honesty is the best policy. Says who? Anyone willing to get laughed at. But the laugh is no laughing matter. It concerns the health and future of a nation. It involves the two-dollar illegal bettor as well as the corporation price-fixer, the college-examination cheater and the payroll-padding Congressman, the expense-account chiseler, the seller of pornography and his schoolboy reader, the bribed judge and the stealing delinquent. All these people may represent a minority. But when, as it appears now, the majority excuse themselves from responsibility by accepting corruption as natural to society ("They all do it"), this society is bordering on total confusion. If the line between right and wrong is finally erased, there is no defense against the power of evil.

Before this happens—and it is by no means far away—it might be well for the schools of the nation to substitute for the much-argued issue of prayer a daily lesson in ethics, law, and responsibility to society that would strengthen the conscience as exercise strengthens muscles. And it would be even better if parents were forced to attend it. For corruption is not something you read about in the papers and leave to courts. We are all involved.

FOR STUDY AND DISCUSSION

Questions on Subject

1. What problem does Mannes address in this essay, and what, in her opinion, has caused it?
2. What does Mannes mean when she says, "If the line between right and wrong is finally erased, there is no defense against the power of evil" (14)?
3. What examples does Mannes use to support her opening statement in paragraph 6? (Glossary: *Example*) Do you agree with her argument in this paragraph? Explain.

4. What solutions does Mannes suggest for the problem of widespread corruption in American society?

Questions on Strategy

1. Mannes begins her essay with a brief narrative. How does this narrative introduce the subject of her essay? How effective do you find this beginning? (Glossary: *Beginnings*)
2. The image of the "thin grey line" is very important in this essay. What purposes does it serve?
3. In terms of cause and effect, what is the function of the questions in paragraph 7? What is the function of this paragraph in the context of the essay?
4. Discuss the transitional links that Mannes makes between paragraphs in this essay. (Glossary: *Transitions*)

Questions on Diction and Vocabulary

1. Why does Mannes characterize the two sides of the "thin grey line" as "They" and "We" (3)? Have you ever used these pronouns to label the two sides in a particular situation? If so, describe the circumstances in which you used them.
2. This essay is informal and conversational in tone. Cite several examples of words and phrases that create this tone. (Glossary: *Tone*)
3. Refer to your desk dictionary to determine the meanings of the following words as they are used in this selection: *cynicism* (1), *perilously* (3), *impotence* (5), *reprisal* (6), *indulgent* (8).

For Classroom Discussion

"The Thin Grey Line" was first published in 1964. In your opinion, have the conditions Mannes describes improved, worsened, or remained the same since that time?

(Note: Activities and Writing Suggestions for Cause and Effect appear on pages 248–249.)

Confessions of a Working Stiff

PATRICK FENTON

Patrick Fenton, a cargo handler for Seaboard World Airlines at John F. Kennedy Airport in New York, tells us in the following essay how he makes his living and what effect his job has on him. Fenton wrote his "confessions" in 1975, when he was thirty-one years old and had worked for the airline for seven years. "Confessions of a Working Stiff" was first published in the April 1975 issue of New York *magazine.*

The Big Ben is hammering out its 5:45 alarm in the half-dark of another Tuesday morning. If I'm lucky, my car down in the street will kick over for me. I don't want to think about that now; all I want to do is roll over into the warm covers that hug my wife. I can hear the wind as it whistles up and down the sides of the building. Tuesday is always the worst day— it's the day the drudgery, boredom, and fatigue start all over again. I'm off from work on Sunday and Monday, so Tuesday is my blue Monday.

I make my living humping cargo for Seaboard World Airlines, one of the big international airlines at Kennedy Airport. They handle strictly all cargo. I was once told that one of the Rockefellers is the major stockholder for the airline, but I don't really think about that too much. I don't get paid to think. The big thing is to beat that race with the time clock every morning of your life so the airline will be happy. The worst thing a man could ever do is to make suggestions about building a better airline. They pay people $40,000 a year to come up with better ideas. It doesn't matter that these ideas never work; it's just that they get nervous when a guy from

South Brooklyn or Ozone Park acts like he actually has a brain.

I throw a Myadec high-potency vitamin into my mouth to ward off one of the ten colds I get every year from humping mailbags out in the cold rain at Kennedy. A huge DC-8 stretch jet waits impatiently for the 8,000 pounds of mail that I will soon feed its empty belly. I wash the Myadec down with some orange juice and grab a brown bag filled with bologna and cheese. Inside the lunch bag there is sometimes a silly note from my wife that says, "I Love You—Guess Who?" It is all that keeps me going to a job that I hate.

I've been going there for seven years now and my job is still the same. It's weary work that makes a man feel used up and worn out. You push and you pull all day long with your back. You tie down pallets loaded with thousands of pounds of freight. You fill igloo-shaped containers with hundreds of boxes that all look the same. If you're assigned to work the warehouse, it's really your hard luck. This is the job all the men hate most. You stack box upon box until the pallet resembles the exact shape of the inside of the plane. You get the same monotonous feeling an adult gets when he plays with a child's blocks. When you finish one pallet, you find another and start the whole dull process over again.

The airline pays me $192 a week for this. After they take out taxes and $5.81 for the pension, I go home with $142. Once a month they take out $10 for term life insurance, and $5.50 for union dues. The week they take out the life insurance is always the worst: I go home with $132. My job will never change. I will fill up the same igloos with the same boxes for the next 34 years of my life, I will hump the same mailbags into the belly of the plane, and push the same 8,000-pound pallets with my back. I will have to do this until I'm 65 years old. Then I'll be free, if I don't die of a heart attack before that, and the airline will let me retire.

In winter the warehouse is cold and damp. There is no heat. The large steel doors that line the warehouse walls stay open most of the day. In the cold months, wind, rain and snow blow across the floor. In the summer the warehouse becomes an oven. Dust and sand from the runways mix with the toxic fumes of fork lifts, leaving a dry, stale taste in your mouth.

The high windows above the doors are covered with a thick, black dirt that kills the sun. The men work in shadows with the constant roar of jet engines blowing dangerously in their ears.

Working the warehouse is a tedious job that leaves a man's mind empty. If he's smart he will spend his days wool-gathering. He will think about pretty girls that he once knew, or some other daydream of warm, dry places where you never had a chill. The worst thing he can do is to think about his problems. If he starts to think about how he is going to pay the mortgage on the $30,000 home that he can't afford, it will bring him down. He will wonder why he comes to the cargo airline every morning of his life, and even on Christmas Day. He will start to wonder why he has to listen to the deafening sound of the jets as they rev up their engines. He will wonder why he crawls on his hands and knees, breaking his back a little bit more every day.

To keep his kids in that great place in the country in the summer, that great place far away from Brooklyn and the South Bronx, he must work every hour of overtime that the airline offers him. If he never turns down an hour, if he works some 600 hours over, he can make about $15,000. To do this he must turn against himself, he must pray that the phone rings in the middle of the night, even though it's snowing out and he doesn't feel like working. He must hump cargo late into the night, eat meatball heroes for supper, drink coffee that starts to taste like oil, and then hope that his car starts when it's time to go home. If he gets sick—well, he better not think about that.

All over Long Island, Ozone Park, Brooklyn, and as far away as the Bronx, men stir in the early morning hours as a new day begins. Every morning is the same as the last. Some of the men drink beer for breakfast instead of coffee. Way out in Bay Shore a cargoman snaps open a can of Budweiser. It's 6 A.M., and he covers the top of the can with his thumb in order to keep down the loud hiss as the beer escapes. He doesn't want to awaken his children as they dream away the morning in the next room. Soon he will swing his Pinto wagon up onto the crowded Long Island Expressway and start the long ride to the job. As he slips the car out of the driveway he tucks another can of beer between his legs.

All the men have something in common: they hate the work 10 they are doing and they drink a little too much. They come to work only to punch a timecard that has their last name on it. At the end of the week they will pick up a paycheck with their last name on it. They will never receive a bonus for a job well done, or even a party. At Christmastime a card from the president of the airline will arrive at each one of their houses. It will say Merry Christmas and have the president's name printed at the bottom of it. They know that the airline will be there long after they are dead. Nothing stops it. It runs non-stop, without sleep, through Christmas Day, New Year's Eve, Martin Luther King's birthday, even the deaths of Presidents.

It's seven in the morning and the day shift is starting to 11 drift in. Huge tractors are backing up to the big-mouth doors of the warehouse. Cattle trucks bring tons of beef to feed its insatiable appetite for cargo. Smoke-covered trailers with re- frigerated units packed deep with green peppers sit with their diesel engines idling. Names like White, Mack, and Kenworth are welded to the front of their radiators, which hiss and moan from the overload. The men walk through the factory-type gates of the parking lot with their heads bowed, oblivious of the shuddering diesels that await them.

Once inside the warehouse they gather in groups of threes 12 and fours like prisoners in an exercise yard. They stand in front of the two time clocks that hang below a window in the manager's office. They smoke and cough in the early morning hour as they await their work assignments. The manager, a nervous-looking man with a stomach that is starting to push out at his belt, walks out with the pink work sheets in his hand.

Eddie, a young Irishman with a mustache, has just bolted 13 in through the door. The manager has his timecard in his hand, holding it so no one else can hit Eddie in. Eddie is four minutes late by the time clock. His name will now go down in the timekeeper's ledger. The manager hands the card to him with a "you'll be up in the office if you don't straighten out" look. Eddie takes the card, hits it in, and slowly takes his place with the rest of the men. He has been out till four in the morning drinking beer in the bars of Ozone Park; the time clock and the manager could blow up, for all he cares. "Jesus," he says to no one in particular, "I hope to Christ they don't put me in the warehouse this morning."

Over in another group, Kelly, a tall man wearing a navy knit hat, talks to the men. "You know, I almost didn't make it in this morning. I passed this green VW on the Belt Parkway. The girl driving it was singing. Jesus, I thought to myself, it must be great going somewhere at 6:30 in the morning that makes you want to sing." Kelly is smiling as he talks. "I often think, why the hell don't you keep on going, Kelly? Don't get off at the cargo exit, stay on. Go anywhere, even if it's only Brooklyn. Christ, if I was a single man I think I would do just that. Some morning I'd pass this damn place by and drive as far away as Riverhead. I don't know what I'd do when I got there—maybe I'd pick up a pound of beefsteak tomatoes from one of those roadside stands or something."

The men laugh at Kelly but they know he is serious. "I feel the same way sometimes," the man next to him says. "I find myself daydreaming a lot lately; this place drives you to that. I get up in the morning and I just don't want to come to work. I get sick when I hit that parking lot. If it wasn't for the kids and the house I'd quit." The men then talk about how hard it is to get work on "the outside." They mention "outside" as if they were in a prison.

Each morning there is an Army-type roll call from the leads. The leads are foremen who must keep the men moving; if they don't, it could mean their jobs. At one time they had power over the men but as time went by the company took away their little bit of authority. They also lost the deep interest, even enjoyment, for the hard work they once did. As the cargo airline grew, it beat this out of them, leaving only apathy. The ramp area is located in the backyard of the warehouse. This is where the huge jets park to unload their 70,000-pound payloads. A crew of men fall in behind the ramp lead as he mopes out of the warehouse. His long face shows the hopelessness of another day.

A brutal rain has started to beat down on the oil-covered 17
concrete of the ramp as the 306 screeches in off the runway.
Its engines scream as they spit off sheets of rain and oil. Two
of the men cover their ears as they run to put up a ladder to
the front of the plane. The airline will give them ear covers
only if they pay for half of them. A lot of the men never buy
them. If they want, the airline will give them two little plugs
free. The plugs don't work and hurt the inside of the ears.

The men will spend the rest of the day in the rain. Some of 18
them will set up conveyor belts and trucks to unload the
thousands of pounds of cargo that sit in the deep belly of the
plane. Then they will feed the awkward bird until it is full
and ready to fly again. They will crawl on their hands and
knees in its belly, counting and humping hundreds of mailbags.
The rest of the men will work up topside on the plane, pushing
8,000-pound pallets with their backs. Like Egyptians building
a pyramid, they will pull and push until the pallet finally gives
in and moves like a massive stone sliding through sand. They
don't complain too much; they know that when the airline
comes up with a better system some of them will go.

The old-timers at the airline can't understand why the 19
younger men stay on. They know what the cargo airline can
do to a man. It can work him hard but make him lazy at the
same time. The work comes in spurts. Sometimes a man will
be pushed for three hours of sweat, other times he will just
stand around bored. It's not the hard work that breaks a man
at the airline, it's the boredom of doing the same job over
and over again.

At the end of the day the men start to move in off the ramp. 20
The rain is still beating down at their backs but they move
slowly. Their faces are red and raw from the rain-soaked wind
that has been snapping at them for eight hours. The harsh
wind moves in from the direction of the city. From the ramp
you can see the Manhattan skyline, gray- and blue-looking,
as it peeks up from the west wall of the warehouse. There is
nothing to block the winter weather as it rolls in like a storm
across a prairie. They head down to the locker room, heads
bowed, like a football team that never wins.

With the workday almost over, the men move between the 21

narrow, gray rows of lockers. Up on the dirty walls that surround the lockers someone has written a couple of four-letter words. There is no wit to the words; they just say the usual. As they strip off their wet gear the men seem to come alive.

"Hey, Arnie! You want to stay four hours? They're asking for overtime down in Export," one of the men yells over the lockers.

Arnie is sitting about four rows over, taking off his heavy winter clothing. He thinks about this for a second and yells back, "What will we be doing?"

"Working the meat trailer." This means that Arnie will be humping huge sides of beef off rows of hooks for four hours. Blood will drip down onto his clothes as he struggles to the front of the trailer. Like most of the men, he needs the extra money, and knows that he should stay. He has Master Charge, Korvettes, Times Square Stores, and Abraham & Straus to pay.

"Nah, I'm not staying tonight. Not if it's working the meat trailer. Don wanted to stop for a few beers at The Owl; maybe I'll stay tomorrow night."

It's four o'clock in the afternoon now—the men have twelve minutes to go before they punch out. The airline has stopped for a few seconds as the men change shifts. Supervisors move frantically across the floor pushing the fresh lot of new men who have just started to come in. They hand out work sheets and yell orders: "Jack, get your men into their rain gear. Put three men in the bellies to finish off the 300 flight. Get someone on the pepper trailers, they've been here all morning."

The morning shift stands around the time clock with three minutes to go. Someone says that Kevin Delahunty has just been appointed to the Fire Department. Kevin, a young Irishman from Ozone Park, has been working the cargo airline for six years. Like most of the men, he has hated every minute of it. The men are openly proud of him as they reach out to shake his hand. Kevin has found a job on "the outside." "Ah, you'll be leaving soon," he tells Pat. "I never thought I'd get out of here either, but you'll see, you're going to make it."

The manager moves through the crowd handing out timecards and stops when he comes to Kevin. Someone told him Kevin is leaving. "Is that right, Delahunty? Well I guess we won't expect you in tomorrow, will we? Going to become a fireman, eh? That means you'll be jumping out of windows like a crazy man. Don't act like you did around here," he adds as he walks back to his office.

The time clock hits 4:12 and the men pour out of the warehouse. Kevin will never be back, but the rest of them will return in the morning to grind out another eight hours. Some of them will head straight home to the bills, screaming children, and a wife who tries to understand them. They'll have a Schaefer or two, then they'll settle down to a night of television.

Some of them will start to fill up the cargo bars that surround Kennedy Airport. They will head to places like Gaylor's on Rockaway Boulevard or The Dew Drop Inn down near Farmers Boulevard. They will drink deep glasses of whiskey and cold mugs of Budweiser. The Dew Drop has a honky-tonk mood of the Old West to it. The barmaid moves around like a modern-day Katie Elder. Like Brandy, she's a fine girl, but she can out-curse any cargoman. She wears a low-cut blouse that reveals most of her breasts. The jukebox will beat out some Country & Western as she says, "Ah, hell, you played my song." The cargomen will hoot and holler as she substitutes some of her own obscene lyrics.

They will drink late into the night, forgetting time clocks, Master Charge, First National City, Korvettes, mortgages, cars that don't start, and jet engines that hurt their ears. They will forget about damp, cold warehouses, winters that get longer and colder every year, minutes that drift by like hours, supervisors that harass, and the thought of growing old on a job they hate. At midnight they will fall dangerously into their cars and make their way up onto the Southern State Parkway. As they ride into the dark night of Long Island they will forget it all until 5:45 the next morning—when the Big Ben will start up the whole grind all over again.

FOR STUDY AND DISCUSSION

Questions on Subject

1. What is Fenton's attitude toward the airline company he works for? What in particular does Fenton dislike about his job? What are the immediate causes for his dissatisfaction? Why does he continue to work for the airline company? (Glossary: *Attitude*)

2. Why, in your opinion, does the airline not do something to improve working conditions for its employees? Why does the airline company "get nervous when a guy from South Brooklyn or Ozone Park acts like he actually has a brain" (2)?

3. What is it, according to Fenton, that breaks a man at the airline?

Questions on Strategy

1. Reread the final sentence of the essay. How is it connected with the first sentence of the essay? Do these sentences together reveal the organization of the essay as a whole? Explain. (Glossary: *Sequence*)

2. What are "leads" (16), and why does Fenton feel it is important to define and to discuss them?

3. Fenton uses concrete details and specific incidents to show rather than merely tell us how awful a job with the airline is. Identify several paragraphs that rely heavily on concrete detail and two or three revealing incidents that dramatize the plight of the workers. Explain how these passages make the cause-and-effect relationship that Fenton sees real for the reader. (Glossary: *Concrete/Abstract* and *Specific/General*)

Questions on Diction and Vocabulary

1. For Fenton and his co-workers, working for the airline is a regimented, prison-like existence. How do Fenton's diction and imagery help to establish this motif?

2. Why do you suppose Fenton depicts the warehouse as having "big-mouth doors" (11) and an "insatiable appetite for cargo" (11) and the plane as being an "awkward bird" (18) with a "deep belly" (18)? (Glossary: *Figures of Speech*)

3. In the title of his essay, Fenton refers to himself as a "working stiff." What does he mean?

4. Comment on the appropriateness of the following similes, which Fenton uses to describe the workers (Glossary: *Appropriateness*):

   a. "like prisoners in an exercise yard" (12)
   b. "like Egyptians building a pyramid" (18)
   c. "like a football team that never wins" (20)

5. Refer to your desk dictionary to determine the meanings of the following words as they are used in this selection: *drudgery* (1), *fatigue* (1), *toxic* (6), *mortgage* (7), *insatiable* (11), *apathy* (16).

For Classroom Discussion

In "Confessions of a Working Stiff," Patrick Fenton discusses the reasons why he hates his job. Not all people, of course, dislike their work. In fact, many people derive considerable satisfaction from the work they do. Discuss the reasons why some jobs are more satisfying than others. Why is it possible for a job to be satisfying for one person and not for another?

(Note: Activities and Writing Suggestions for Cause and Effect appear on pages 248–249.)

How TV Violence Damages Your Children

VICTOR B. CLINE

Victor B. Cline, professor of psychology at the University of Utah, received his Ph.D. from the University of California at Berkeley in 1953. Cline's research interests include interpersonal perception, psychotherapy, the effects of media violence and pornography, successful marriage, values, and delinquency. In 1974 he edited a collection of essays, Where Do We Draw the Line? An Exploration into Media Violence, Pornography, and Censorship.

In this selection, first published in the February 1975 issue of Ladies' Home Journal, *Cline assesses the effects of television violence on children.*

ITEM: Shortly after a Boston TV station showed a movie depicting a group of youths dousing a derelict with gasoline and setting him afire for "kicks," a woman was burned to death in that city—turned into a human torch under almost identical circumstances.

ITEM: Several months ago, NBC-TV presented in early-evening, prime viewing time a made-for-TV film, *Born Innocent*, which showed in explicit fashion the sexual violation of a young girl with a broom handle wielded by female inmates in a juvenile detention home. Later a California mother sued NBC and San Francisco TV station KRON for $11,000,000, charging that this show had inspired three girls, ages 10 to 15, to commit a similar attack on her 9-year-old daughter and an 8-year-old friend three days after the film was aired.

ITEM: A 14-year-old boy, after watching rock star Alice Cooper engage in a mock hanging on TV, attempted to reproduce the stunt and killed himself in the process.

ITEM: Another boy laced the family dinner with ground glass 4
after seeing it done on a television crime show.

ITEM: A British youngster died while imitating his TV hero, 5
Batman. The boy was hanged while leaping from a cabinet in a garden shed. His neck became caught in a nylon loop hanging from the roof. His father blamed the TV show for his death— and for encouraging children to attempt the impossible.

These are just a sampling of many well-documented instances 6
of how TV violence can cause antisocial behavior—instances that are proving that TV violence is hazardous to your child's health.

TV broadcasters can no longer plead that they are unaware 7
of the potential adverse effects of such programs as *Born Innocent*. During the last decade, two national violence commissions and an overwhelming number of scientific studies have continually come to one conclusion: televised and filmed violence can powerfully teach, suggest—even legitimatize— extreme antisocial behavior, and can in some viewers trigger specific aggressive or violent behavior. The research of many behavioral scientists has shown that a definite cause-effect relationship exists between violence on TV and violent behavior in real life.

When U.S. Surgeon General Jesse Steinfeld appeared before 8
the U.S. Senate subcommittee reviewing two years of scientific research on the issue, he bluntly concluded, "The overwhelming consensus and the unanimous Scientific Advisory Committee's report indicate that televised violence, indeed, does have an adverse effect on certain members of our society. . . . It is clear to me that the causal relationship between televised violence and antisocial behavior is sufficient to warrant appropriate and immediate remedial action. . . . There comes a time when the data are sufficient to justify action. That time has come."

The Federal Communications Commission was ordered by 9
Congress to come up with a report by December 31, 1974, on how children can be protected from televised violence (and sex). Hopefully, some concrete proposals will develop.

The television moguls have repeatedly paraded before various 10

Congressional subcommittees over the last ten years, solemnly promising to reduce the overall amount of violence programmed, especially in time slots that had large numbers of child viewers. However, if we look at the data compiled throughout the 1960's and early 1970's, we find very little change in the average number of violent episodes per program broadcast by all three networks. In one study, the staff of U.S. Congressman John M. Murphy of New York found NBC leading the pack with violent sequences in 71 percent of its primetime shows, followed by ABC with 67 percent and CBS with 57 percent.

With more and more mega-violent films coming to TV from the commercial theater market, as well as the increasing violence injected into made-for-TV movies, we find that the promise of television has been shamelessly ignored. In too many TV films, we see a glorification of violence that makes heroes of killers. The primary motivation for all of this is money and the fierce scramble for ratings. Thus the television industry's "repentance" for past wrongs, occurring after major national tragedies such as the assassination of the Kennedy brothers and Martin Luther King, Jr., with the transient public outrage and demand for change, has been all ritual with little substance.

We are a great free society with the power to shape our destiny and create almost any social-cultural environment we wish, but as the late President John F. Kennedy put it, "We have the power to make this the best generation in the history of mankind, or the last." If one looks at crime statistics, we find that we are by far the most violent of all the great Western nations. Our homicide rate is about ten times greater than, say, the Scandinavian countries', or four times greater than Scotland's or Australia's. There are more murders per year on the island of Manhattan or in the city of Philadelphia than in the entire United Kingdom, with its nearly 60,000,000 people. Violent crime has been increasing at six to ten times the rate of population growth in this country. And interestingly, if one analyzes the content of TV programs in England, we find that their rate of televised violence is half that of ours; in the Scandinavian countries it is much less even than that.

Thus one of the major social-cultural differences between

the United States with its high homicide and violence rates and those countries with low violence rates is the amount of violence screened on public television.

"Monkey See, Monkey Do"

Much of the research that has led to the conclusion that TV 14 and movie violence could cause aggressive behavior in some children has stemmed from work in the area of imitative learning or modeling which, reduced to its simplest expression, might be termed "monkey see, monkey do." Research by Stanford psychologist Albert Bandura has shown that even brief exposure to novel aggressive behavior *on a one-time basis* can be repeated in free play by as high as 88 percent of the young children seeing it on TV. Dr. Bandura also demonstrated that even a single viewing of a novel aggressive act could be recalled and produced by children six months later, without any inter- vening exposure. Earlier studies have estimated that the average child between the ages of 5 and 15 will witness, during this 10-year period, the violent destruction of more than 13,400 fellow humans. This means that through several hours of TV- watching, a child may see more violence than the average adult experiences in a lifetime. Killing is as common as taking a walk, a gun more natural than an umbrella. Children are thus taught to take pride in force and violence and to feel ashamed of ordinary sympathy.

According to the Nielsen Television Index, preschoolers 15 watch television an average of 54 hours a week. During one year, children of school age spend more time in front of a TV set than they do in front of a teacher; in fact, they spend more time watching TV than any other type of waking activity in their lives.

So we might legitimately ask, What are the major lessons, 16 values and attitudes that television teaches our children? Con- tent analyses of large numbers of programs broadcast during children's viewing hours suggest that the major message taught in TV entertainment is that violence is the way to get what you want.

Who Are the "Good Guys"?

Another major theme that many TV studies have shown to occur repeatedly is that violence is acceptable if the victim "deserved" it. This, of course, is a very dangerous and insidious philosophy. It suggests that aggression, while reprehensible in criminals, is acceptable for the "good guys" who have right on their side. But, of course, nearly every person feels that he or she is "right." And often the "good guys" are criminals whom the film happens to depict sympathetically, as in *The Godfather*. Who is "good" and who is "bad" merely depends on whose side you're on.

Studies by McLeod and Associates of boys and girls in junior and senior high school found that the more the youngster watched violent television fare, the more aggressive he or she was likely to be. Other studies revealed that the amount of television violence watched by children (especially boys) at age 9 influenced the degree to which they were aggressive 10 years later, at age 19.

The problem becomes increasingly serious because, even if your child is not exposed to a lot of media violence, the youngster still could become the *victim or target* of aggression by a child who is stimulated by the violence that he or she sees on TV.

And criminals are too frequently shown on TV as daring heroes. In the eyes of many young viewers, these criminals possess all that's worth having in life—fast cars, beautiful, admiring women, super-potent guns, modish clothes, etc. In the end they die like heroes—almost as martyrs—but then only to appease the "old folks" who insist on "crime-does-not-pay" endings.

The argument that you can't get high ratings for your show unless it is hyped up with violence is, of course, not true—as 20 years of *I Love Lucy* and, more recently, *All in the Family*, *Sanford and Son*, *The Waltons* and scores of other shows have demonstrated. Action shows featuring themes of human conflict frequently have appeal, yet even they needn't pander to the antisocial side of man's nature or legitimatize evil.

The hard scientific evidence clearly demonstrates that watching television violence, sometimes for only a few hours, and in some studies even for a few minutes, can and often does instigate aggressive behavior that would not otherwise occur. If only 1 percent of the possibly 40,000,000 people who saw *The Godfather* on TV were stimulated to commit an aggressive act, this would involve 400,000 people. Or if it were only one in 10,000, it would involve 4,000 people—plus their victims.

Some parents believe that if their children are suitably loved, 23 properly brought up and emotionally well-balanced, they will not be affected by TV violence. However, psychiatrist Frederic Wertham responds to this by noting that all children are impressionable and therefore susceptible. We flatter ourselves if we think that our social conditions, our family life, our education and our entertainment are so far above reproach that only emotionally sick children can get into trouble. As Dr. Wertham points out, if we believe that harm can come only to the predisposed child, this leads to a contradictory and irresponsible attitude on the part of adults. Constructive TV programs are praised for giving children constructive ideas, but we deny that destructive scenes give children destructive ideas.

It should also be noted that the "catharsis theory" in vogue 24 a few years ago, which suggested that seeing violence is good for children because it allows them vicariously to discharge their hostile feelings, has been convincingly discarded. Just the opposite has been found to be true. Seeing violence stimulates children aggressively; it also shows them how to commit aggressive acts.

The author of this article has conducted research studying 25 the "desensitization" of children to TV violence and its potential effects.

In our University of Utah laboratories, we set up two six- 26 channel physiographs which had the capacity to measure emotional responsiveness in children while they watched violent TV shows. When most of our subjects saw violent films, those instruments measuring heart action, respiration, perspiration, etc., all hooked up to the autonomic nervous system, did indeed record strong emotional arousal. We studied 120 boys between the ages of 5 and 14. Half had seen little or no

TV in the previous two years (hence had seen little media violence), and the other half had seen an average of 42 hours of TV a week for the past two years (hence a lot of violence). As our violent film, we chose an eight-minute sequence from the Kirk Douglas prizefighting film, *The Champion*, which had been shown many times on TV reruns but which none of the boys tested had ever seen. We considered other, more violent films, but they were too brutal, we felt, to be shown to children—even for experimental purposes. The boxing match seemed like a good compromise. Nobody was killed or seriously injured. Nothing illegal occurred. Yet the fight did depict very graphically human aggression that was emotionally arousing.

These two groups of boys watched our film while we recorded their emotional responses on the physiograph. The results showed that the boys with a history of heavy violence watching were significantly less aroused emotionally by what they saw— they had become habituated or "desensitized" to violence. To put it another way, our findings suggested that the heavy TV watchers appeared to be somewhat desensitized or "turned off" to violence, suggesting the possibility of an emotional blunting or less "conscience and concern" in the presence of witnessed violence. This means that they had developed a tolerance for it, and possibly an indifference toward human life and suffering. They were no longer shocked or horrified by it. It suggested to us the many instances of "bystander apathy," in which citizens in large urban areas have witnessed others being assaulted, yet did not come to their rescue or try to secure aid or help. Or incidents such as the My Lai massacre, in which American soldiers killed Vietnamese civilians. This suggests an unfeeling, indifferent, noncaring, dehumanized response to suffering or distress.

In any event, our research has presented the first empirical evidence that children who are exposed to a lot of TV violence do to some extent become blunted emotionally or desensitized to it.

Since our children are an important national resource, these findings suggest that we should teach them wisely. The kinds of fantasies to which we expose them may make a great deal of difference as to what kind of adults they become, and whether we will survive as a society.

The author, who is a psychotherapist and who treats many 30 damaged children and families, was then faced with the problem of what to do about his own TV set and his own children, who regularly watched TV and had their favorite programs. The evidence had been stacking up in my laboratory—so what should I do about it at home? The thing that finally turned me from being the permissive, tolerant, "good-guy" dad to the concerned parent was the realization that whenever my children looked at TV for any lengthy period, especially violent action shows, they became frequently touchy, cross and irritable. Instead of playing outside, even on beautiful days, discharging tensions in healthy interaction with others, they sat passive for hours, too often hypnotized by whatever appeared on the tube. Frequently, homework didn't get done, chores were neglected, etc. One Saturday morning I was shocked to find my bright, 15-year-old son watching cartoons for four straight hours, having let all chores and other responsibilities go. It was then that we finally decided to turn off the TV set on a relatively permanent basis.

"No TV" Is a Turn-on

When we announced this decision, we found ourselves faced 31 with a family revolt. There was much wailing and gnashing of teeth. It was as if the alcoholic had been deprived of his bottle, or as if we had suddenly announced that no more food would be served at our table.

However, the "storm" lasted only one week. Interestingly, 32 during that week, the children went outside and played with each other and the neighbors much more, a lot more good books got read, homework was done on time, chores got finished, and the children got along with each other better. And very interestingly, the complaints about "no TV" suddenly stopped at the end of that week. Now, several years later, we do occasionally look at TV—some sports specials, a good movie, something required for school, even a mystery. But it's almost never on school nights—and it is no longer an issue in our home. Nobody feels deprived. It's now just not a major part of our lifestyle.

It should be stated, in all fairness, that television has the potential for great good—to teach children pro-social values and behavior, such as sharing with others, controlling one's impulses, solving problems through reason and discussion, being kind and thoughtful. Such programs as *The Waltons* suggest to me that such content can have wide popular appeal and be commercially marketable—if done with talent, care and commitment. In other words, television could be used for far more constructive programming than we have seen in the past. For the time being, parents should, in my judgment, be very cautious about what they expose their children to on television (as well as in movies). If something particularly objectionable is broadcast during children's prime-time hours, there are three things that can be done: (1) turn the television set off; (2) phone your local station expressing your concern; (3) write to the program's sponsor, indicating your objections (the firm's address will be found on the label of his merchandise).

The evidence is clear: a child's mind can be polluted and corrupted just as easily as his body can be poisoned by contaminants in the environment. Children are essentially powerless to deal with such problems. This means that the responsibility for effecting change rests with every adult citizen. Meaning you. Meaning me. Meaning us.

FOR STUDY AND DISCUSSION

Questions on Subject

1. What, according to Cline, is the relationship between violence on television and violent behavior in American life? What types of evidence does he present to support his analysis? (Glossary: *Supporting Evidence*)
2. Cline briefly recounts the research done by Stanford University psychologist Albert Bandura in the area of "imitative learning or modeling" (14). What, exactly, is imitative learning or modeling, and how is it related to the five "items" which Cline uses in the beginning of his essay?
3. What is the "catharsis theory" (24)? Why, according to Cline, has it been discarded?

4. What solutions does Cline offer that will help to minimize the harmful effects of TV on children? Are his solutions realistic? Why, or why not? Can you offer any alternatives?

Questions on Strategy

1. Cline opens his essay with a series of five "Items." Why do you suppose Cline uses the word *Item* to label each incident he recounts? Does each "Item" show that the crime or mishap it presents was the result of watching television? Explain.
2. What is the relationship between the opening "Items" and the rest of the essay? (Glossary: *Beginnings*)
3. For what audience has Cline written this essay? How do you know? Explain. (Glossary: *Audience*)
4. Does Cline present sufficient evidence in paragraph 12 to support the generalization he makes in paragraph 13? Explain. (Glossary: *Supporting Evidence*)
5. In paragraphs 30 through 32, Cline tells of being "faced with the problem of what to do about his own TV set and his own children, who regularly watched TV and had their favorite programs" (30). Why does he give us this narrative, and how does it relate to the essay as a whole? (Glossary: *Unity*)

Questions on Diction and Vocabulary

1. Analyze the diction used to describe the activities of "television moguls" (10) in paragraphs 7 through 11. Which words are particularly connotative, and what do they tell you about Cline's attitude toward the television industry? (Glossary: *Connotation*)
2. Refer to your desk dictionary to determine the meanings of the following words as they are used in this selection: *depicting* (1), *wielded* (2), *pander* (21), *instigate* (22), *susceptible* (23), *reproach* (23), *predisposed* (23), *empirical* (28).

For Classroom Discussion

Victor B. Cline argues that television is a major cause of violence among children. Discuss in class other possible causes of violent behavior among children. Are these causes as plausible as television? Why, or why not?

(Note: Activities and Writing Suggestions for Cause and Effect appear on pages 248–249.)

Three Mile Island

BARRY COMMONER

*Barry Commoner was born in Brooklyn, New York, in 1917
and received degrees from Columbia and Harvard universities. Trained as a biologist, he has taught at a number of
colleges and universities and is currently University Professor of Environmental Science at Washington University
in St. Louis and Director of the Center for Biology and
Natural Systems. In recent years he has become an out-
spoken environmentalist and a highly respected critic of
nuclear power. He is a champion of nonhazardous renewable
alternative sources of energy.*

In the following essay, taken from his book The Politics
of Energy, *Commoner examines the technological difficulties
that in 1979 caused a near disaster at the Three Mile Island
nuclear facility in Harrisburg, Pennsylvania.*

The high and growing cost of nuclear power plants is due not
so much to the difficulties associated with the technology that
it has in common with non-nuclear plants—that is, the conversion of energy of steam into electricity—but rather to its
unique feature, the use of fission to supply the heat needed to
produce steam. The accident at Harrisburg showed that a failure
in the steam-to-electricity section of the plant that would have
caused very little trouble in a conventional power plant came
close to producing a catastrophic disaster in the nuclear one
and has shut down the plant for a long time, and possibly
permanently.

The Three Mile Island Power Plant produced the steam
needed to drive its electric turbines in a pressurized-water
reactor. In such a reactor, water is circulated through the reactor's

234

fuel core, where—because it is under pressure—it is heated far above its normal boiling point by the heat generated by the fission reaction. The superheated water flows through the reactor's "primary loop" into a heat exchanger where it brings water, which circulates in a "secondary loop," to the boiling point, and the resulting steam flows into the turbine to generate electricity. The spent steam is recondensed and pumped back to the heat exchanger, where it is again converted to steam, and so on. A third loop of cooling water is used to condense the steam, carrying off the excess heat to a cooling tower where it is finally released into the air. This arrangement is much more complex than the design of a conventional power system, where the steam generated in the boiler passes directly into the turbine. In this type of nuclear plant the water that circulates through the reactor (which is equivalent to the boiler in a conventional plant) becomes intensely radioactive, and the complex successive circulation loops are essential to keep that radioactivity from leaving the reactor.

On March 28, 1979, at 3:53 A.M., a pump at the Harrisburg plant failed. Because the pump failed, the reactor's heat was not drawn off in the heat exchanger and the very hot water in the primary loop overheated. The pressure in the loop increased, opening a release valve that was supposed to counteract such an event. But the valve stuck open and the primary loop system lost so much water (which ended up as a highly radioactive pool, six feet deep, on the floor of the reactor building) that it was unable to carry off all the heat generated within the reactor core. Under these circumstances, the intense heat held within the reactor could, in theory, melt its fuel rods, and the resulting "meltdown" could then carry a hugely radioactive mass through the floor of the reactor. The reactor's emergency cooling system, which is designed to prevent this disaster, was then automatically activated; but when it was, apparently, turned off too soon, some of the fuel rods overheated. This produced a bubble of hydrogen gas at the top of the reactor. (The hydrogen is dissolved in the water in order to react with oxygen that is produced when the intense reactor radiation splits water molecules into their atomic constituents. When heated, the dissolved hydrogen bubbles out of the solution.) This bubble blocked the flow of cooling water so that despite the action of the emergency cooling system the reactor core was again in danger of melting down. Another danger was that the gas might contain enough oxygen to cause an explosion that could rupture the huge containers that surround the reactor and release a deadly cloud of radioactive material into the surrounding countryside. Working desperately, technicians were able to gradually reduce the size of the gas bubble using a special apparatus brought in from the atomic laboratory at Oak Ridge, Tennessee, and the danger of a catastrophic release of radioactive materials subsided. But the sealed-off plant was now so radioactive that no one could enter it for many months—or, according to some observers, for years—without being exposed to a lethal dose of radiation.

Some radioactive gases did escape from the plant, prompting the Governor of Pennsylvania, Richard Thornburgh, to ask that pregnant women and children leave the area five miles around the plant. Many other people decided to leave as well, and within a week 60,000 or more residents had left the area, drawing money from their banks and leaving state offices and a local hospital shorthanded.

Like the horseshoe nail that lost a kingdom, the failure of a pump at the Three Mile Island Nuclear Power Plant may have lost the entire industry. It dramatized the vulnerability of the complex system that is embodied in the elaborate technology of nuclear power. In that design, the normally benign and easily controlled process of producing steam to drive an electric generator turned into a trigger for a radioactive catastrophe. . . .

FOR STUDY AND DISCUSSION

Questions on Subject

1. What is a "meltdown" (3)? What were the causes of the two potential "meltdown" situations at the Three Mile Island nuclear power plant?
2. To what degree does Commoner attribute the problems at Three Mile Island to human error?

3. A causal chain of events occurs when one cause brings about one or more effects which, in turn, can cause other effects and so on. Discuss the causal chain of events in the Three Mile Island accident as described by Commoner.

Questions on Strategy

1. In paragraph 2 Commoner explains how a nuclear power plant works. How does this description of the process function within the context of the essay? (Glossary: *Unity*)
2. In paragraphs 1 and 2 Commoner compares and contrasts the technology of conventional and nuclear power plants. What is the purpose of this comparison and contrast? (Glossary: *Unity*)
3. In paragraph 3 Commoner provides a detailed causal analysis of the events at Three Mile Island. Commoner does more than establish the chronological sequence of these events; his intention is to establish a causal relationship among them. Which words and phrases in paragraph 3 indicate cause-and-effect relationships?

Questions on Diction and Vocabulary

1. In the first sentence of paragraph 5 Commoner uses an analogy. To what does he allude in the first half of the analogy? What is the purpose of the analogy? (Glossary: *Analogy*)
2. Refer to your desk dictionary to determine the meanings of the following words as they are used in this selection: *fission* (1), *conventional* (1), *turbine* (2), *constituents* (3), *benign* (5).

For Classroom Discussion

Discuss the impact of the Three Mile Island accident on the development of nuclear power and alternate energy sources in the United States. In what ways do you think the events at Three Mile Island and the subsequent investigations and reports have changed our attitude toward the risks we are willing to take in order to satisfy our energy needs?

(Note: Activities and Writing Suggestions for Cause and Effect appear on pages 248–249.)

Marriage as a Wretched Institution

MERVYN CADWALLADER

Mervyn Cadwallader has taught sociology and humanities at San Jose State College and has directed its experimental program in humanities and sciences. In the following essay he tells of the pressures that contemporary society exerts on the institution of marriage. A veteran of three "happy marriages" himself, Cadwallader examines what he feels are some of the causes for the soaring divorce rate in the United States and offers several alternatives to the traditional marriage. "Marriage as a Wretched Institution" first appeared in the November 1966 issue of The Atlantic Monthly.

Our society expects us all to get married. With only rare exceptions we all do just that. Getting married is a rather complicated business. It involves mastering certain complex hustling and courtship games, the rituals and the ceremonies that celebrate the act of marriage, and finally the difficult requirements of domestic life with a husband or wife. It is an enormously elaborate round of activity, much more so than finding a job, and yet while many resolutely remain unemployed, few remain unmarried.

Now all this would not be particularly remarkable if there were no question about the advantages, the joys, and the rewards of married life, but most Americans, even young Americans, know or have heard that marriage is a hazardous affair. Of course, for all the increase in divorce, there are still young marriages that work, unions made by young men and women intelligent or fortunate enough to find the kind of mates they want, who know that they want children and how to love them when they come, or who find the artful blend between giving and receiving. It is not these marriages that concern us here, and that is not the trend in America today. We are concerned with the increasing number of others who, with mixed intentions and varied illusions, grope or fling themselves into marital disaster. They talk solemnly and sincerely about working to make their marriage succeed, but they are very aware of the countless marriages they have seen fail. But young people in particular do not seem to be able to relate the awesome divorce statistics to the probability of failure of their own marriage. And they rush into it, in increasing numbers, without any clear idea of the reality that underlies the myth.

Parents, teachers, and concerned adults all counsel against premature marriage. But they rarely speak the truth about marriage as it really is in modern middle-class America. The truth as I see it is that contemporary marriage is a wretched institution. It spells the end of voluntary affection, of love freely given and joyously received. Beautiful romances are transmuted into dull marriages, and eventually the relationship becomes constricting, corrosive, grinding, and destructive. The beautiful love affair becomes a bitter contract.

The basic reason for this sad state of affairs is that marriage was not designed to bear the burdens now being asked of it by the urban American middle class. It is an institution that evolved over centuries to meet some very specific functional needs of a nonindustrial society. Romantic love was viewed as tragic, or merely irrelevant. Today it is the titillating prelude to domestic tragedy, or, perhaps more frequently, to domestic grotesqueries that are only pathetic.

Marriage was not designed as a mechanism for providing friendship, erotic experience, romantic love, personal fulfillment, continuous lay psychotherapy, or recreation. The Western European family was not designed to carry a lifelong load of highly emotional romantic freight. Given its present structure, it simply has to fail when asked to do so. The very idea of an irrevocable contract obligating the parties concerned to a lifetime of romantic effort is utterly absurd.

Other pressures of the present era have tended to overburden marriage with expectations it cannot fulfill. Industrialized, urbanized America is a society which has lost the sense of community. Our ties to our society, to the bustling multitudes that make up this dazzling kaleidoscope of contemporary America, are as formal and superficial as they are numerous. We all search for community, and yet we know that the search is futile. Cut off from the support and satisfactions that flow from community, the confused and searching young American can do little but place all of his bets on creating a community in microcosm, his own marriage.

And so the ideal we struggle to reach in our love relationship is that of complete candor, total honesty. Out there all is phony, but within the romantic family there are to be no dishonest games, no hypocrisy, no misunderstanding. Here we have a painful paradox, for I submit that total exposure is probably always mutually destructive in the long run. What starts out as a tender coming together to share one's whole person with the beloved is transmuted by too much togetherness into attack and counterattack, doubt, disillusionment, and ambivalence. The moment the once-upon-a-time lover catches a glimpse of his own hatred, something precious and fragile is shattered. And soon another brave marriage will end.

The purposes of marriage have changed radically, yet we cling desperately to the outmoded structures of the past. Adult Americans behave as though the more obvious the contradiction between the old and the new, the more sentimental and irrational should be their advice to young people who are going steady or are engaged. Our schools, both high schools and colleges, teach sentimental rubbish in their marriage and family courses. The texts make much of a posture of hard-nosed objectivity that is neither objective nor hard-nosed. The basic structure of Western marriage is never questioned, alternatives are not proposed or discussed. Instead, the prospective young bride and bridegroom are offered housekeeping advice and told to work hard at making their marriage succeed. The chapter on sex, complete with ugly diagrams of the male and female genitals, is probably wedged in between a chapter on budgets and life insurance. The message is that if your marriage fails, you have been weighed in the domestic balance and found wanting. Perhaps you did not master the fifth position for sexual intercourse, or maybe you bought cheap term life rather than a preferred policy with income protection and retirement benefits. If taught honestly, these courses would alert the teen-ager and young adult to the realities of matrimonial life in the United States and try to advise them on how to survive marriage if they insist on that hazardous venture.

But teen-agers and young adults do insist upon it in greater and greater numbers with each passing year. And one of the reasons they do get married with such astonishing certainty is because they find themselves immersed in a culture that is preoccupied with and schizophrenic about sex. Advertising, entertainment, and fashion are all designed to produce and then to exploit sexual tension. Sexually aroused at an early age and asked to postpone marriage until they become adults, they have no recourse but to fill the intervening years with courtship rituals and games that are supposed to be sexy but sexless. Dating is expected to culminate in going steady, and that is the beginning of the end. The dating game hinges on an important exchange. The male wants sexual intimacy, and the female wants social commitment. The game involves bartering sex for security amid the sweet and heady agitations of a romantic entanglement. Once the game reaches the going-steady stage, marriage is virtually inevitable. The teen-ager finds himself driven into a corner, and the one way to legitimize his sex play and assuage the guilt is to plan marriage. 9

Another reason for the upsurge in young marriages is the real cultural break between teen-agers and adults in our society. This is a recent phenomenon. In my generation there was no teen culture. Adolescents wanted to become adults as soon as possible. The teen-age years were a time of impatient waiting, as teen-age boys tried to dress and act like little men. Adolescents sang the adults' songs ("South of the Border," "The Music Goes Round and Round," "Mairzy Doats"—notice I didn't say 10 anything about the quality of the music), saw their movies, listened to their radios, and waited confidently to be allowed in. We had no money, and so there was no teen-age market. There was nothing to do then but get it over with. The boundary line was sharp, and you crossed it when you took your first serious job, when you passed the employment test.

Now there is a very definite adolescent culture, which is in many ways hostile to the dreary culture of the adult world. In its most extreme form it borrows from the beats and turns the middle-class value system inside out. The hip teen-ager on Macdougal Street or Telegraph Avenue can buy a costume and go to a freak show. It's fun to be an Indian, a prankster, a beat, or a swinging troubadour. He can get stoned. That particular trip leads to instant mysticism.

Even in less extreme forms, teen culture is weighted against the adult world of responsibility. I recently asked a roomful of eighteen-year-olds to tell me what an adult is. Their deliberate answer, after hours of discussion, was that an adult is someone who no longer plays, who is no longer playful. Is Bob Dylan an adult? No, never! Of course they did not want to remain children, or teens, or adolescents; but they did want to remain youthful, playful, free of squares, and free of responsibility. The teen-ager wants to be old enough to drive, drink, screw, and travel. He does not want to get pushed into square maturity. He wants to drag the main, be a surf bum, a ski bum, or dream of being a bum. He doesn't want to go to Vietnam, or to IBM, or to buy a split-level house in Knotty Pines Estates.

This swing away from responsibility quite predictably produces friction between the adolescent and his parents. The clash of cultures is likely to drive the adolescent from the home, to persuade him to leave the dead world of his parents and strike out on his own. And here we find the central paradox of young marriages. For the only way the young person can escape from his parents is to assume many of the responsibilities that he so reviles in the life-style of his parents. He needs a job and an apartment. And he needs some kind of emotional substitute, some means of filling the emotional vacuum that leaving home has caused. And so he goes steady, and sooner rather than later, gets married to a girl with similar inclinations.

When he does this, he crosses the dividing line between 14 the cultures. Though he seldom realizes it at the time, he has taken the first step to adulthood. Our society does not have a conventional "rite of passage." In Africa the Masai adolescent takes a lion test. He becomes an adult the first time he kills a lion with a spear. Our adolescents take the domesticity test. When they get married they have to come to terms with the system in one way or another. Some brave individuals continue to fight it. But most simply capitulate.

The cool adolescent finishing high school or starting college 15 has a skeptical view of virtually every institutional sector of his society. He knows that government is corrupt, the military dehumanizing, the corporations rapacious, the churches organized hypocrisy, and the schools dishonest. But the one area that seems to be exempt from his cynicism is romantic love and marriage. When I talk to teen-agers about marriage, that cool skepticism turns to sentimental dreams right out of *Ladies' Home Journal* or the hard-hitting pages of *Reader's Digest*. They all mouth the same vapid platitudes about finding happiness through sharing and personal fulfillment through giving (each is to give 51 percent). They have all heard about divorce, and most of them have been touched by it in some way or another. Yet they insist that their marriage will be different.

So, clutching their illusions, young girls with ecstatic screams 16 of joy lead their awkward brooding boys through the portals of the church into the land of the Mustang, Apartment 24, Macy's, Sears, and the ubiquitous drive-in. They have become members in good standing of the adult world.

The end of most of these sentimental marriages is quite 17 predictable. They progress, in most cases, to varying stages of marital ennui, depending on the ability of the couple to adjust to reality; most common are (1) a lackluster standoff, (2) a bitter business carried on for the children, church, or neighbors, or (3) separation and divorce, followed by another search to find the right person.

Divorce rates have been rising in all Western countries. In 18 many countries the rates are rising even faster than in the United States. In 1910 the divorce rate for the United States was 87 per 1,000 marriages. In 1965 the rate had risen to an estimated figure of well over 300 per 1,000 in many parts of the country. At the present time some 40 percent of all brides are between the ages of fifteen and eighteen; half of these marriages break up within five years. As our population becomes younger and the age of marriage continues to drop, the divorce rate will rise to significantly higher levels.

What do we do, what can we do, about this wretched and disappointing institution? In terms of the immediate generation, the answer probably is, not much. Even when subjected to the enormous strains I have described, the habits, customs, traditions, and taboos that make up our courtship and marriage cycle are uncommonly resistant to change. Here and there creative and courageous individuals can and do work out their own unique solutions to the problem of marriage. Most of us simply suffer without understanding and thrash around blindly in an attempt to reduce the acute pain of a romance gone sour. In time, all of these individual actions will show up as a trend away from the old and toward the new, and the bulk of sluggish moderates in the population will slowly come to accept this trend as part of social evolution. Clearly, in middle-class America, the trend is ever toward more romantic courtship and marriage, earlier premarital sexual intercourse, earlier first marriages, more extramarital affairs, earlier first divorces, more frequent divorces and remarriages. The trend is away from stable lifelong monogamous relationships toward some form of polygamous male-female relationship. Perhaps we should identify it as serial or consecutive polygamy, simply because Americans in significant numbers are going to have more than one husband or more than one wife. Attitudes and laws that make multiple marriages (in sequence, of course) difficult for the romantic and sentimental among us are archaic obstacles that one learns to circumvent with the aid of weary judges and clever attorneys.

Now, the absurdity of much of this lies in the fact that we pretend that marriages of short duration must be contracted for life. Why not permit a flexible contract perhaps for one to two or more years, with periodic options to renew? If a couple grew disenchanted with their life together, they would not feel trapped for life. They would not have to anticipate and then go through the destructive agonies of divorce. They would not have to carry about the stigma of marital failure, like the mark of Cain on their foreheads. Instead of a declaration of war, they could simply let their contract lapse, and while still friendly, be free to continue their romantic quest. Sexualized romanticism is now so fundamental to American life—and is bound to become even more so—that marriage will simply have to accommodate itself to it in one way or another. For a great proportion of us it already has.

What of the children in a society that is moving inexorably 21 toward consecutive plural marriages? Under present arrangements in which marriages are ostensibly lifetime contracts and then are dissolved through hypocritical collusions or messy battles in court, the children do suffer. Marriage and divorce turn lovers into enemies, and the child is left to thread his way through the emotional wreckage of his parents' lives. Financial support of the children, mere subsistence, is not really a problem in a society as affluent as ours. Enduring emotional support of children by loving, healthy, and friendly adults is a serious problem in America, and it is a desperately urgent problem in many families where divorce is unthinkable. If the bitter and poisonous denouement of divorce could be avoided by a frank acceptance of short-term marriages, both adults and children would benefit. Any time husbands and wives and ex-husbands and ex-wives treat each other decently, generously, and respectfully, their children will benefit.

The braver and more critical among our teen-agers and 22 youthful adults will still ask, But if the institution is so bad, why get married at all? This is a tough one to deal with. The social pressures pushing any couple who live together into marriage are difficult to ignore even by the most resolute rebel. It can be done, and many should be encouraged to carry out their own creative experiments in living together in a relationship that is wholly voluntary. If the demands of society to conform seem overwhelming, the couple should know that simply to be defined by others as married will elicit married-like behavior in themselves, and that is precisely what they want to avoid.

How do you marry and yet live like gentle lovers, or at least like friendly roommates? Quite frankly, I do not know the answer to that question.

FOR STUDY AND DISCUSSION

Questions on Subject

1. Cadwallader says that "marriage is a wretched institution" (3). What, in his opinion, accounts for this "sad state of affairs" (4)?
2. Why, according to Cadwallader, do people marry? What is his attitude toward their reasons for marriage? Why do you feel a couple should marry? (Glossary: *Attitude*)
3. Why does Cadwallader feel that "the divorce rate will rise to significantly higher levels" (18)? Do you agree? Why, or why not?
4. Why, according to Cadwallader, does our society expect us to get married? Do you feel any of these pressures personally?
5. What does Cadwallader offer as a solution to the "problem of marriage" (19)? Where is that solution best stated? Is Cadwallader's solution realistic? Why, or why not? Explain.

Questions on Strategy

1. Identify and discuss some immediate and ultimate causes of divorce that Cadwallader presents.
2. Cadwallader's essay has three parts:

   a. a discussion of marriage as a wretched institution
   b. a causal analysis of the reasons why people marry and divorce
   c. a presentation of possible alternatives to the basic structure of marriage

   Identify each of these parts in the essay by paragraph number, and explain how they are unified. (Glossary: *Unity*)
3. How has Cadwallader limited and focused the subject of his essay? Why do you suppose such limitations were necessary?
4. What is the function of the last paragraph in the essay? (Glossary: *Endings*)

Questions on Diction and Vocabulary

1. Cadwallader examines many causal relationships in his essay. Identify key words or phrases such as "reason" (4) and "predictably produces" (13), and explain how each indicates a causal relationship.
2. At one time, people who divorced carried with them "the stigma of marital failure" (20). What connotations do the words *divorce* and *divorced* carry with them today? (Glossary: *Connotation*)
3. Refer to your desk dictionary to determine the meanings of the following words as they are used in this selection: *rituals* (1), *corrosive* (3), *candor* (7), *capitulate* (14), *archaic* (19), *collusions* (21), *elicit* (22).

For Classroom Discussion

How would you respond to Cadwallader's charge that teenagers want all the freedoms accorded adults in our society but none of the responsibilities that accompany these rights and privileges?

(Note: Activities and Writing Suggestions for Cause and Effect appear on pages 248–249.)

Activities and Writing Suggestions for Cause and Effect

ACTIVITIES

1. Superstitions are examples of a common fault in logical thinking known as *post hoc, ergo propter hoc* ("after this, therefore because of this"). Avoid this fault by being careful not to see one event as causing another just because one event precedes another. Discuss Huck's analysis of the events he describes in the following passage from Mark Twain's *The Adventures of Huckleberry Finn*.

   > I've always reckoned that looking at the new moon over your left shoulder is one of the carelessest and foolishest things a body can do. Old Hank Bunker done it once, and bragged about it; and in less than two years he got drunk and fell off of the shot-tower and spread himself out so that he was just kind of a layer, as you may say; and they slid him edgeways between two barn doors for a coffin, and buried him so, so they say, but I didn't see it. Pap told me. But anyway, it all come of looking at the moon that way, like a fool.

2. There is often more than one cause for an event. Make a list of at least six possible causes for each of the following:

   a. a quarrel with a friend
   b. an upset victory in football
   c. doing well on an exam
   d. an automobile accident

   Examine each of your lists, and identify the causes in each list which seem most probable. Which of these are immediate causes and which are ultimate causes? Compare your lists with those prepared by your classmates. What conclusions about the relationship between causes and effects can you draw?

3. Consider each of the following sentences, and select one for use as the controlling idea for a brief essay. Discuss the types of evidence that you would need to develop adequately the causal relationship implied by the controlling idea.

   a. Cities make me feel lonely.
   b. Exams can be an education in themselves.
   c. Traveling can be a frustrating experience.
   d. Dieting can be dangerous to your health.

WRITING SUGGESTIONS

1. Write an essay in which you analyze the most significant reasons why you went to college. You may wish to discuss such matters as your family background, your high-school experience, people and events that influenced your decision, and your goals in college as well as in later life.

2. It is interesting to think of ourselves in terms of the influences that have caused us to be what we are. Write an essay in which you discuss two or three of what you consider the most important influences on your life. Below are some areas you may wish to consider in planning and writing your paper:

   a. a parent
   b. a book or movie
   c. a member of the clergy
   d. a teacher
   e. a hero
   f. a friend
   g. a youth organization
   h. a coach
   i. your neighborhood
   j. your ethnic background

3. Decisions often involve cause-and-effect relationships; that is, a person usually weighs the possible results of an action before deciding to act. Write an essay in which you consider the possible effects that would result from one decision or another in one of the following controversies:

   a. taxing cars on the basis of fuel consumption
   b. reinstituting the military draft
   c. legalizing marijuana
   d. mandatory licensing of handguns

8

ARGUMENTATION

To argue is to attempt to convince your reader to agree with your point of view, to make a given decision, or to pursue a particular course of action. Because the writer of an argument is interested in explaining a subject as well as in advocating a particular view, argumentation frequently adopts the other rhetorical strategies. Nevertheless, it is the writer's attempt to convince, not explain, that is of primary importance in an argumentative essay.

A writer can appeal to an audience in many ways. In logical argumentation, the writer makes a reasoned appeal, one which aims at a reader's rational or intellectual faculties. A writer can also use varying degrees of persuasion and, thereby, appeal to a reader's emotions and prejudices. *Logical argument* changes a reader's thinking, whereas *persuasive argument* changes a reader's feelings. The degree to which one or the other of these appeals is emphasized in a piece of writing depends on the writer's subject, specific purpose in using argumentation, and intended audience. While you may occasionally need to make emotional appeals to your readers, most often in your college work you will need to rely on the fundamental techniques of logical argumentation.

Inasmuch as argumentation may incorporate exposition, narration, and description, an argumentative essay can take many

250

forms. Argumentative essays do, however, have a number of features in common.

Somewhere near the beginning of an argumentative essay, you should identify the issue to be discussed, explain why you feel it is important, and point out what interest you and your reader share in the issue. Because it is unlikely that all readers will agree with your particular position, you may wish to acknowledge the merits of their strongest objections and explain why you feel your position is more valid.

Then, in the body of your essay, you should organize the various points of your argument. You may move from your least important point to your most important point, from the most familiar to the least familiar, from the easiest to accept or comprehend to the most difficult. For each point in your argument, you should provide appropriate supporting evidence—facts and statistics, illustrative examples and narratives, or quotations from authorities. This evidence should be logical, and it should be presented in a reasoned way, by induction or deduction. *Inductive reasoning,* the more common in argumentation, moves from a set of specific examples to a general statement. Inductive reasoning is the method of the detective, who gathers facts, analyzes them, and derives a conclusion from them. *Deductive reasoning,* on the other hand, moves from a general statement to a specific conclusion and works on the model of the syllogism, a simple three-part argument that consists of a major premise, a minor premise, and a conclusion. For example, notice how the following syllogism works:

a. All humans are mortal. (major premise)
b. Judy is a human. (minor premise)
c. Judy is mortal. (conclusion)

In constructing your argument, you should be careful to avoid *logical fallacies,* flaws in your reasoning that will render your argument invalid. A discussion of logical fallacies together with examples of the more common fallacies appears in the Glossary.

In the conclusion of your essay, you should briefly restate your position. Besides persuading your reader to your point of view, you may also encourage some specific course of action.

Above all, your conclusion should not surprise your reader; it should follow naturally from the points you have presented in the body of your essay.

In the essays in this section, the authors use argumentation to address issues concerning the quality of life. For example, Rachel Carson argues against the uncontrolled use of lethal chemicals; Norman Cousins argues against living a life without dignity or sensitivity; and Alvin Toffler argues for controlled technological progress. Each author in the section is interested not only in explaining his or her views on the subject but also in advocating a particular position or course of action.

The Obligation to Endure

RACHEL CARSON

Rachel Carson (1907–1964), zoologist and accomplished writer, has written much about the marine world. Her delightfully warm and sensitive interpretations of scientific data in Under the Sea Wind, The Sea Around Us, *and* The Edge of the Sea *made these books very popular. But it was* Silent Spring, *her study of herbicides and insecticides, that made Carson a controversial figure. Once denounced as an alarmist, she is now recognized as having been a powerful force in the ecology movement.*

In "The Obligation to Endure," the second chapter of Silent Spring *(1962), Carson argues for a more responsible use of pesticides.*

The history of life on earth has been a history of interaction   1
between living things and their surroundings. To a large extent,
the physical form and the habits of the earth's vegetation and
its animal life have been molded by the environment. Considering the whole span of earthly time, the opposite effect, in
which life actually modifies its surroundings, has been relatively
slight. Only within the moment of time represented by the
present century has one species—man—acquired significant
power to alter the nature of his world.

During the past quarter century this power has not only   2
increased to one of disturbing magnitude but it has changed
in character. The most alarming of all man's assaults upon the
environment is the contamination of air, earth, rivers, and sea
with dangerous and even lethal materials. This pollution is for
the most part irrecoverable; the chain of evil it initiates not
only in the world that must support life but in living tissues

is for the most part irreversible. In this now universal contamination of the environment, chemicals are the sinister and little recognized partners of radiation in changing the very nature of the world—the very nature of its life. Strontium 90, released through nuclear explosions into the air, comes to earth in rain or drifts down as fallout, lodges in soil, enters the grass or corn or wheat grown there, and in time takes up its abode in the bones of a human being, there to remain until his death. Similarly, chemicals sprayed on croplands or forests or garden lie long in soil, entering into living organisms, passing from one to another in a chain of poisoning and death. Or they pass mysteriously by underground streams until they emerge and through the alchemy of air and sunlight, combine into new forms that kill vegetation, sicken cattle, and work unknown harm on those who drink from once pure wells. As Albert Schweitzer has said, "Man can hardly even recognize the devils of his own creation."

It took hundreds of millions of years to produce the life that now inhabits the earth—eons of time in which that developing and evolving and diversifying life reached a state of adjustment and balance with its surroundings. The environment, rigorously shaping and directing the life it supported, contained elements that were hostile as well as supporting. Certain rocks gave out dangerous radiation; even within the light of the sun, from which all life draws its energy, there were short-wave radiations with power to injure. Given time—time not in years but in millennia—life adjusts, and a balance has been reached. For time is the essential ingredient; but in the modern world there is no time.

The rapidity of change and the speed with which new situations are created follow the impetuous and heedless pace of man rather than the deliberate pace of nature. Radiation is no longer merely the background radiation of rocks, the bombardment of cosmic rays, the ultraviolet of the sun that have existed before there was any life on earth; radiation is now the unnatural creation of man's tampering with the atom. The chemicals to which life is asked to make its adjustment are no longer merely the calcium and silica and copper and all the rest of the minerals washed out of the rocks and carried in rivers to the sea; they are the synthetic creations of man's inventive mind, brewed in his laboratories, and having no counterparts in nature.

To adjust to these chemicals would require time on the scale that is nature's; it would require not merely the years of a man's life but the life of generations. And even this, were it by some miracle possible, would be futile, for the new chemicals come from our laboratories in an endless stream; almost five hundred annually find their way into actual use in the United States alone. The figure is staggering and its implications are not easily grasped—500 new chemicals to which the bodies of men and animals are required somehow to adapt each year, chemicals totally outside the limits of biologic experience.

Among them are many that are used in man's war against nature. Since the mid-1940's over 200 basic chemicals have been created for use in killing insects, weeds, rodents, and other organisms described in the modern vernacular as "pests"; and they are sold under several thousand different brand names.

These sprays, dusts, and aerosols are now applied almost universally to farms, gardens, forests, and homes—nonselective chemicals that have the power to kill every insect, the "good" and the "bad," to still the song of birds and the leaping of fish in the streams, to coat the leaves with a deadly film, and to linger on in soil—all this though the intended target may be only a few weeds or insects. Can anyone believe it is possible to lay down such a barrage of poisons on the surface of the earth without making it unfit for all life? They should not be called "insecticides," but "biocides."

The whole process of spraying seems caught up in an endless spiral. Since DDT was released for civilian use, a process of escalation has been going on in which ever more toxic materials must be found. This has happened because insects, in a triumphant vindication of Darwin's principle of the survival of the fittest, have evolved super races immune to the particular insecticide used, hence a deadlier one has always to be developed—and then a deadlier one than that. It has happened also because destructive insects often undergo a "flareback," or resurgence, after spraying, in numbers greater than before.

Thus the chemical war is never won, and all life is caught in its violent crossfire.

Along with the possibility of the extinction of mankind by nuclear war, the central problem of our age has therefore become the contamination of man's total environment with such substances of incredible potential for harm—substances that accumulate in the tissues of plants and animals and even penetrate the germ cells to shatter or alter the very material of heredity upon which the shape of the future depends.

Some would-be architects of our future look toward a time when it will be possible to alter the human germ plasm by design. But we may easily be doing so now by inadvertence for many chemicals, like radiation, bring about gene mutations. It is ironic to think that man might determine his own future by something so seemingly trivial as the choice of an insect spray.

All this has been risked—for what? Future historians may well be amazed by our distorted sense of proportion. How could intelligent beings seek to control a few unwanted species by a method that contaminated the entire environment and brought the threat of disease and death even to their own kind? Yet this is precisely what we have done. We have done it, moreover, for reasons that collapse the moment we examine them. We are told that the enormous and expanding use of pesticides is necessary to maintain farm production. Yet is our real problem not one of *overproduction*? Our farms, despite measures to remove acreages from production and to pay farmers *not* to produce, have yielded such a staggering excess of crops that the American taxpayer in 1962 is paying out more than one billion dollars a year as the total carrying cost of the surplus-food storage program. And is the situation helped when one branch of the Agriculture Department tries to reduce production while another states, as it did in 1958, "It is believed generally that reduction of crop acreages under provisions of the Soil Bank will stimulate interest in use of chemicals to obtain maximum production on the land retained in crops."

All this is not to say there is no insect problem and no need of control. I am saying, rather, that control must be geared to realities, not to mythical situations, and that the methods employed must be such that they do not destroy us along with the insects.

The problem whose attempted solution has brought such a 13 train of disaster in its wake is an accompaniment of our modern way of life. Long before the age of man, insects inhabited the earth—a group of extraordinarily varied and adaptable beings. Over the course of time since man's advent, a small percentage of the more than half a million species of insects have come into conflict with human welfare in two principal ways: as competitors for the food supply and as carriers of human disease.

Disease-carrying insects become important where human 14 beings are crowded together, especially under conditions where sanitation is poor, as in time of natural disaster or war or in situations of extreme poverty and deprivation. Then control of some sort becomes necessary. It is a sobering fact, however, that the method of massive chemical control has had only limited success, and also threatens to worsen the very conditions it is intended to curb.

Under primitive agricultural conditions the farmer had few 15 insect problems. These arose with the intensification of agri-culture—the devotion of immense acreages to a single crop. Such a system set the stage for explosive increases in specific insect populations. Single-crop farming does not take advantage of the principles by which nature works; it is agriculture as an engineer might conceive it to be. Nature has introduced great variety into the landscape, but man has displayed a passion for simplifying it. Thus he undoes the built-in checks and balances by which nature holds the species within bounds. One important natural check is a limit on the amount of suitable habitat for each species. Obviously then, an insect that lives on wheat can build up its population to much higher levels on a farm devoted to wheat than on one in which wheat is intermingled with other crops to which the insect is not adapted.

The same thing happens in other situations. A generation 16 or more ago, the towns of large areas of the United States lined their streets with the noble elm tree. Now the beauty they hopefully created is threatened with complete destruction as disease sweeps through the elms, carried by a beetle that would have only limited chance to build up large populations and to spread from tree to tree if the elms were only occasional trees in a richly diversified planting.

Another factor in the modern insect problem is one that must be viewed against a background of geologic and human history: the spreading of thousands of different kinds of organisms from their native homes to invade new territories. This worldwide migration has been studied and graphically described by the British ecologist Charles Elton in his recent book *The Ecology of Invasions*. During the Cretaceous Period, some hundred million years ago, flooding seas cut many land bridges between continents and living things found themselves confined in what Elton calls "colossal separate nature reserves." There, isolated from others of their kind, they developed many new species. When some of the land masses were joined again, about 15 million years ago, these species began to move out into new territories—a movement that is not only still in progress but is now receiving considerable assistance from man.

The importation of plants is the primary agent in the modern spread of species, for animals have almost invariably gone along with the plants, quarantine being a comparatively recent and not completely effective innovation. The United States Office of Plant Introduction alone has introduced almost 200,000 species and varieties of plants from all over the world. Nearly half of the 180 or so major insect enemies of plants in the United States are accidental imports from abroad, and most of them have come as hitchhikers on plants.

In new territory, out of reach of the restraining hand of the natural enemies that kept down its numbers in its native land, an invading plant or animal is able to become enormously abundant. Thus it is no accident that our most troublesome insects are introduced species.

These invasions, both the naturally occurring and those dependent on human assistance, are likely to continue indefinitely. Quarantine and massive chemical campaigns are only extremely expensive ways of buying time. We are faced, according to Dr. Elton, "with a life-and-death need not just to find new technological means of suppressing this plant or that animal"; instead we need the basic knowledge of animal populations and their relations to their surroundings that will "promote an even balance and damp down the explosive power of outbreaks and new invasions."

Much of the necessary knowledge is now available but we 21 do not use it. We train ecologists in our universities and even employ them in our governmental agencies but we seldom take their advice. We allow the chemical death rain to fall as though there were no alternative, whereas in fact there are many, and our ingenuity could soon discover many more if given opportunity.

Have we fallen into a mesmerized state that makes us accept 22 as inevitable that which is inferior or detrimental, as though having lost the will or the vision to demand that which is good? Such thinking, in the words of the ecologist Paul Shepard, "idealizes life with only its head out of water, inches above the limits of toleration of the corruption of its own environment. . . . Why should we tolerate a diet of weak poisons, a home in insipid surroundings, a circle of acquaintances who are not quite our enemies, the noise of motors with just enough relief to prevent insanity? Who would want to live in a world which is just not quite fatal?"

Yet such a world is pressed upon us. The crusade to create 23 a chemically sterile, insect-free world seems to have engendered a fanatic zeal on the part of many specialists and most of the so-called control agencies. On every hand there is evidence that those engaged in spraying operations exercise a ruthless power. "The regulatory entomologists . . . function as prosecutor, judge and jury, tax assessor and collector and sheriff to enforce their own orders," said Connecticut entomologist Neely Turner. The most flagrant abuses go unchecked in both state and federal agencies.

It is not my contention that chemical insecticides must never 24 be used. I do contend that we have put poisonous and biologically potent chemicals indiscriminately into the hands of persons largely or wholly ignorant of their potentials for harm.

We have subjected enormous numbers of people to contact with these poisons, without their consent and often without their knowledge. If the Bill of Rights contains no guarantee that a citizen shall be secure against lethal poisons distributed either by private individuals or by public officials, it is surely only because our forefathers, despite their considerable wisdom and foresight, could conceive of no such problem.

I contend, furthermore, that we have allowed these chemicals to be used with little or no advance investigation of their effect on soil, water, wildlife, and man himself. Future generations are unlikely to condone our lack of prudent concern for the integrity of the natural world that supports all life.

There is still very limited awareness of the nature of the threat. This is an era of specialists, each of whom sees his own problem and is unaware of or intolerant of the larger frame into which it fits. It is also an era dominated by industry, in which the right to make a dollar at whatever cost is seldom challenged. When the public protests, confronted with some obvious evidence of damaging results of pesticide applications, it is fed little tranquilizing pills of half truth. We urgently need an end to these false assurances, to the sugar coating of unpalatable facts. It is the public that is being asked to assume the risks that the insect controllers calculate. The public must decide whether it wishes to continue on the present road, and it can do so only when in full possession of the facts. In the words of Jean Rostand, "The obligation to endure gives us the right to know."

FOR STUDY AND DISCUSSION

Questions on Subject

1. Humans in the twentieth century have acquired the power to modify their environment. Why does Rachel Carson find this power so disturbing?
2. What is the "chain of evil" (2) that pollution initiates?
3. Why are the "pace of nature" (4) and the "pace of man" (4) in conflict? What problems are caused by this conflict?

4. Carson devotes much of her essay to a critical examination of the use of insecticides to control the insect population. What are her attitudes toward chemical insecticides and insect control?
5. What is the significance of the title that Carson has given this essay?

Questions on Strategy

1. What is Carson's thesis, and where is it stated? (Glossary: *Thesis*)
2. How does Carson organize her essay? (Outlining the essay will help you determine its organization.) What devices does the author use to unify the various parts? (Glossary: *Coherence*)
3. What types of evidence does Carson use to support her argument? Are you convinced by her evidence? Why or why not? (Glossary: *Supporting Evidence*)
4. An effective strategy in argumentation is to anticipate and refute an opponent's arguments. Where in this essay does Carson employ this strategy? How effective is her use of the strategy?
5. What is the function of the questions that begin paragraphs 11 and 22? (Glossary: *Rhetorical Question*)

Questions on Diction and Vocabulary

1. Carson's essay in large part examines "man's war against nature" (6). Identify those words and phrases that Carson uses to develop and sustain the image of warfare. How appropriate, in your opinion, is this dominant image?
2. What is the connotative value of the italicized words or phrases in each of the following excerpts from the essay?

    a. considering the whole span of *earthly time* (1)
    b. the *chain of evil* it initiates (2)
    c. chemicals are the *sinister* and little recognized *partners* of radiation (2)
    d. through the *alchemy* of air and sunlight (2)
    e. man has displayed a *passion* for simplifying it (15)
    f. most of them have come as *hitchhikers* on plants (18)
    g. we allow the *chemical death rain* to fall (21)
    h. it is surely only because our *forefathers* (24)
    i. it is fed little *tranquilizing pills of half truth* (26)
    j. *sugar coating* of unpalatable facts (26)

3. Do you feel that Carson's statement that nonselective chemicals

"should not be called 'insecticides,' but 'biocides' " (7) is justified? Explain.

4. Refer to your desk dictionary to determine the meanings of the following words as they are used in this selection: *impetuous* (4), *toxic* (8), *habitat* (15), *ingenuity* (21), *insipid* (22), *flagrant* (23), *potent* (24).

For Classroom Discussion

In 1962, Rachel Carson argued that "we have put poisonous and biologically potent chemicals indiscriminately into the hands of persons largely or wholly ignorant of their potentials for harm" (24). The validity of her charge is everywhere evident today. Discuss specific examples of chemical abuse that have been brought to our attention in recent years. How has the public responded to these reports?

(Note: Activities and Writing Suggestions for Argumentation appear on pages 295–298.)

The Declaration of Independence

THOMAS JEFFERSON

President, governor, statesman, diplomat, lawyer, architect, philosopher, thinker, and writer, Thomas Jefferson was one of the most important figures in the early history of our country. He was born in Albemarle County, Virginia, in 1743 and attended the College of William and Mary. After being admitted to law practice in 1767, he began his long and illustrious career of public service to the colonies and, later, the new republic.

In 1776 Jefferson drafted the Declaration of Independence. Although it was revised by Benjamin Franklin and his colleagues in the Continental Congress, the document retains in its sound logic and forceful and direct style the unmistakable qualities of Jefferson's prose. In 1809, after two terms as president, Jefferson retired to Monticello, a home he designed and helped to build. Ten years later he founded the University of Virginia. Jefferson died at Monticello on July 4, 1826, the fiftieth anniversary of the signing of the Declaration of Independence.

When in the course of human events, it becomes necessary for 1
one people to dissolve the political bands which have connected them with another, and to assume among the Powers of the earth, the separate and equal station to which the Laws of Nature and of Nature's God entitle them, a decent respect to the opinions of mankind requires that they should declare the causes which impel them to the separation.

We hold these truths to be self-evident, that all men are created equal, that they are endowed by their Creator with certain unalienable Rights, that among these are Life, Liberty and the pursuit of Happiness. That to secure these rights, Governments are instituted among Men deriving their just powers from the consent of the governed. That whenever any Form of Government becomes destructive of these ends, it is the Right of the People to alter or to abolish it, and to institute new Government, laying its foundation on such principles and organizing its powers in such form, as to them shall seem most likely to effect their Safety and Happiness. Prudence, indeed, will dictate that Governments long established should not be changed for light and transient causes; and accordingly all experience hath shown, that mankind are more disposed to suffer, while evils are sufferable, than to right themselves by abolishing the forms to which they are accustomed. But when a long train of abuses and usurpations pursuing invariably the same Object evinces a design to reduce them under absolute Despotism, it is their right, it is their duty, to throw off such government, and to provide new Guards for their future security. Such has been the patient sufferance of these Colonies; and such is now the necessity which constrains them to alter their former Systems of Government. The history of the present King of Great Britain is a history of repeated injuries and usurpations, all having in direct object the establishment of an absolute Tyranny over these States. To prove this, let Facts be submitted to a candid world.

He has refused his Assent to Laws, the most wholesome and necessary for the public good.

He has forbidden his Governors to pass Laws of immediate and pressing importance, unless suspended in their operation till his Assent should be obtained; and when so suspended, he has utterly neglected to attend to them.

He has refused to pass other Laws for the accommodation of large districts of people, unless those people would relinquish the right of Representation in the Legislature, a right inestimable to them and formidable to tyrants only.

He has called together legislative bodies at places unusual, uncomfortable, and distant from the depository of their Public

Records, for the sole purpose of fatiguing them into compliance with his measures.

He has dissolved Representative Houses repeatedly, for op- 7
posing with manly firmness his invasions on the rights of the people.

He has refused for a long time, after such dissolutions, to 8
cause others to be elected; whereby the Legislative Powers, incapable of Annihilation, have returned to the People at large for their exercise; the State remaining in the mean time exposed to all the dangers of invasion from without, and convulsions within.

He has endeavoured to prevent the population of these States; 9
for that purpose obstructing the Laws of Naturalization of Foreigners; refusing to pass others to encourage their migration hither, and raising the conditions of new Appropriations of Lands.

He has obstructed the Administration of Justice, by refusing 10
his Assent to Laws for establishing Judiciary Powers.

He has made Judges dependent on his Will alone, for the 11
tenure of their offices, and the amount and payment of their salaries.

He has erected a multitude of New Offices, and sent hither 12
swarms of Officers to harass our People, and eat out their substance.

He has kept among us, in time of peace, Standing Armies 13
without the Consent of our Legislature.

He has affected to render the Military independent of and 14
superior to the Civil Power.

He has combined with others to subject us to jurisdictions 15
foreign to our constitution, and unacknowledged by our laws; giving his Assent to their acts of pretended Legislation:

For quartering large bodies of armed troops among us: 16

For protecting them, by a mock Trial, from Punishment for 17
any Murders which they should commit on the Inhabitants of these States:

For cutting off our Trade with all parts of the world: 18

For imposing Taxes on us without our Consent: 19

For depriving us in many cases, of the benefits of Trial by 20
Jury:

For transporting us beyond Seas to be tried for pretended offenses:

For abolishing the free System of English Laws in a Neighbouring Province, establishing therein an Arbitrary government, and enlarging its boundaries so as to render it at once an example and fit instrument for introducing the same absolute rule into these Colonies:

For taking away our Charters, abolishing our most valuable Laws, and altering fundamentally the Forms of our Governments:

For suspending our own Legislatures, and declaring themselves invested with Power to legislate for us in all cases whatsoever.

He has abdicated Government here, by declaring us out of his Protection and waging War against us.

He has plundered our seas, ravaged our Coasts, burnt our towns and destroyed the Lives of our people.

He is at this time transporting large Armies of foreign Mercenaries to compleat works of death, desolation and tyranny, already begun with circumstances of Cruelty & perfidy scarcely paralleled in the most barbarous ages, and totally unworthy the Head of a civilized nation.

He has constrained our fellow Citizens taken Captive on the high Seas to bear Arms against their Country, to become the executioners of their friends and Brethren, or to fall themselves by their Hands.

He has excited domestic insurrections amongst us, and has endeavoured to bring on the inhabitants of our frontiers, the merciless Indian Savages, whose known rule of warfare, is an undistinguished destruction of all ages, sexes and conditions.

In every stage of these Oppressions We Have Petitioned for Redress in the most humble terms: Our repeated petitions have been answered only by repeated injury. A Prince, whose character is thus marked by every act which may define a Tyrant, is unfit to be the ruler of a free People.

Not have We been wanting in attention to our British brethren. We have warned them from time to time of attempts by their legislature to extend an unwarrantable jurisdiction over us. We have reminded them of the circumstances of our emigration and settlement here. We have appealed to their native justice and magnanimity and we have conjured them by the ties of our common kindred to disavow these usurpations, which would inevitably interrupt our connections and correspondence. They too have been deaf to the voice of justice and of consanguinity. We must, therefore acquiesce in the necessity, which denounces our Separation, and hold them, as we hold the rest of mankind, Enemies in War, in Peace Friends.

We, therefore, the Representatives of the United States of America, in General Congress, Assembled, appealing to the Supreme Judge of the world for the rectitude of our intentions, do, in the Name, and by Authority of the good People of these Colonies, solemnly publish and declare, That these United Colonies are, and of Right ought to be Free and Independent States; that they are Absolved from all Allegiance to the British Crown, and that all political connection between them and the State of Great Britain, is and ought to be totally dissolved; and that as Free and Independent States, they have full power to levy War, conclude Peace, contract Alliances, establish Commerce, and to do all other Acts and Things which Independent States may of right do. And for the support of this Declaration, with a firm reliance on the protection of Divine Providence, we mutually pledge to each other our lives, our Fortunes and our sacred Honor.

32

FOR STUDY AND DISCUSSION

Questions on Subject

1. Where, according to Jefferson, do rulers get their authority? What does Jefferson believe is the purpose of government?
2. In paragraphs 3 through 29, Jefferson lists the many ways King George has wronged the colonists. Which of these "injuries and usurpations" do you feel are just cause for the colonies to declare their independence?
3. In paragraph 2, Jefferson presents certain "self-evident" truths. What are these truths, and how are they related to the intent of his argument?

4. What are the specific points of Jefferson's declaration in the final paragraph?

Questions on Strategy

1. The Declaration of Independence is a deductive argument; it is, therefore, possible to present it in the form of a syllogism. What are the major premise, the minor premise, and the conclusion of Jefferson's argument? (Glossary: *Syllogism*)
2. The list of charges against the king is given as evidence in support of Jefferson's minor premise. Does he offer any evidence in support of his major premise? Why, or why not? (Glossary: *Supporting Evidence*)
3. How, specifically, does Jefferson refute the possible charge that the colonists had not tried to solve their problems by less drastic means?
4. In the context of Jefferson's argument, what is the function of paragraph 31?
5. Identify several instances in which Jefferson uses parallel structure, and explain what he achieves by using it. (Glossary: *Parallelism*)

Questions on Diction and Vocabulary

1. While the basic structure of the Declaration of Independence reflects sound deductive reasoning, Jefferson's language, particularly when he lists the charges against the king, tends to be emotional. Identify as many examples of this emotional language as you can, and discuss possible reasons why Jefferson uses this emotionally charged language in his argument.
2. Comment on the connotative value of each of the italicized words in the following excerpts from this selection (Glossary: *Connotation*):

   a. necessary for one people to *dissolve* the political bands (1)
   b. it is their *duty* (2)
   c. let Facts be submitted to a *candid* world (2)
   d. sole purpose of *fatiguing* them into compliance (6)
   e. wanting in attention to our British *brethren* (31)

3. Refer to your desk dictionary to determine the meanings of the following words as they are used in this selection: *prudence* (2), *usurpations* (2), *convulsions* (8), *abdicated* (25), *perfidy* (27), *conjured* (31), *consanguinity* (31), *acquiesce* (31), *rectitude* (32).

For Classroom Discussion

Why, in your opinion, have so many individuals and groups used the Declaration of Independence as a model for the redress of their own grievances?

(Note: Activities and Writing Suggestions for Argumentation appear on pages 295–298.)

The Right to Die

NORMAN COUSINS

Norman Cousins was born in New Jersey in 1915, and after attending Columbia University he began a long and industrious career as a journalist and writer. Cousins has taught at a number of universities and colleges and has won many awards for his service to education and the world community. He is perhaps best known, however, as the editor of Saturday Review, *a position he held for thirty-eight years. His numerous books include* The Last Defense in a Nuclear Age, The Celebration of Life, The Quest for Immortality, *and most recently* Anatomy of An Illness as Perceived by the Patient: Reflections on Healing and Regeneration, *his widely read account of how he coped with a nearly fatal illness.*

"The Right to Die" was first published in Saturday Review *in 1975.*

The world of religion and philosophy was shocked recently when Henry P. Van Dusen and his wife ended their lives by their own hands. Dr. Van Dusen had been president of Union Theological Seminary; for more than a quarter-century he had been one of the luminous names in Protestant theology. He enjoyed world status as a spiritual leader. News of the self-inflicted death of the Van Dusens, therefore, was profoundly disturbing to all those who attach a moral stigma to suicide and regard it as a violation of God's laws.

Dr. Van Dusen had anticipated this reaction. He and his wife left behind a letter that may have historic significance. It was very brief, but the essential point it made is now being widely discussed by theologians and could represent the beginning of a reconsideration of traditional religious attitudes toward self-inflicted death. The letter raised a moral issue: does an individual have the obligation to go on living even when the beauty and meaning and power of life are gone?

Henry and Elizabeth Van Dusen had lived full lives. In recent 3
years, they had become increasingly ill, requiring almost continual medical care. Their infirmities were worsening, and they realized they would soon become completely dependent for even the most elementary needs and functions. Under these circumstances, little dignity would have been left in life. They didn't like the idea of taking up space in a world with too many mouths and too little food. They believed it was a misuse of medical science to keep them technically alive.

They therefore believed they had the right to decide when 4
to die. In making that decision, they weren't turning against life as the highest value; what they were turning against was the notion that there were no circumstances under which life should be discontinued.

An important aspect of human uniqueness is the power of 5
free will. In his books and lectures, Dr. Van Dusen frequently spoke about the exercise of this uniqueness. The fact that he used his free will to prevent life from becoming a caricature of itself was completely in character. In their letter, the Van Dusens sought to convince family and friends that they were not acting solely out of despair or pain.

The use of free will to put an end to one's life finds no 6
sanction in the theology to which Pitney Van Dusen was committed. Suicide symbolizes discontinuity; religion symbolizes continuity, represented at its quintessence by the concept of the immortal soul. Human logic finds it almost impossible to come to terms with the concept of nonexistence. In religion, the human mind finds a larger dimension and is relieved of the ordeal of a confrontation with non-existence.

Even without respect to religion, the idea of suicide has been 7
abhorrent throughout history. Some societies have imposed severe penalties on the families of suicides in the hope that the individual who sees no reason to continue his existence may be deterred by the stigma his self-destruction would inflict on

loved ones. Other societies have enacted laws prohibiting suicide on the grounds that it is murder. The enforcement of such laws, of course, has been an exercise in futility.

Customs and attitudes, like individuals themselves, are largely shaped by the surrounding environment. In today's world, life can be prolonged by science far beyond meaning or sensibility. Under these circumstances, individuals who feel they have nothing more to give to life, or to receive from it, need not be applauded, but they can be spared our condemnation.

The general reaction to suicide is bound to change as people come to understand that it may be a denial, not an assertion, of moral or religious ethics to allow life to be extended without regard to decency or pride. What moral or religious purpose is celebrated by the annihilation of the human spirit in the triumphant act of keeping the body alive? Why are so many people more readily appalled by an unnatural form of dying than by an unnatural form of living?

"Nowadays," the Van Dusens wrote in their last letter, "it is difficult to die. We feel that this way we are taking will become more usual and acceptable as the years pass.

"Of course, the thought of our children and our grandchildren makes us sad, but we still feel that this is the best way and the right way to go. We are both increasingly weak and unwell and who would want to die in a nursing home?

"We are not afraid to die. . . ."

Pitney Van Dusen was admired and respected in life. He can be admired and respected in death. "Suicide," said Goethe, "is an incident in human life which, however much disputed and discussed, demands the sympathy of every man, and in every age must be dealt with anew."

Death is not the greatest loss in life. The greatest loss is what dies inside us while we live. The unbearable tragedy is to live without dignity or sensitivity.

FOR STUDY AND DISCUSSION

Questions on Subject

1. What basic question did the Van Dusens' suicide letter raise?
2. What position does Cousins take with respect to the central question raised by the Van Dusens' letter? Where is his position stated?
3. Why, according to Cousins, has the idea of suicide been so "abhorrent throughout history" (7)? Why does he feel that this general reaction to suicide will change?
4. Many people throughout history have committed suicide. Why does Cousins find the suicides of the Van Dusens so interesting?

Questions on Strategy

1. Cousins argues inductively in this essay. Trace the development of his argument. Where does he move from his evidence to his generalization?
2. In what ways does Cousins use the case of the Van Dusens' suicides to support his argument?
3. In paragraph 9 Cousins asserts that "the general reaction to suicide is bound to change." How does he support this generalization?

Questions on Diction and Vocabulary

1. In reference to the Van Dusens, Cousins uses the phrase "self-inflicted death" (1, 2). Elsewhere in the essay he uses the word *suicide*. What distinction, if any, does Cousins appear to be making?
2. Comment on the connotative value of the italicized words or phrases in each of the following excerpts (Glossary: *Connotation*):

   a. one of the *luminous* names in Protestant theology (1)
   b. to keep them *technically alive* (3)
   c. to prevent life from becoming a *caricature* of itself (5)
   d. what moral or religious purpose is *celebrated* (9)

3. Refer to your desk dictionary to determine the meanings of the following words as they are used in this selection: *stigma* (1), *sanction* (6), *quintessence* (6), *annihilation* (9), *appalled* (9).

For Classroom Discussion

If you wished to take issue with Cousins's arguments, what main points would you make? What evidence would you need to support these points?

(Note: Activities and Writing Suggestions for Argumentation appear on pages 295–298.)

Health and High Voltage

KELLY DAVIS

Kelly Davis was born in Mt. Kisco, New York, and received two degrees from Syracuse University, one in fine arts and another in journalism. Currently, she is the director of the Council of Parks Friends, an environmental group concerned with parks and public land. She is responsible for developing nature centers and educational programs at parks in central New York. Davis writes a regular column for Central New York Environment, *a bimonthly newspaper.*

"Health and High Voltage" first appeared in the July-August 1978 issue of the Sierra Club Bulletin.

Extra-high-voltage (EHV) transmission lines are on the march across North America; 1400 miles of lines are already in operation in the Midwest and 2500 miles in Quebec. There is an extra-high-voltage DC line running from Oregon to Los Angeles. More EHV lines are planned; five lines will crisscross New York, connecting with others in the Northeast. Electricity from coal-burning plants in Wyoming, Montana and North and South Dakota will be carried by massive lines and steel towers to the cities of the Northwest.

A transmission line is simply a pipeline for electricity. In the case of a water pipeline, more water will flow through the pipe as water pressure increases. The same is true of electricity. It is transmitted more economically at high voltages; the more power carried, the less current lost along the lines.

We've come a long way from the early low-voltage lines strung on telephone poles. The newest transmission lines carry 765,000 volts (765 kilovolts, or kV) of electricity from power plant to transformer, and they represent only a modest advance in transmission technology. Plans are under way to build lines that will carry 1.2 million and 1.5 million volts. But as voltages have increased, the utility companies' understanding of the effects of these new transmission lines hasn't advanced much from the days when they still used wooden poles. The lines are designed under the assumption that they will not affect the people who work or live near them. Evidence is accumulating, however, that extra-high-voltage lines increase biological stress capable of causing hypertension, ulcers, and abnormal growths. The electric fields are a danger to wild animals, migratory birds and livestock pastured near the right-of-way. The lines are noisy, especially when damp from rain, snow or fog. Crops growing near them have shown abnormal growth patterns. Uninsulated wires, carrying thousands of volts of electricity as low as 48 feet overhead, can cause potentially harmful shocks.

Robert Becker, a physician and director of the Orthopedic-Biophysics Laboratory at the Syracuse, New York, Veterans Administration Hospital–Upstate Medical Center, has been researching the effects of low-frequency electric fields (60 Hz) for fifteen years. Testifying at health and safety hearings for proposed lines in New York, he said that exposure to the fields can produce physiological and functional changes in humans— anything from increased irritability and fatigue to raised cholesterol levels, hypertension and ulcers. Studies of rats exposed to low-level electric fields showed tumor growths and abnormalities in development. Dr. Becker believes we are performing unauthorized medical experiments by exposing people to the electromagnetic fields surrounding the transmission lines.

American utility companies do not take the health hazards of extra-high-voltage lines seriously, but the Russians do. Soviet investigators studied the health of 45 people who had worked in 400kV and 500kV switchyards for about four years. Of the 45 subjects, all but four had some type of disorder. The workers complained of headaches, unusual fatigue, sluggishness and reduced sexual potency. These symptoms occurred during and shortly after field exposure and subsided after the workers stayed away from the lines for a while.

The Russians have instituted strict rules for workers on their lines. Workers must be protected by shields or other devices while working. Workers may spend only limited periods of time near the lines. Conditions the Russians consider dangerous extend beyond the limits to the right-of-way, and use of this area is forbidden. In contrast, American utility companies promote use of the right-of-way for farming and recreation.

An American power company representative has claimed that there have been no "outstanding complaints" against lines currently in operation in this country—although many citizens have, in fact, complained. But even the absence of such complaints, according to Dr. Andrew Marino, a biophysicist working with Dr. Becker, would not prove that electric fields are not dangerous. If very dramatic things happened, says Dr. Marino, such as people falling down from shocks, then the effects of the lines would be more obvious and complaints more frequent. But the public might not yet know about subtle effects of extra-high-voltage lines—effects that they might not even associate with the power lines. 7

In view of the Russian findings and his own studies, Dr. Marino called for a public research program comparable to the Russians' to investigate the specific effects of transmission lines. In view of the vast environmental impact of proposed new lines, Marino thinks it is difficult to justify doing anything less. 8

The power companies have put only a minuscule amount of money into research. The Electric Power Research Institute is conducting a study of the effect of electrical fields on workers, but it has not produced any finished reports on transmission lines and the people living near them. One EPRI report relied solely upon the unsubstantiated opinion of an examining physician that individuals examined were normal. No data were cited, nor were any controls employed. Yet this study is used by American power companies as evidence of the absence of harmful effects of transmission lines. 9

The power companies concede that it is possible for the lines to cause electric shocks by inducing currents in metal objects such as wire fences, but they insist that such shocks are little more than nuisances, like the static charges one experiences after walking across certain carpets. Farmers who live and work near the lines in Ohio think differently. "It's like being zapped 10 by 110-volt household current," said one. He stated that even 400 to 500 feet from the line, the shocks can be quite severe. "I wouldn't send my boys [sixteen and eighteen years old] to work under the lines alone," he added.

The power companies can ground all stationary objects such as metal buildings, roofs and fences that they think may be a shock hazard; the companies also suggest the use of grounding chains for vehicles that regularly use the right-of-way. But farmers have found that the grounding methods do not always succeed in warding off strong shocks. Farmers must take care in getting off farm machinery near the lines. School buses have to be warned not to pick up or discharge children near them. People using pacemakers must be warned that the lines can interfere with their operation.

The most hazardous shocks, those that can do physical harm, are the ones that rise above the "let-go" threshold, the point at which a person loses voluntary muscle control. The threshold is about 9 milliamperes (mA, a standard measure of volts against resistance) for men, 6mA for women and 4.5mA for children. With lines operating at 800kV (lines operate within 5% of stated capacity) and a 48-foot clearance, a tractor-trailer would be subjected to 6.5mA and a school bus to 4.2mA under the lines. The Russians have recommended a maximum exposure of 4.0. To meet this requirement, clearances of about 70 feet would be needed.

To minimize the environmental impact of all transmission lines, siting guidelines have been set by the Department of the Interior, the Department of Agriculture, the Federal Power Commission and others. Transmission routes, they say, should avoid scenic, historic and recreational areas, prime farm and timber lands, population centers and areas of valuable natural resources. Where, then, to put the towers? The power companies naturally want the cheapest route, and farmlands are flat, relatively bare and offer easy access for construction vehicles. Since it is cheaper to keep the lines as straight as possible, the power companies will buy an easement through a farm rather than move the towers to the edge of a property.

It is estimated that 30 miles of lines with a right-of-way 250 feet wide require 1000 acres—and the 765kV lines need a right-of-way at least 500 feet wide to operate safely.

The towers supporting the 765kV lines are 135 to 200 feet tall, four or more to a mile, with a "wingspread" of 100 feet. Each tower leg is four feet in diameter, set in five-foot-wide concrete bases. 15

The construction vehicles and access roads of the utility companies compact the earth. It can take from four to six years to restore the damaged land to its original productivity. Drainage patterns may change because of construction and maintenance crew activity. 16

Farmers have noted changes in corn planted under the lines; the height of the stalks is not affected, but the ears do not mature. Cattle pastured under the lines lose as many as half their calves. The egg-laying capacity of hens also has been significantly altered. As one farmer put it, "What are they going to do when our farms die, eat electricity?" 17

Power lines produce a continuous humming and crackling sound that turns into a loud roar when they get wet. The noise 400 feet away from the line sounds like a small waterfall. Power companies have said that one of the key factors in assessing public acceptability of the lines will be the noise. Company figures show 53dB(A) (decibels as perceived by human hearing) at the edge of a 250-foot right-of-way, but others say it is nearer 70dB(A). At 60dB(A), one must shout in order to be heard. 18

A nationally known expert on noise from Stanford University, Dr. Karl Kryter, says that sleep disturbances will occur in some people when the level reaches only 34dB(A). Long-term effect of exposure to the noise from extra-high-voltage transmission lines is not known. Americans are exposed to twice as much noise today as twenty years ago. Clinical evidence shows that excessive exposure to noise constricts the arteries, increases the heartbeat and dilates the pupils of the eye. 19

Building heavier lines with more cables per bundle would reduce noise as well as radio and TV interference but would be more costly. Cables for 765kV transmission are made of aluminum reinforced with steel. They consist of a bundle of four conductors, each about 1.3 inches in diameter, approximately 20

18 inches apart; each circuit is composed of three parallel conductor bundles.

The utilities will build the lightest lines acceptable. In some cases, power companies have come to the agencies for permits only after spending large sums of money on equipment. Faced with a *fait accompli,* power commissions rarely demand costly changes in design.

What are the alternatives to a nationwide grid of potentially dangerous, environmentally unsound, land-gulping power lines? Should we delay certification of all proposed extra-high-voltage lines until an adequate research program has resolved questions of their safety?

Transmission lines are used to carry electricity from generating source to consumer. Locating the two closer together, as energy experts such as Amory Lovins have suggested, would eliminate the need for many of the lines. Advocates of decentralized energy call for more smaller local plants and less reliance on energy generated in one region and consumed in another. One problem is that it is cheaper to burn coal at a mine and transport electricity on expensive lines than to ship the coal to plants nearer cities, where compliance with clean-air laws may be more difficult. But should cities be allowed to escape the consequences of their energy consumption in this way?

Extra-high-voltage lines are also well suited to transmitting the high outputs of electricity from nuclear power plants and, in fact, may be designed with that use in mind.

Utilities will argue that increasing the "interties" among their power systems reduces the need for extra capacity within individual systems, thus requiring fewer power plants; the interties permit moving energy from places with excess capacity to areas where power is short because of heavy peak demands or equipment failure.

Where transmission of electricity cannot be avoided, better planning would create a safer and more efficient system. More research and investment is necessary to develop national safety standards. Superconductors (metals that carry power without heat or energy loss) could make present 345kV lines more effective, and eliminate the need for higher-voltage lines; towers can be designed to be more attractive; noise and shock hazards can be reduced.

But the ultimate answer to more and potentially dangerous lines is the conservation of energy. Power companies have a vested interest in expanding their business. The more power they sell, the more profit they make, since state regulations fix profit margins for utility companies at a percentage of total investment. 27

Forecasts of electricity demand should be made by independent agencies. We should insist that incentives for conservation of energy be built into rate systems. We should support the decentralization of power systems, the development of alternative—and safer—sources of energy closer to the people who will eventually use the energy. In these ways we can resist the degradation of the land by higher-voltage power lines. 28

FOR STUDY AND DISCUSSION

Questions on Subject

1. Why have utility companies begun to use extra-high-voltage transmission lines to carry electricity?
2. Identify the potential health and environmental hazards associated with extra-high-voltage transmission lines?
3. Why does Davis find fault with the American utility companies?
4. What solutions to the prospect of "a nationwide grid of potentially dangerous . . . power lines" (22) does Davis suggest? What, in Davis's view, is "the ultimate answer" (27)?

Questions on Strategy

1. The first two paragraphs of Davis's essay are not argumentative. What is their function? (Glossary: *Beginnings*)
2. In arguing her position on extra-high-voltage transmission lines, Davis uses definition, comparison and contrast, cause and effect, and description. Identify passages in which she uses each of these strategies, and explain how each is used within her argument. (Glossary: *Definition, Comparison and Contrast, Cause and Effect,* and *Description*)

3. In terms of content and organization, which paragraph controls Davis's essay? (Glossary: *Thesis* and *Unity*)
4. Davis claims that the harmful effects of extra-high-voltage transmission lines are (1) biological stress, (2) electric fields, (3) noise, (4) abnormal growth patterns in crops, and (5) harmful shocks. What types of evidence does she use to substantiate her claims? (Glossary: *Supporting Evidence*)
5. Davis anticipates and answers possible counterarguments to her own views. Identify several passages in which she does this, and explain how this strategy helps her argument.

Questions on Diction and Vocabulary

1. What evidence do you find in Davis's diction to suggest that her attitude toward utilities is less than objective? (Glossary: *Attitude*)
2. Identify the analogy that Davis uses early in the essay, and explain how it works. (Glossary: *Analogy*)
3. Refer to your desk dictionary to determine the meanings of the following words as they are used in this selection: *hypertension* (3), *physiological* (4), *inducing* (10), *decibels* (18), *clinical* (19), *fait accompli* (21), *vested* (27).

For Classroom Discussion

In "Health and High Voltage" Davis obviously feels that safety, health, and environmental concerns should take precedence over economic factors. While most people would agree in principle with Davis's position, why are our principles and practices often so far apart?

(Note: Activities and Writing Suggestions for Argumentation appear on pages 295–298.)

Taming Technology

ALVIN TOFFLER

Alvin Toffler, born in 1928, has been a Washington-based correspondent and an editor for Fortune. *In addition to contributing numerous articles to leading periodicals, he has written* The Culture Consumers *and has edited* The Schoolhouse in the City. *After years of research into "future shock," a term Toffler coined, he published the best-selling book* Future Shock *in 1970. Translated into twenty languages, the book made both Toffler and the concept famous. Since 1970 Toffler has been in great demand as a lecturer on speculative sociology and has edited* The Futurists, Learning for Tomorrow, *and* The Eco-Spasm Report. The Third Wave, *his latest book, appeared in 1980.*

In this selection, which has been excerpted from Future Shock, *Toffler argues for various ways in which man might bring the accelerative thrust of technology under control.*

Future shock—the disease of change—can be prevented. But it will take drastic social, even political action. No matter how individuals try to pace their lives, no matter what psychic crutches we offer them, no matter how we alter education, the society as a whole will still be caught on a runaway treadmill until we capture control of the accelerative thrust itself. 1

The high velocity of change can be traced to many factors. Population growth, urbanization, the shifting proportions of young and old—all play their part. Yet technological advance is clearly a critical node in the network of causes; indeed, it may be the node that activates the entire net. One powerful strategy in the battle to prevent mass future shock, therefore, involves the conscious regulation of technological advance. 2

We cannot and must not turn off the switch of technological progress. Only romantic fools babble about returning to a "state of nature." A state of nature is one in which infants shrivel and die for lack of elementary medical care, in which malnutrition stultifies the brain, in which, as Hobbes reminded us, the typical life is "poor, nasty, brutish, and short." To turn our back on technology would be not only stupid but immoral.

Given that a majority of men still figuratively live in the twelfth century, who are we even to contemplate throwing away the key to economic advance? Those who prate anti-technological nonsense in the name of some vague "human values" need to be asked "which humans?" To deliberately turn back the clock would be to condemn billions to enforced and permanent misery at precisely the moment in history when their liberation is becoming possible. We clearly need not less but more technology.

At the same time, it is undeniably true that we frequently apply new technology stupidly and selfishly. In our haste to milk technology for immediate economic advantage, we have turned our environment into a physical and social tinderbox.

The speed-up of diffusion, the self-reinforcing character of technological advance, by which each forward step facilitates not one but many additional further steps, the intimate link-up between technology and social arrangements—all these create a form of psychological pollution, a seemingly unstoppable acceleration of the pace of life.

This psychic pollution is matched by the industrial vomit that fills our skies and seas. Pesticides and herbicides filter into our foods. Twisted automobile carcasses, aluminum cans, non-returnable glass bottles and synthetic plastics form immense kitchen middens in our midst as more and more of our detritus resists decay. We do not even begin to know what to do with our radioactive wastes—whether to pump them into the earth, shoot them into outer space, or pour them into the oceans.

Our technological powers increase, but the side effects and potential hazards also escalate. We risk thermopollution of the oceans themselves, overheating them, destroying immeasurable quantities of marine life, perhaps even melting the polar icecaps. On land we concentrate such large masses of population in such small urban-technological islands, that we threaten to use up the air's oxygen faster than it can be replaced, conjuring up the possibility of new Saharas where the cities are now. Through such disruptions of the natural ecology, we may literally, in the words of biologist Barry Commoner, be "destroying this planet as a suitable place for human habitation." . . .

. . . Technological questions can no longer be answered in technological terms alone. They are political questions. Indeed, they affect us more deeply than most of the superficial political issues that occupy us today. This is why we cannot continue to make technological decisions in the old way. We cannot permit them to be made haphazardly, independently of one another. We cannot permit them to be dictated by short-run economic considerations alone. We cannot permit them to be made in a policy vacuum. And we cannot casually delegate responsibility for such decisions to businessmen, scientists, engineers or administrators who are unaware of the profound consequences of their own actions.

To capture control of technology, and through it gain some influence over the accelerative thrust in general, we must, therefore, begin to submit new technology to a set of demanding tests before we unleash it in our midst. We must ask a whole series of unaccustomed questions about any innovation before giving it a clean bill of sale.

First, bitter experience should have taught us by now to look far more carefully at the potential physical side effects of any new technology. Whether we are proposing a new form of power, a new material, or a new industrial chemical, we must attempt to determine how it will alter the delicate ecological balance upon which we depend for survival. Moreover, we must anticipate its indirect effects over great distances in both time and space. Industrial waste dumped into a river can turn up hundreds, even thousands of miles away in the ocean.

DDT may not show its effects until years after its use. So much has been written about this that it seems hardly necessary to belabor the point further.

Second, and much more complex, we must question the long-term impact of a technical innovation on the social, cultural and psychological environment. The automobile is widely believed to have changed the shape of our cities, shifted home ownership and retail trade patterns, altered sexual customs and loosened family ties. In the Middle East, the rapid spread of transistor radios is credited with having contributed to the resurgence of Arab nationalism. The birth control pill, the computer, the space effort, as well as the invention and diffusion of such "soft" technologies as systems analysis, all have carried significant social changes in their wake.

We can no longer afford to let such secondary social and cultural effects just "happen." We must attempt to anticipate them in advance, estimating, to the degree possible, their nature, strength and timing. Where these effects are likely to be seriously damaging, we must also be prepared to block the new technology. It is as simple as that. Technology cannot be permitted to rampage through the society.

It is quite true that we can never know all the effects of any action, technological or otherwise. But it is not true that we are helpless. It is, for example, sometimes possible to test new technology in limited areas, among limited groups, studying its secondary impacts before releasing it for diffusion. We could, if we were imaginative, devise living experiments, even volunteer communities, to help guide our technological decisions. Just as we may wish to create enclaves of the past where the rate of change is artificially slowed, or enclaves of the future in which individuals can pre-sample future environments, we may also wish to set aside, even subsidize, special high-novelty communities in which advanced drugs, power sources, vehicles, cosmetics, appliances and other innovations are experimentally used and investigated.

A corporation today will routinely field test a product to make sure it performs its primary function. The same company will market test the product to ascertain whether it will sell.

But, with rare exception, no one post-checks the consumer or the community to determine what the human side effects have been. Survival in the future may depend on our learning to do so.

Even when life-testing proves unfeasible, it is still possible 16 for us systematically to anticipate the distant effects of various technologies. Behavioral scientists are rapidly developing new tools, from mathematical modeling and simulation to so-called Delphi analyses, that permit us to make more informed judgments about the consequences of our actions. We are piecing together the conceptual hardware needed for the social evaluation of technology; we need but to make use of it.

Third, an even more difficult and pointed question: Apart 17 from actual changes in the social structure, how will a proposed new technology affect the value system of the society? We know little about value structures and how they change, but there is reason to believe that they, too, are heavily impacted by technology. Elsewhere I have proposed that we develop a new profession of "value impact forecasters"—men and women trained to use the most advanced behavioral science techniques to appraise the value implications of proposed technology.

At the University of Pittsburgh in 1967 a group of distin- 18 guished economists, scientists, architects, planners, writers, and philosophers engaged in a day-long simulation intended to advance the art of value forecasting. At Harvard, the Program on Technology and Society has undertaken work relevant to this field. At Cornell and at the Institute for the Study of Science in Human Affairs at Columbia, an attempt is being made to build a model of the relationship between technology and values, and to design a game useful in analyzing the impact of one on the other. All these initiatives, while still extremely primitive, give promise of helping us assess new technology more sensitively than ever before.

Fourth and finally, we must pose a question that until now 19 has almost never been investigated, and which is, nevertheless, absolutely crucial if we are to prevent widespread future shock. For each major technological innovation we must ask: What are its accelerative implications?

The problems of adaptation already far transcend the difficulties of coping with this or that invention or technique. Our problem is no longer the innovation, but the chain of innovations, not the supersonic transport, or the breeder reactor, or the ground effect machine, but entire inter-linked sequences of such innovations and the novelty they send flooding into the society.

Does a proposed innovation help us control the rate and direction of subsequent advance? Or does it tend to accelerate a host of processes over which we have no control? How does it affect the level of transience, the novelty ratio, and the diversity of choice? Until we systematically probe these questions, our attempts to harness technology to social ends—and to gain control of the accelerative thrust in general—will prove feeble and futile.

Here, then, is a pressing intellectual agenda for the social and physical sciences. We have taught ourselves to create and combine the most powerful of technologies. We have not taken pains to learn about their consequences. Today these consequences threaten to destroy us. We must learn, and learn fast.

The challenge, however, is not solely intellectual; it is political as well. In addition to designing new research tools—new ways to understand our environment—we must also design creative new political institutions for guaranteeing that these questions are, in fact, investigated; and for promoting or discouraging (perhaps even banning) certain proposed technologies. We need, in effect, a machinery for screening machines.

A key political task of the next decade will be to create this machinery. We must stop being afraid to exert systematic social control over technology. Responsibility for doing so must be shared by public agencies and the corporations and laboratories in which technological innovations are hatched.

Any suggestion for control over technology immediately raises scientific eyebrows. The specter of ham-handed governmental interference is invoked. Yet controls over technology need not imply limitations on the freedom to conduct research.

What is at issue is not discovery but diffusion, not invention but application. Ironically, as sociologist Amitai Etzioni points out, "many liberals who have fully accepted Keynesian economic controls take a laissez-faire view of technology. Theirs are the arguments once used to defend laissez-faire economics: that any attempt to control technology would stifle innovation and initiative."

Warnings about overcontrol ought not be lightly ignored. 26 Yet the consequences of lack of control may be far worse. In point of fact, science and technology are never free in any absolute sense. Inventions and the rate at which they are applied are both influenced by the values and institutions of the society that gives rise to them. Every society, in effect, does pre-screen technical innovations before putting them to widespread use.

The haphazard way in which this is done today, however, 27 and the criteria on which selection is based, need to be changed. In the West, the basic criterion for filtering out certain technical innovations and applying others remains economic profitability. In communist countries, the ultimate tests have to do with whether the innovation will contribute to overall economic growth and national power. In the former, decisions are private and pluralistically decentralized. In the latter, they are public and tightly centralized.

Both systems are now obsolete—incapable of dealing with 28 the complexity of super-industrial society. Both tend to ignore all but the most immediate and obvious consequences of technology. Yet, increasingly, it is these non-immediate and non-obvious impacts that must concern us. "Society must so organize itself that a proportion of the very ablest and most imaginative of scientists are continually concerned with trying to foresee the long-term effects of new technology," writes O. M. Solandt, chairman of the Science Council of Canada. "Our present method of depending on the alertness of individuals to foresee danger and to form pressure groups that try to correct mistakes will not do for the future."

One step in the right direction would be to create a techno- 29 logical ombudsman—a public agency charged with receiving, investigating, and acting on complaints having to do with the irresponsible application of technology.

Who should be responsible for correcting the adverse effects of technology? The rapid diffusion of detergents used in home washing machines and dishwashers intensified water purification problems all over the United States. The decisions to launch detergents on the society were privately taken, but the side effects have resulted in costs borne by the taxpayer and (in the form of lower water quality) by the consumer at large.

The costs of air pollution are similarly borne by taxpayer and community even though, as is often the case, the sources of pollution are traceable to individual companies, industries or government installations. Perhaps it is sensible for de-pollution costs to be borne by the public as a form of social overhead, rather than by specific industries. There are many ways to allocate the cost. But whichever way we choose, it is absolutely vital that the lines of responsibility are made clear. Too often no agency, group or institution has clear responsibility.

A technology ombudsman could serve as an official sounding board for complaints. By calling press attention to companies or government agencies that have applied new technology irresponsibly or without adequate forethought, such an agency could exert pressure for more intelligent use of new technology. Armed with the power to initiate damage suits where necessary, it could become a significant deterrent to technological irresponsibility.

But simply investigating and apportioning responsibility after the fact is hardly sufficient. We must create an environmental screen to protect ourselves against dangerous intrusions as well as a system of public incentives to encourage technology that is both safe and socially desirable. This means governmental and private machinery for reviewing major technological advances *before* they are launched upon the public.

Corporations might be expected to set up their own "consequence analysis staffs" to study the potential effects of the innovations they sponsor. They might, in some cases, be required not merely to test new technology in pilot areas but to make a public report about its impact before being permitted to spread the innovation through the society at large. Much responsibility should be delegated to industry itself. The less centralized the controls the better. If self-policing works, it is preferable to external, political controls.

Where self-regulation fails, however, as it often does, public 35 intervention may well be necessary, and we should not evade the responsibility. In the United States, Congressman Emilio Q. Daddario, chairman of the House Subcommittee on Science, Research and Development, has proposed the establishment of a Technology Assessment Board within the federal government. Studies by the National Academy of Sciences, the National Academy of Engineering, the Legislative Reference Service of the Library of Congress, and by the science and technology program of the George Washington University are all aimed at defining the appropriate nature of such an agency. We may wish to debate its form; its need is beyond dispute.

The society might also set certain general principles for 36 technological advance. Where the introduction of an innovation entails undue risk, for example, it might require that funds be set aside by the responsible agency for correction of adverse effects should they materialize. We might also create a "technological insurance pool" to which innovation-diffusing agencies might pay premiums.

Certain large-scale ecological interventions might be delayed 37 or prohibited altogether—perhaps in line with the principle that if an incursion on nature is too big and sudden for its effects to be monitored and possibly corrected, it should not take place. For example, it has been suggested that the Aswan Dam, far from helping Egyptian agriculture, might someday lead to salinization of the land on both banks of the Nile. This could prove disastrous. But such a process would not occur overnight. Presumably, therefore, it can be monitored and prevented. By contrast, the plan to flood the entire interior of Brazil is fraught with such instant and imponderable ecological effects that it should not be permitted at all until adequate monitoring can be done and emergency corrective measures are available.

At the level of social consequences, a new technology might 38 be submitted for clearance to panels of behavioral scientists—psychologists, sociologists, economists, political scientists—who would determine, to the best of their ability, the probable strength of its social impact at different points in time. Where an innovation appears likely to entail seriously disruptive consequences, or to generate unrestrained accelerative pressures, these facts need to be weighed in a social cost-benefit accounting procedure. In the case of some high-impact innovations, the technological appraisal agency might be empowered to seek restraining legislation, or to obtain an injunction forcing delay until full public discussion and study is completed. In other cases, such innovations might still be released for diffusion—provided ample steps were taken in advance to offset their negative consequences. In this way, the society would not need to wait for disaster before dealing with its technology-induced problems.

By considering not merely specific technologies, but their relationship to one another, the time lapse between them, the proposed speed of diffusion, and similar factors, we might eventually gain some control over the pace of change as well as its direction.

Needless to say, these proposals are themselves fraught with explosive social consequences, and need careful assessment. There may be far better ways to achieve the desired ends. But the time is late. We simply can no longer afford to hurtle blindfolded toward super-industrialism. The politics of technology control will trigger bitter conflict in the days to come. But conflict or no, technology must be tamed, if the accelerative thrust is to be brought under control. And the accelerative thrust must be brought under control, if future shock is to be prevented.

FOR STUDY AND DISCUSSION

Questions on Subject

1. To what does Toffler attribute the "high velocity of change" (2)? How does he feel that the pace of change can be controlled?
2. What reasons does Toffler give for believing that "technological

questions can no longer be answered in technological terms alone" (9)? In what terms, according to Toffler, should they be addressed?

3. Why does Toffler feel the need to create what he calls a "technology ombudsman" (32)? What would be the duties and responsibilities of a technology ombudsman? Does Toffler think that this person alone could tame technology? Explain.

4. What is an "environmental screen" (33)? How would it work?

Questions on Strategy

1. Toffler argues that "we must ask a whole series of unaccustomed questions about any innovation before giving it a clean bill of sale" (10). What questions does Toffler feel need to be asked? Do these questions and his discussion of them make his argument more persuasive? Explain.

2. How does Toffler dispel commonly held fears about governmental controls over technology?

3. In arguing for the taming of technology, Toffler proposes some possible courses of action. What are his proposals? How do they impress you? Would they have had the same impact had they been placed earlier in the essay? Explain.

4. In the course of his argument, Toffler asks a number of rhetorical questions. What does he achieve by asking these questions? (Glossary: *Rhetorical Question*)

Questions on Diction and Vocabulary

1. In "Taming Technology," Toffler uses many words and phrases like *future shock* (1), *accelerative thrust* (1), *speed-up* (6), *urban-technological islands* (8), and *super-industrialism* (40). Cite other examples of such words and phrases in this essay. Does his use of technological jargon help or hinder his argument? Explain.

2. Refer to your desk dictionary to determine the meanings of the following words as they are used in this selection: *velocity* (2), *urbanization* (2), *stultifies* (3), *immoral* (3), *diffusion* (6), *escalate* (8), *appraise* (17), *transcend* (20), *allocate* (31), *incentives* (33), *injunction* (38).

For Classroom Discussion

Today many people, especially the environmentalists, do not have a favorable opinion of industry and technology. In fact, some have gone so far as to suggest that industrial development be limited. Discuss the various arguments that can be made in favor of technology.

(Note: Activities and Writing Suggestions for Argumentation appear on pages 295–298.)

Activities and Writing Suggestions for Argumentation

ACTIVITIES

1. William V. Haney of Northwestern University has developed the following test to determine your ability to analyze accurately the evidence presented. After completing Haney's test, discuss your answers with other members of the class.

THE UNCRITICAL INFERENCE TEST

DIRECTIONS

1. You will read a brief story. Assume that all of the information presented in the story is definitely accurate and true. Read the story carefully. You may refer back to the story whenever you wish.
2. You will then read statements about the story. Answer them in numerical order. DO NOT GO BACK to fill in answers or to change answers. This will only distort your test score.
3. After you read carefully each statement, determine whether the statement is:

   a. "T"—meaning: On the basis of the information presented in the story the statement is DEFINITELY TRUE.
   b. "F"—meaning: On the basis of the information presented in the story the statement is DEFINITELY FALSE.
   c. "?"—meaning: The statement MAY be true (or false) but on the basis of the information presented in the story you cannot be definitely certain. (If any part of the statement is doubtful, mark the statement "?".)

4. Indicate your answer by circling either "T" or "F" or "?" opposite the statement.

THE STORY

Babe Smith has been killed. Police have rounded up six suspects, all of whom are known gangsters. All of them are known to have been near the scene of the killing at the approximate time that it occurred. All had substantial motives for wanting Smith killed. However, one of these suspected gangsters, Slinky Sam, has positively been cleared of guilt.

STATEMENTS ABOUT THE STORY

1. Slinky Sam is known to have been near the scene   T   F   ?
   of the killing of Babe Smith.
2. All six of the rounded-up gangsters were known to   T   F   ?
   have been near the scene of the murder.
3. Only Slinky Sam has been cleared of guilt.   T   F   ?
4. All six of the rounded-up suspects were near the   T   F   ?
   scene of Smith's killing at the approximate time
   that it took place.
5. The police do not know who killed Smith.   T   F   ?
6. All six suspects are known to have been near the   T   F   ?
   scene of the foul deed.
7. Smith's murderer did not confess of his own free   T   F   ?
   will.
8. Slinky Sam was not cleared of guilt.   T   F   ?
9. It is known that the six suspects were in the   T   F   ?
   vicinity of the cold-blooded assassination.

2. Choose one of the following position statements for an exercise in argumentation:

   a. More parking spaces should be provided on campus for students.
   b. Too much land is being set aside as park land.
   c. Athletic facilities for women should be equal to those for men.
   d. Capital punishment is an ineffective deterrent to crime.
   e. States should be able to control population growth and/or immigration.
   f. Residency requirements for tuition are unfair.

   List the types of information and evidence you would need to write an argumentative essay on the topic you choose. Indicate where or from whom you might obtain this information.

3. Write a paragraph concisely summarizing the main points of one of the essays in this section. What does your summary reveal about the way the author has structured his or her argument?

4. The effectiveness of an argument largely depends on the writer's awareness of audience. For example, if a writer wished to argue for the use of technology to solve environmental problems, that argu-

ment would have to be more convincing—that is, more carefully reasoned and more factual—for an audience of environmentalists than for an audience of industrialists. Consider the following proposition:

> Students should be represented on the Board of Trustees of your college or university.

How would you argue this proposition for each of the following audiences?

a. the student body
b. the faculty
c. the alumni
d. the administration

5. Choose from your local newspaper an editorial about a controversial issue. Outline the argument used in the editorial. Now assume that you have been offered equal space in the newspaper to present an opposing viewpoint. Consider the types of evidence you would present in a counterargument, and write an outline for your rebuttal.

WRITING SUGGESTIONS

1. Think of a product that you like and want to use even though it has an annoying feature. Write a letter of complaint in which you attempt to persuade the manufacturer to improve the product. Your letter should include the following points:

   a. a statement concerning the nature of the problem
   b. evidence supporting or explaining your complaint
   c. suggestions for improving the product

2. Select one of the position statements listed below, and write an argumentative essay in which you defend that statement:

   a. Living in a dormitory is (is not) as attractive as living off campus.
   b. Grain sales should (should not) be used as a political weapon.
   c. Student government shows (does not show) that the democratic process is effective.
   d. America should (should not) be a refuge for the oppressed.
   e. School spirit is (is not) as important as it ever was.
   f. Interest in religion is (is not) increasing in the United States.
   g. We have (have not) brought air pollution under control in the United States.

h. The need to develop alternative energy sources is (is not) serious.
i. America's great cities are (are not) thriving.
j. Youth organizations do (do not) build character.
k. We have (have not) found effective means to dispose of nuclear or chemical wastes.
l. Fair play is (is not) a thing of the past.
m. Human life is (is not) valued in a technological society.
n. The consumer does (does not) need to be protected.
o. The family farm in America is (is not) in danger of extinction.
p. Grades do (do not) encourage learning.
q. America is (is not) a violent society.
r. Television is (is not) a positive cultural force in America.
s. America should (should not) feel a commitment to the starving peoples of the world.
t. The federal government should (should not) regulate all utilities.

9

ESSAYS FOR FURTHER ANALYSIS

Let's Suppose . . .

ISAAC ASIMOV

Suppose the whole world became industrialized and that industry and science worked very carefully and very well. How many people could such a world support? Different limits have been suggested, but the highest figure I have seen is 20 billion. How long will it be before the world contains so many people?

For the sake of argument, and to keep things simple, let's suppose the demographic growth rate will stay as it is now at two per cent per annum. At this rate, it will take 35 years for the population to double, so it will take the present world population of 3.8 billion 70 years to reach the 15.2 billion mark. Then, fifteen more years will bring the world population to our 20 billion. In other words, at the present growth rate our planet will contain all the people that an industrialized world may be able to support by about 2060 A.D. That is not a pleasant outlook for only 85 years from now.

Suppose we decide to hope for the best. Let us suppose that a change *will* take place in the next 70 years and that there will be a new age in which population can continue rising to a far higher level than we think it can now. This means that there will be a new and higher limit, but before that is reached, still another change will take place, and so on. Let's suppose that this sort of thing can just keep on going forever.

Is there any way of setting a limit past which nothing can raise the human population no matter how many changes take place?

Suppose we try to invent a real limit; something so huge that no one can imagine a population rising past it. Suppose we imagine that there are so many men and women and children in the world, that altogether they weigh as much as the whole planet does. Surely you can't expect there can be more people than that.

Let us suppose that the average human being weighs 60   6
kilogrammes. If that's the case then 100,000,000,000,000,000,-
000,000 people would weigh as much as the whole Earth does.
That number of people is 30,000,000,000,000 times as many
people as there are living now.

It may seem to you that the population can go up a long,   7
long time before it reaches the point where there are 30,000,-
000,000,000 times as many people in the world as there are
today. Let's think about that, though. Let us suppose that the
population growth-rate stays at 2.0 per cent so that the number
of people in the world continues to double every 35 years.
How long, then, will it take for the world's population to
weigh as much as the entire planet?

The answer is—not quite 1,600 years. This means that by   8
3550 A.D., the human population would weigh as much as the
entire Earth. Nor is 1,600 years a long time. It is considerably
less time than has passed since the days of Julius Caesar.

Do you suppose that perhaps in the course of the next 1,600   9
years, it will be possible to colonize the Moon and Mars, and
the other planets of the Solar system? Do you think that we
might get many millions of people into the other world in the
next 1,600 years and thus lower the population of the Earth
itself?

Even if that were possible, it wouldn't give us much time.   10
If the growth-rate stays at 2.0 per cent, then in a little over
2,200 years—say, by 4220 A.D.—the human population would
weigh as much as the entire Solar system, including the Sun.

We couldn't escape to the stars, either. Even if we could   11
reach them; even if we could reach *all* of them; population
would reach a limit. If the growth-rate stays at 2.0 per cent,
then in 4,700 years—by about 6700 A.D.—the human population
would weigh as much as the entire Universe.

So you see we can't go on forever at the rate we are going.   12
The population rise is going to have to stop somewhere. We
just can't keep that 2.0 per cent growth-rate for thousands of
years. We just can't, no matter what we do.

Let's try again, and let's be more reasonable. Suppose we   13
go back to considering the density of population on Earth.

Right now, the average density of population on Earth is 25 per km². If the population of the world doubles then the average density of population also doubles, since the area of the world's surface stays the same. This means that at a population growth-rate of 2.0 per cent per year, the average density of population in the world will double every 35 years.

In that case, if the growth-rate stays where it is, how long will it take for the average density of population to become 18,600/km²? Such a density is almost 750 times as high as the present density, but it will be reached, at the present growth-rate, in just about 340 years.

Of course, this density is reached only if human beings are confined to the land surface of the world. Perhaps human beings will learn to live on the bottom of the ocean, or on great platforms floating on the sea. There is more than twice as much ocean surface as there is land surface and that would give more room for people.

That wouldn't do much good, however. At the present growth-rate, it would take only 45 additional years to fill the ocean surface, too. In 385 years, the average density of population would be 18,600/km² over land and sea both. That would be by about 2320 A.D.

But a density of 18,600/km² is the average density of population of the island of Manhattan.

Imagine a world in which the average density everywhere, over land and sea alike—*everywhere*—in Antarctica and Greenland, over the oceans and along the mountains, over the entire face of the globe—was equal to that of Manhattan. There would have to be skyscrapers everywhere. There would be hardly any open space. There would be no room for wilderness or for any plants and animals except those needed by human beings.

Very few people would imagine a world like that could be comfortable, yet at the present growth-rate we will reach such a world in only 385 years.

But let's not pick Manhattan. Let's try the Netherlands. It is a pleasant, comfortable nation, with open land and gardens and farms. It has a standard of living that is very high and yet its average population density is 400/km². How long would it take for our population to increase to the point where the average density of the surface of the world, sea and land, would be 400/km²?

The answer is 200 years, by about 2175 A.D.   22

You see, then, that if we don't want to go past the average   23
population density of the Netherlands, we can't keep our present growth-rate going even for hundreds of years, let alone thousands.

In fact, we might still be arguing in an unreasonable way.   24
Can we really expect to have a world-wide Netherlands in the next 200 years?

No one really believes that mankind can spread out over   25
the ocean bottom or the ocean top in the next 200 years. It is much more likely that man will stay on land. To be sure, there may be some people who would be living off shore in special structures, on the sea or under it. They would make up only a small fraction of all mankind. Almost everybody will be living on land.

Then, too, not every place on land is desirable. It isn't at all   26
likely that there will be very many people living in Antarctica or in Greenland or in the Sahara Desert or along the Himalaya Mountain range over the next 200 years. There may be some people living there, more people than are living there now, but they will represent only a small fraction of the total population of the Earth.

In fact, most of the Earth's land surface isn't very suitable   27
for large populations. At the present moment, most of the Earth's population is squeezed into that small portion of Earth's land surface that is not too mountainous, too dry, too hot, too cold, or too uncomfortable generally. In fact, two-thirds of the world's population is to be found on a little over $\frac{1}{13}$ of the land surface of the planet. About 2,500,000,000 people are living on 11,000,000 sq. km. of land that can best support a high population.

The average density on the 11,000,000 square kilometres of   28
the best land is 230/km², while the average density on the rest of the land surface is just under 10/km².

Suppose the population continues to increase at the present   29
growth-rate and the distribution remains the same. In that

case, after 30 years, the average population density of the less pleasant parts of the Earth will reach the $19/km^2$ figure, but the density of the 11,000,000 square kilometres of best land will be $400/km^2$.

In other words, we will reach a kind of world-wide Netherlands density-figure, for as far as we can go, in only about 30 years.

But will all the world be as well-organized and as prosperous as the Netherlands is now? Some of the reasons why the Netherlands is as well off as it is now, are that it has a stable government, a highly-educated population, and a well-organized industrial system.

This is not true of all nations and they need not expect to be as well off as the Netherlands when they are as crowded as the Netherlands. Indeed, if they have an agricultural way of life and a poorly-educated people, who don't have long traditions of stable government, then a population as dense as that of the Netherlands now is, would only bring misery.

In other words, the world can't keep going at the present growth-rate, even for tens of years, let alone for hundreds or thousands.

The matter of a population limit is not a problem for the future, then. We might just as well realize that the world is just about reaching its population limit *now*.

Of course, this entire argument is based on the supposition that the population growth-rate will stay the same as it is now. If the growth-rate drops, that obviously will give us more time before the limit is reached. If it drops to zero, the limit will never be reached. Even a 1 per cent per year population increase, however, is enough to bring disaster. So we can't just sit back and do nothing. We will have to do something.

An 18-Year-Old Looks Back on Life

JOYCE MAYNARD

Every generation thinks it's special—my grandparents because 1
they remember horses and buggies, my parents because of the
Depression. The over-30's are special because they knew the
Red Scare of Korea, Chuck Berry and beatniks. My older sister
is special because she belonged to the first generation of teen-
agers (before that, people in their teens were *adolescents*), when
being a teen-ager was still fun. And I—I am 18, caught in the
middle. Mine is the generation of unfulfilled expectations.
"When you're older," my mother promised, "you can wear
lipstick." But when the time came, of course, lipstick wasn't
being worn. "When we're big, we'll dance like that," my
friends and I whispered, watching Chubby Checker twist on
"American Bandstand." But we inherited no dance steps, ours
was a limp, formless shrug to watered-down music that rarely
made the feet tap. "Just wait till we can vote," I said, bursting
with 10-year-old fervor, ready to fast, freeze, march and die
for peace and freedom as Joan Baez, barefoot, sang "We Shall
Overcome." Well, now we can vote, and we're old enough to
attend rallies and knock on doors and wave placards, and
suddenly it doesn't seem to matter any more.

My generation is special because of what we missed rather 2
than what we got, because in a certain sense we are the first
and the last. The first to take technology for granted. (What
was a space shot to us, except an hour cut from Social Studies
to gather before a TV in the gym as Cape Canaveral counted
down?) The first to grow up with TV. My sister was 8 when
we got our set, so to her it seemed magic and always somewhat
foreign. She had known books already and would never really
replace them. But for me, the TV set was, like the kitchen sink
and the telephone, a fact of life.

We inherited a previous generation's hand-me-downs and took in the seams, turned up the hems, to make our new fashions. We took drugs from the college kids and made them a high-school commonplace. We got the Beatles, but not those lovable look-alikes in matching suits with barber cuts and songs that made you want to cry. They came to us like a bad joke—aged, bearded, discordant. And we inherited the Vietnam war just after the crest of the wave—too late to burn draft cards and too early not to be drafted. The boys of 1953—my year—will be the last to go.

So where are we now? Generalizing is dangerous. Call us the apathetic generation and we will become that. Say times are changing, nobody cares about prom queens and getting into the college of his choice any more—say that (because it sounds good, it indicates a trend, gives a symmetry to history) and you make a movement and a unit out of a generation unified only in its common fragmentation. If there is a reason why we are where we are, it comes from where we have been.

Like overanxious patients in analysis, we treasure the traumas of our childhood. Ours was more traumatic than most. The Kennedy assassination has become our myth: Talk to us for an evening or two—about movies or summer jobs or Nixon's trip to China or the weather—and the subject will come up ("Where were *you* when you heard?"), as if having lived through Jackie and the red roses, John-John's salute and Oswald's on-camera murder justifies our disenchantment.

We haven't all emerged the same, of course, because our lives were lived in high-school corridors and drive-in hamburger joints as well as in the pages of *Time* and *Life*, and the images on the TV screen. National events and personal memory blur so that, for me, November 22, 1963, was a birthday party that had to be called off and Armstrong's moonwalk was my first full can of beer. If you want to know who we are now; if you wonder how we'll vote, or whether we will, or whether, 10 years from now, we'll end up just like all those other generations that thought they were special—with 2.2 kids and a house in Connecticut—if that's what you're wondering, look to the past because, whether we should blame it or not, we do.

I didn't know till years later that they called it the Cuban 7
Missile Crisis. But I remember Castro. (We called him Castor
Oil and were awed by his beard—beards were rare in those
days.) We might not have worried so much (what would the
Communists want with our small New Hampshire town?)
except that we lived 10 miles from an air base. Planes buzzed
around us like mosquitoes that summer. People talked about
fallout shelters in their basements and one family on our street
packed their car to go to the mountains. I couldn't understand
that. If everybody was going to die, I certainly didn't want to
stick around, with my hair falling out and—later—a plague of
thalidomide-type babies. I wanted to go quickly, with my
family.

Dying didn't bother me so much—I'd never known anyone 8
who died, and death was unreal, fascinating. (I wanted Doctor
Kildare to have more terminal cancer patients and fewer love
affairs.) What bothered me was the business of immortality.
Sometimes, the growing-up sort of concepts germinate slowly,
but the full impact of death hit me like a bomb, in the night.
Not only would my body be gone—that I could take—but I
would cease to think. That I would no longer be a participant
I had realized before; now I saw that I wouldn't even be an
observer. What especially alarmed me about The Bomb (always
singular like, a few years later, The Pill) was the possibility of
total obliteration. All traces of me would be destroyed. There
would be no grave and, if there were, no one left to visit it.

Newly philosophical, I pondered the universe. If the earth 9
was in the solar system and the solar system was in the galaxy
and the galaxy was in the universe, what was the universe
in? And if the sun was just a dot—the head of a pin—what
was I? We visited a planetarium that year, in third grade, and
saw a dramatization of the sun exploding. Somehow the image
of that orange ball zooming toward us merged with my image
of The Bomb. The effect was devastating, and for the first time
in my life—except for Easter Sundays, when I wished I went
to church so I could have a fancy new dress like my Catholic
and Protestant friends—I longed for religion.

I was 8 when Joan Baez entered our lives, with long, black, 10
beatnik hair and a dress made out of a burlap bag. When we

got her first record (we called her Joan *Baze* then—soon she was simply Joan) we listened all day, to "All My Trials" and "Silver Dagger" and "Wildwood Flower." My sister grew her hair and started wearing sandals, making pilgrimages to Harvard Square. I took up the guitar. We loved her voice and her songs but, even more, we loved the idea of Joan, like the 15th-century Girl of Orleans, burning at society's stake, marching along or singing, solitary, in a prison cell to protest segregation. She was the champion of nonconformity and so—like thousands of others—we joined the masses of her fans.

I knew she must but somehow I could never imagine Jackie Kennedy going to the bathroom. She was too cool and poised and perfect. We had a book about her, filled with color pictures of Jackie painting, in a spotless yellow linen dress, Jackie on the beach with Caroline and John-John, Jackie riding elephants in India and Jackie, in a long white gown, greeting Khrushchev like Snow White welcoming one of the seven dwarfs. (No, I wasn't betraying Joan in my adoration. Joan was beautiful but human, like us; Jackie was magic.) When, years later, she married Rumpelstiltskin, I felt like a child discovering, in his father's drawer, the Santa Claus suit. And, later still, reading some *Ladies' Home Journal* exposé ("Jacqueline Onassis's secretary tells all . . .") I felt almost sick. After the first few pages I put the magazine down. I wasn't interested in the fragments, only in the fact that the glass had broken.

If I had spent at the piano the hours I gave to television, on all those afternoons when I came home from school, I would be an accomplished pianist now. Or if I'd danced, or read, or painted. . . . But I turned on the set instead, every day, almost, every year, and sank into an old green easy chair, smothered in quilts, with a bag of Fritos beside me and a glass of milk to wash them down, facing life and death with Dr. Kildare, laughing at Danny Thomas, whispering the answers—out loud sometimes—with "Password" and "To Tell the Truth." Looking back over all those afternoons, I try to convince myself they weren't wasted. I must have learned something; I must, at least, have changed.

What I learned was certainly not what TV tried to teach me. From the reams of trivia collected over years of quiz shows, I remember only the questions, never the answers. I loved "Leave It to Beaver" for the messes Beaver got into, not for the inevitable lecture from Dad at the end of each show. I saw every episode two or three times, witnessed Beaver's aging, his legs getting longer and his voice lower, only to start all over again with young Beaver every fall. (Someone told me recently that the boy who played Beaver Cleaver died in Vietnam. The news was a shock—I kept coming back to it for days until another distressed Beaver fan wrote to tell me that it wasn't true after all.)

I got so I could predict punch lines and endings, not really   14
knowing whether I'd seen the episode before or only watched one like it. There was the bowling-ball routine, for instance: Lucy, Dobie Gillis, Pete and Gladys—they all used it. Somebody would get his finger stuck in a bowling ball (Lucy later updated the gimmick using Liz Taylor's ring) and then they'd have to go to a wedding or give a speech at the P.T.A. or have the boss to dinner, concealing one hand all the while. We weren't supposed to ask questions like "Why don't they just tell the truth?" These shows were built on deviousness, on the longest distance between two points, and on a kind of symmetry which decrees that no loose ends shall be left untied, no lingering doubts allowed. (The Surgeon General is off the track in worrying about TV violence, I think. I grew up in the days before lawmen became peacemakers. What carries over is not the gunfights but the memory that everything always turned out all right.) Optimism shone through all those half hours I spent in the dark shadows of the TV room—out of evil shall come good.

Most of all, the situation comedies steeped me in American   15
culture. I emerged from years of TV viewing indifferent to the museums of France, the architecture of Italy, the literature of England. A perversely homebound American, I pick up paperbacks in bookstores, checking before I buy to see if the characters have foreign names, whether the action takes place in London or New York. Vulgarity and banality fascinate me. More intellectual friends (who watch no TV) can't understand what I see in "My Three Sons." "Nothing happens," they say. "The characters are dull, plastic, faceless. Every show is the

same." I guess that's why I watch them—boring repetition is, itself, a rhythm—a steady pulse of flashing Coca-Cola signs, McDonald's Golden Arches and Howard Johnson roofs.

I don't watch TV as an anthropologist, rising loftily above my subject to analyze. Neither do I watch, as some kids now tune in to reruns of "The Lone Ranger" and "Superman" (in the same spirit they enjoy comic books and pop art) for their camp. I watch in earnest. How can I do anything else? Five thousand hours of my life have gone into this box.

There were almost no blacks in our school. They were Negroes then; the word *black* was hard to say at first. *Negro* got hard to say for a while too, so I said nothing at all and was embarrassed. If you had asked me, at 9, to describe Cassius Clay, I would have taken great, liberal pains to be color-blind, mentioning height, build, eye color and shoe size, disregarding skin. I knew black people only from newspapers and the TV screen—picket lines, National Guardsmen at the doors of schools. (There were few black actors on TV then, except for Jack Benny's Rochester.) It was easy, in 1963, to embrace the Negro cause. Later, faced with cold stares from an all-black table in the cafeteria or heckled by a Panther selling newspapers, I first became aware of the fact that maybe the little old lady didn't want to be helped across the street. My visions of black-and-white-together look at me now like shots from "To Sir With Love." If a black is friendly to me, I wonder, as other blacks might, if he's a sellout.

I had no desire to scream or cry or throw jelly beans when I first saw the Beatles on the Ed Sullivan Show. An eighth-grader would have been old enough to revert to childhood, but I was too young to act anything but old. So mostly we laughed at them. We were in fifth grade, the year of rationality, the calm before the storm. We still screamed when the boys came near us (which they rarely did) and said they had cooties. Barbie dolls tempted us. That was the year when I got my first Barbie. Perhaps they were produced earlier, but they didn't reach New Hampshire till late that fall, and the stores were always sold out. So at the close of our doll-playing careers there was a sudden dramatic switch from lumpy, round-bellied Betsy Wetsys and stiff-legged little-girl dolls to slim, curvy

Barbie, just 11 inches tall, with a huge, expensive wardrobe that included a filmy black negligee and a mouth that made her look as if she'd just swallowed a lemon.

Barbie wasn't just a toy, but a way of living that moved us 19 suddenly from tea parties to dates with Ken at the Soda Shoppe. Our short careers with Barbie, before junior high sent her to the attic, built up our expectations for teen-age life before we had developed the sophistication to go along with them. Children today are accustomed to having a tantalizing youth culture all around them. (They play with Barbie in the nursery school.) For us, it broke like a cloudburst, without preparation. Caught in the deluge, we were torn—wanting to run for shelter but tempted, also, to sing in the rain.

Marijuana and the class of '71 moved through high school 20 together. When we came in, as freshmen, drugs were still strange and new; marijuana was smoked only by a few marginal figures while those in the mainstream guzzled beer. It was called pot then—the words grass and dope came later; hash and acid and pills were almost unheard of. By my sophomore year, lots of the seniors and even a few younger kids were trying it. By the time I was a junior—in 1969—grass was no longer reserved for the hippies; basketball players and cheer-leaders and boys with crew-cuts and boys in black-leather jackets all smoked. And with senior year—maybe because of the nostalgia craze—there was an odd liquor revival. In my last month of school, a major bust led to the suspension of half a dozen boys. They were high on beer.

Now people are saying that the drug era is winding down. 21 (It's those statisticians with their graphs again, charting social phenomena like the rise and fall of hemlines.) I doubt if it's real, this abandonment of marijuana. But the frenzy is gone, certainly, the excitement and the fear of getting caught and the worry of where to get good stuff. What's happened to dope is what happens to a new record: you play it constantly, full volume, at first. Then, as you get to know the songs, you play them less often, not because you're tired of them exactly, but just because you know them. They're with you always, but quietly, in your head.

My position was a difficult one, all through those four years 22 when grass took root in Oyster River High. I was on the side of all those things that went along with smoking dope—the clothes, the music, the books, the candidates. More and more of my friends smoked, and many people weren't completely my friends, I think, because I didn't. Drugs took on a dispro-portionate importance. Why was it I could spend half a dozen evenings with someone without his ever asking me what I thought of Beethoven or Picasso but always, in the first half hour, he'd ask whether I smoked?

It became—like hair length and record collection—a symbol of who you were, and you couldn't be all the other things— progressive and creative and free-thinking—without taking that crumpled roll of dry, brown vegetation and holding it to your lips. You are what you eat—or what you smoke, or what you don't smoke. And when you say "like—you know," you're speaking the code, and suddenly the music of the Grateful Dead and the poetry of Bob Dylan and the general brilliance of Ken Kesey all belong to you as if, in those three fuzzy, mumbled words, you'd created art yourself and uttered the wisdom of the universe.

The freshman women's dorm at Yale has no house mother. We have no check-in hours or drinking rules or punishments for having boys in our rooms past midnight. A guard sits by the door to offer, as they assured us at the beginning of the year, physical—not moral—protection. All of which makes it easy for many girls who feel, after high-school curfews and dating regulations, suddenly liberated. (The first week of school last fall, many girls stayed out all night, every night, displaying next morning the circles under their eyes the way some girls show off engagement rings.)

We all received the "Sex at Yale" book, a thick, black pamphlet filled with charts and diagrams and a lengthy discussion of contraceptive methods. And at the first women's assembly, the discussion moved quickly from course-signing-up proce-dures to gynecology, where it stayed for much of the evening. Somebody raised her hand to ask where she could fill her pill prescription, someone else wanted to know about abortions. There was no standing in the middle any more—you had to either take out a pen and paper and write down the phone numbers they gave out or stare stonily ahead, implying that those were numbers *you* certainly wouldn't be needing. From then on it seemed the line had been drawn.

But of course the problem is that no lines, no barriers, ex- 26 ist. Where, five years ago a girl's decisions were made for her (she had to be in at 12 and, if she was found—in—with her boyfriend . . .): today the decision rests with her alone. She is surrounded by knowledgeable, sexually experienced girls and if *she* isn't willing to sleep with her boyfriend, somebody else will. It's peer-group pressure, 1972 style—the embarrassment of virginity.

Everyone is raised on nursery rhymes and nonsense stories. 27 But it used to be that when you grew up, the nonsense disappeared. Not for us—it is at the core of our music and literature and art and, in fact, of our lives. Like characters in an Ionesco play, we take absurdity unblinking. In a world where military officials tell us "We had to destroy the village in order to save it," Dylan lyrics make an odd kind of sense. They aren't meant to be understood; they don't jar our sensibilities because we're used to *non sequiturs*. We don't take anything too seriously these days. (Was it a thousand earthquake victims or a million? Does it matter?) The casual butcher's-operation in the film M*A*S*H and the comedy in Vonnegut and the album cover showing John and Yoko, bareback, are all part of the new absurdity. The days of the Little Moron joke and the elephant joke and the knock-knock joke are gone. It sounds melodramatic, but the joke these days is life.

You're not supposed to care too much any more. Reactions 28 have been scaled down from screaming and jelly-bean-throwing to nodding your head and maybe—if the music really gets to you (and music's the only thing that does any more)—tapping a finger. We need a passion transfusion, a shot of energy in the veins. It's what I'm most impatient with, in my generation—this languid, I-don't-give-a-s——ism that stems in part, at least, from a culture of put-ons in which any serious expression of emotion is branded sentimental and old-fashioned. The fact that we set such a premium on being cool reveals a lot about my generation; the idea is not to care. You can hear it in the speech of college students today: cultivated monotones, low volume, punctuated with four-letter words that come off sounding only bland. I feel it most of all on Saturday morning, when the sun is shining and the crocuses are about to bloom and, walking through the corridors of my dorm, I see there isn't anyone awake.

I'm basically an optimist. Somehow, no matter what the latest population figures say, I feel everything will work out—just like on TV. I may doubt man's fundamental goodness, but I believe in his power to survive. I say, sometimes, that I wonder if we'll be around in 30 years, but then I forget myself and speak of "when I'm 50. . . ." Death has touched me now— from Vietnam and Biafra and a car accident that makes me buckle my seat belt—but like negative numbers and the sound of a dog whistle (too high-pitched for human ears), it's not a concept I can comprehend. I feel immortal while all the signs around me proclaim that I'm not.

We feel cheated, many of us—the crop of 1953—which is why we complain about inheriting problems we didn't cause. (Childhood notions of justice, reinforced by Perry Mason, linger on. Why should I clean up someone else's mess? Who can I blame?) We're excited also, of course: I can't wait to see how things turn out. But I wish I weren't quite so involved. I wish it weren't my life that's being turned into a suspense thriller.

When my friends and I were little, we had big plans. I would be a famous actress and singer, dancing on the side. I would paint my own sets and compose my own music, writing the script and the lyrics and reviewing the performance for the *New York Times*. I would marry and have three children (they don't allow us dreams like that any more) and we would live, rich and famous (donating lots to charity, of course, and periodically adopting orphans), in a house we designed ourselves. When I was older I had visions of good works. I saw myself in South American rain forests and African deserts, feeding the hungry and healing the sick with an obsessive selflessness, I see now, as selfish, in the end, as my original plans for stardom.

Now my goal is simpler. I want to be happy. And I want comfort—nice clothes, a nice house, good music and good food, and the feeling that I'm doing some little thing that matters. I'll vote and I'll give to charity, but I won't give myself. I feel a sudden desire to buy land—not a lot, not as a business investment, but just a small plot of earth so that whatever they do to the country I'll have a place where I can go—a kind of fallout shelter, I guess. As some people prepare for their old age, so I prepare for my 20's. A little house, a comfortable chair, peace and quiet—retirement sounds tempting.

My People

CHIEF SEATTLE

Yonder sky that has wept tears of compassion upon my people for centuries untold, and which to us appears changeless and eternal, may change. Today is fair. Tomorrow may be overcast with clouds. My words are like the stars that never change. Whatever Seattle says the great chief at Washington can rely upon with as much certainty as he can upon the return of the sun or the seasons. The White Chief says that Big Chief at Washington sends us greetings of friendship and goodwill. That is kind of him for we know he has little need of our friendship in return. His people are many. They are like the grass that covers vast prairies. My people are few. They resemble the scattering trees of a storm-swept plain. The great, and—I presume—good, White Chief sends us word that he wishes to buy our lands but is willing to allow us enough to live comfortably. This indeed appears just, even generous, for the Red Man no longer has rights that he need respect, and the offer may be wise also, as we are no longer in need of an extensive country. . . . I will not dwell on, nor mourn over, our untimely decay, nor reproach our paleface brothers with hastening it, as we too may have been somewhat to blame.

Youth is impulsive. When our young men grow angry at some real or imaginary wrong, and disfigure their faces with black paint, it denotes that their hearts are black, and then they are often cruel and relentless, and our old men and old women are unable to restrain them. Thus it has ever been. Thus it was when the white men first began to push our forefathers further westward. But let us hope that the hostilities between us may never return. We would have everything to lose and nothing to gain. Revenge by young men is considered gain, even at the cost of their own lives, but old men who stay at home in times of war, and mothers who have sons to lose, know better.

Our good father at Washington—for I presume he is now our ³
father as well as yours, since King George has moved his
boundaries further north—our great good father, I say, sends
us word that if we do as he desires he will protect us. His brave
warriors will be to us a bristling wall of strength, and his
wonderful ships of war will fill our harbors so that our ancient
enemies far to the northward—the Hydas and Tsimpsians—will
cease to frighten our women, children, and old men. Then in
reality will he be our father and we his children. But can that
ever be? Your God is not our God! Your God loves your people
and hates mine. He folds his strong and protecting arms
lovingly about the paleface and leads him by the hand as a
father leads his infant son—but He has forsaken His red
children—if they really are his. Our God, the Great Spirit,
seems also to have forsaken us. Your God makes your people
wax strong every day. Soon they will fill the land. Our people
are ebbing away like a rapidly receding tide that will never
return. The white man's God cannot love our people or He
would protect them. They seem to be orphans who can look
nowhere for help. How then can we be brothers? How can your
God become our God and renew our prosperity and awaken in
us dreams of returning greatness? If we have a common heavenly
father He must be partial—for He came to his paleface children.
We never saw Him. He gave you laws but He had no word for
His red children whose teeming multitudes once filled this vast
continent as stars fill the firmament. No; we are two distinct
races with separate origins and separate destinies. There is
little in common between us.

To us the ashes of our ancestors are sacred and their resting ⁴
place is hallowed ground. You wander far from the graves of
your ancestors and seemingly without regret. Your religion was
written upon tables of stone by the iron finger of your God so
that you could not forget. The Red Man could never comprehend
nor remember it. Our religion is the traditions of our ancestors—
the dreams of our old men, given them in solemn hours of
night by the Great Spirit; and the visions of our sachems; and
it is written in the hearts of our people.

Your dead cease to love you and the land of their nativity as ⁵
soon as they pass the portals of the tomb and wander way

beyond the stars. They are soon forgotten and never return. Our dead never forget the beautiful world that gave them being.

Day and night cannot dwell together. The Red man has ever fled the approach of the White Man, as the morning mist flees before the morning sun. However, your proposition seems fair and I think that my people will accept it and will retire to the reservation you offer them. Then we will dwell apart in peace, for the words of the Great White Chief seem to be the words of nature speaking to my people out of dense darkness.

It matters little where we pass the remnant of our days. They will not be many. A few more moons; a few more winters—and not one of the descendants of the mighty hosts that once moved over this broad land or lived in happy homes, protected by the Great Spirit, will remain to mourn over the graves of a people once more powerful and hopeful than yours. But why should I mourn at the untimely fate of my people? Tribe follows tribe, and nation follows nation, like the waves of the sea. It is the order of nature, and regret is useless. Your time of decay may be distant, but it will surely come, for even the White Man whose God walked and talked with him as friend with friend, cannot be exempt from the common destiny. We may be brothers after all. We will see.

We will ponder your proposition, and when we decide we will let you know. But should we accept it, I here and now make this condition that we will not be denied the privilege without molestation of visiting at any time the tombs of our ancestors, friends and children. Every part of this soil is sacred in the estimation of my people. Every hillside, every valley, every plain and grove, has been hallowed by some sad or happy event in days long vanished. . . . The very dust upon which you now stand responds more lovingly to their footsteps than to yours, because it is rich with the blood of our ancestors and our bare feet are conscious of the sympathetic touch. . . . Even the little children who lived here and rejoiced here for a brief season will love these somber solitudes and at eventide they greet shadowy returning spirits. And when the last Red Man shall have perished, and the memory of my tribe shall have become a myth among the White Men, these shores will swarm with the invisible dead of my tribe, and when your children's children think themselves alone in the field, the store, the shop, upon the highway, or in the silence of the pathless woods, they will not be alone. . . . At night when the streets of your cities and villages are silent and you think them deserted, they will throng with the returning hosts that once filled and still love this beautiful land. The White Man will never be alone.

Let him be just and deal kindly with my people, for the dead are not powerless. Dead, did I say? There is not death, only a change of worlds. 9

Once More to the Lake

E. B. WHITE

August 1941

One summer, along about 1904, my father rented a camp on a lake in Maine and took us all there for the month of August. We all got ringworm from some kittens and had to rub Pond's Extract on our arms and legs night and morning, and my father rolled over in a canoe with all his clothes on; but outside of that the vacation was a success and from then on none of us ever thought there was any place in the world like that lake in Maine. We returned summer after summer—always on August 1 for one month. I have since become a salt-water man, but sometimes in summer there are days when the restlessness of the tides and the fearful cold of the sea water and the incessant wind that blows across the afternoon and into the evening make me wish for the placidity of a lake in the woods. A few weeks ago this feeling got so strong I bought myself a couple of bass hooks and a spinner and returned to the lake where we used to go, for a week's fishing and to revisit old haunts.

I took along my son, who had never had any fresh water up his nose and who had seen lily pads only from train windows. On the journey over to the lake I began to wonder what it would be like. I wondered how time would have marred this unique, this holy spot—the coves and streams, the hills that the sun set behind, the camps and the paths behind the camps. I was sure that the tarred road would have found it out, and I wondered in what other ways it would be desolated. It is strange how much you can remember about places like that once you allow your mind to return into the grooves that lead back. You remember one thing, and that suddenly reminds you of another thing. I guess I remembered clearest of all the early mornings, when the lake was cool and motionless, remembered how the bedroom smelled of the lumber it was made of and of the wet woods whose scent entered through the screen. The partitions in the camp were thin and did not extend clear to the top of the rooms, and as I was always the first up I would dress softly so as not to wake the others, and sneak out into the sweet outdoors and start out in the canoe, keeping close along the shore in the long shadows of the pines. I remembered being very careful never to rub my paddle against the gunwale for fear of disturbing the stillness of the cathedral.

The lake had never been what you would call a wild lake. There were cottages sprinkled around the shores, and it was in farming country although the shores of the lake were quite heavily wooded. Some of the cottages were owned by nearby farmers, and you would live at the shore and eat your meals at the farmhouse. That's what our family did. But although it wasn't wild, it was a fairly large and undisturbed lake and there were places in it that, to a child at least, seemed infinitely remote and primeval. 3

I was right about the tar: it led to within half a mile of the shore. But when I got back there, with my boy, and we settled into a camp near a farmhouse and into the kind of summertime I had known, I could tell that it was going to be pretty much the same as it had been before—I knew it, lying in bed the first morning, smelling the bedroom and hearing the boy sneak quietly out and go off along the shore in a boat. I began to sustain the illusion that he was I, and therefore, by simple transposition, that I was my father. This sensation persisted, kept cropping up all the time we were there. It was not an entirely new feeling, but in this setting it grew much stronger. I seemed to be living a dual existence. I would be in the middle of some simple act, I would be picking up a bait box or laying down a table fork, or I would be saying something, and suddenly it would be not I but my father who was saying the words or making the gesture. It gave me a creepy sensation. 4

We went fishing the first morning. I felt the same damp moss covering the worms in the bait can, and saw the dragonfly alight on the tip of my rod as it hovered a few inches from the surface of the water. It was the arrival of this fly that convinced me beyond any doubt that everything was as it always had 5 been, that the years were a mirage and that there had been no years. The small waves were the same, chucking the rowboat under the chine as we fished at anchor, and the boat was the same boat, the same color green and the ribs broken in the same places, and under the floorboards the same fresh-water leavings and débris—the dead helgramite, the wisps of moss, the rusty discarded fishhook, the dried blood from yesterday's catch. We stared silently at the tips of our rods, at the dragonflies that came and went. I lowered the tip of mine into the water, tentatively, pensively dislodging the fly, which darted two feet away, poised, darted two feet back, and came to rest again a little farther up the rod. There had been no years between the ducking of this dragonfly and the other one—the one that was part of memory. I looked at the boy, who was silently watching his fly, and it was my hands that held his rod, my eyes watching. I felt dizzy and didn't know which rod I was at the end of.

We caught two bass, hauling them in briskly as though they were mackerel, pulling them over the side of the boat in a businesslike manner without any landing net, and stunning them with a blow on the back of the head. When we got back for a swim before lunch, the lake was exactly where we had left it, the same number of inches from the dock, and there was only the merest suggestion of a breeze. This seemed an utterly enchanted sea, this lake you could leave to its own devices for a few hours and come back to, and find that it had not stirred, this constant and trustworthy body of water. In the shallows, the dark, water-soaked sticks and twigs, smooth and old, were undulating in clusters on the bottom against the clean ribbed sand, and the track of the mussel was plain. A school of minnows swam by, each minnow with its small individual shadow, doubling the attendance, so clear and sharp in the sunlight. Some of the other campers were in swimming, along the shore, one of them with a cake of soap, and the water felt thin and clear and unsubstantial. Over the years there had been this person with the cake of soap, this cultist, and here he was. There had been no years.

Up to the farmhouse to dinner through the teeming, dusty field, the road under our sneakers was only a two-track road.

The middle track was missing, the one with the marks of the hooves and the splotches of dried, flaky manure. There had always been three tracks to choose from in choosing which track to walk in; now the choice was narrowed down to two. For a moment I missed terribly the middle alternative. But the way led past the tennis court, and something about the way it lay there in the sun reassured me; the tape had loosened along the backline, the alleys were green with plantains and other weeds, and the net (installed in June and removed in September) sagged in the dry noon, and the whole place steamed with midday heat and hunger and emptiness. There was a choice of pie for dessert, and one was blueberry and one was apple, and the waitresses were the same country girls, there having been no passage of time, only the illusion of it as in a dropped curtain—the waitresses were still fifteen; their hair had been washed, that was the only difference—they had been to the movies and seen the pretty girls with the clean hair.

Summertime, oh, summertime, pattern of life indelible, the 8 fadeproof lake, the woods unshatterable, the pasture with the sweetfern and the juniper forever and ever, summer without end; this was the background, and the life along the shore was the design, the cottagers with their innocent and tranquil design, their tiny docks with the flagpole and the American flag floating against the white clouds in the blue sky, the little paths over the roots of the trees leading from camp to camp and the paths leading back to the outhouses and the can of lime for sprinkling, and at the souvenir counters at the store the miniature birch-bark canoes and the postcards that showed things looking a little better than they looked. This was the American family at play, escaping the city heat, wondering whether the newcomers in the camp at the head of the cove were "common" or "nice," wondering whether it was true that the people who drove up for Sunday dinner at the farmhouse were turned away because there wasn't enough chicken.

It seemed to me, as I kept remembering all this, that those 9 times and those summers had been infinitely precious and worth saving. There had been jollity and peace and goodness. The arriving (at the beginning of August) had been so big a business in itself, at the railway station the farm wagon drawn up, the first smell of the pine-laden air, the first glimpse of the smiling farmer, and the great importance of the trunks and your father's enormous authority in such matters, and the feel of the wagon under you for the long ten-mile haul, and at the top of the last long hill catching the first view of the lake after eleven months of not seeing this cherished body of water. The shouts and cries of the other campers when they saw you, and the trunks to be unpacked, to give up their rich burden. (Arriving was less exciting nowadays, when you sneaked up in your car and parked it under a tree near the camp and took out the bags and in five minutes it was all over, no fuss, no loud wonderful fuss about trunks.)

Peace and goodness and jollity. The only thing that was wrong now, really, was the sound of the place, an unfamiliar nervous sound of the outboard motors. This was the note that jarred, the one thing that would sometimes break the illusion and set the years moving. In those other summertimes all motors were inboard; and when they were at a little distance, the noise they made was a sedative, an ingredient of summer sleep. They were one-cylinder and two-cylinder engines, and some were make-and-break and some were jump-spark, but they all made a sleepy sound across the lake. The one-lungers throbbed and fluttered, and the twin-cylinder ones purred and purred, and that was a quiet sound, too. But now the campers all had outboards. In the daytime, in the hot mornings, these motors made a petulant, irritable sound; at night, in the still evening when the afterglow lit the water, they whined about one's ears like mosquitoes. My boy loved our rented outboard, and his great desire was to achieve single-handed mastery over it, and authority, and he soon learned the trick of choking it a little (but not too much), and the adjustment of the needle valve. Watching him I would remember the things you could do with the old one-cylinder engine with the heavy flywheel, how you could have it eating out of your hand if you got really close to it spiritually. Motorboats in those days didn't have clutches, and you would make a landing by shutting off the motor at the proper time and coasting in with a dead rudder. But there was a way of reversing them, if you learned the trick, by cutting the switch and putting it on again exactly on the final dying revolution of the flywheel, so that it would kick back against compression and begin reversing. Approaching a dock in a strong following breeze, it was difficult to slow up sufficiently by the ordinary coasting method, and if a boy felt he had complete mastery over his motor, he was tempted to keep it running beyond its time and then reverse it a few feet from the dock. It took a cool nerve, because if you threw the switch a twentieth of a second too soon you would catch the flywheel when it still had speed enough to go up past center, and the boat would leap ahead, charging bull-fashion at the dock.

We had a good week at the camp. The bass were biting well and the sun shone endlessly, day after day. We would be tired at night and lie down in the accumulated heat of the little bedrooms after the long hot day and the breeze would stir almost imperceptibly outside and the smell of the swamp drift in through the rusty screens. Sleep would come easily and in the morning the red squirrel would be on the roof, tapping out his gay routine. I kept remembering everything, lying in bed in the mornings—the small steamboat that had a long rounded stern like the lip of a Ubangi, and how quietly she ran on the moonlight sails, when the older boys played their mandolins and the girls sang and we ate doughnuts dipped in sugar, and how sweet the music was on the water in the shining night, and what it had felt like to think about girls then. After breakfast we would go up to the store and the things were in the same place—the minnows in a bottle, the plugs and spinners disarranged and pawed over by the youngsters from the boys' camp, the Fig Newtons and the Beeman's gum. Outside, the road was tarred and cars stood in front of the store. Inside, all was just as it had always been, except there was more Coca-Cola and not so much Moxie and root beer and birch beer and sarsaparilla. We would walk out with the bottle of pop apiece and sometimes the pop would backfire up our noses and hurt. We explored the streams, quietly, where the turtles slid off the sunny logs and dug their way into the soft bottom; and we lay on the town wharf and fed worms to the tame bass. Everywhere we went I had trouble making out which was I, the one walking at my side, the one walking in my pants.

11

One afternoon while we were there at that lake a thunderstorm came up. It was like the revival of an old melodrama that I had seen long ago with childish awe. The second-act climax of the drama of the electrical disturbance over a lake in America had not changed in any important respect. This was the big scene, still the big scene. The whole thing was so familiar, the first feeling of oppression and heat and a general air around camp of not wanting to go very far away. In mid-afternoon (it was all the same) a curious darkening of the sky, and a lull in everything that had made life tick; and then the way the boats suddenly swung the other way at their moorings with the coming of a breeze out of the new quarter, and the premonitory rumble. Then the kettle drum, then the snare, then the bass drum and cymbals, then crackling light against the dark, and the gods grinning and licking their chops in the hills. Afterward the calm, the rain steadily rustling in the calm lake, the return of light and hope and spirits, and the campers running out in joy and relief to go swimming in the rain, their bright cries perpetuating the deathless joke about how they were getting simply drenched, and the children screaming with delight at the new sensation of bathing in the rain, and the joke about getting drenched linking the generations in a strong indestructible chain. And the comedian who waded in carrying an umbrella.

When the others went swimming, my son said he was going in, too. He pulled his dripping trunks from the line where they had hung all through the shower and wrung them out. Languidly, and with no thought of going in, I watched him, his hard little body, skinny and bare, saw him wince slightly as he pulled up around his vitals the small, soggy, icy garment. As he buckled the swollen belt, suddenly my groin felt the chill of death.

The Subway

TOM WOLFE

In a way, of course, the subway is the living symbol of all
that adds up to lack of status in New York. There is a sense
of madness and disorientation at almost every express stop.
The ceilings are low, the vistas are long, there are no landmarks,
the lighting is an eerie blend of fluorescent tubing, electric
light bulbs and neon advertising. The whole place is a gross
assault in the senses. The noise of the trains stopping or
rounding curves has a high-pitched harshness that is difficult
to describe. People feel no qualms about pushing whenever it
becomes crowded. Your tactile sense takes a crucifying you
never dreamed possible. The odors become unbearable when
the weather is warm. Between platforms, record shops broadcast
45 r.p.m. records with metallic tones and lunch counters serve
the kind of hot dogs in which you bite through a tensile,
rubbery surface and then hit a soft, oleaginous center like
cottonseed meal, and the customers sit there with pastry and
bread flakes caked around their mouths, belching to themselves
so that their cheeks pop out flatulently now and then.

The underground spaces seem to attract every eccentric
passion. A small and ancient man with a Bible, an American
flag and a megaphone haunts the subways of Manhattan. He
opens the Bible and quotes from it in a strong but old and
monotonous voice. He uses the megaphone at express stops,
where the noise is too great for his voice to be heard ordinarily,
and calls for redemption.

Also beggars. And among the beggars New York's status
competition is renewed, there in the much-despised subway.
On the Seventh Avenue IRT line the competition is maniacal.
Some evenings the beggars ricochet off one another between
stops, calling one another ——s and ——s and telling each
other to go find their own —— car. A mere blind man with a

cane and a cup is mediocre business. What is demanded is entertainment. Two boys, one of them with a bongo drum, get on and the big boy, with the drum, starts beating on it as soon as the train starts up, and the little boy goes into what passes for a native dance. Then, if there is room, he goes into a tumbling act. He runs from one end of the car, first in the direction the train is going, and does a complete somersault in the air, landing on his feet. Then he runs back the other way and does a somersault in the air, only this time against the motion of the train. He does this several times both ways, doing some native dancing in between. This act takes so long that it can be done properly only over a long stretch, such as the run between 42nd Street and 72nd Street. After the act is over, the boys pass along the car with Dixie cups, asking for contributions.

The Dixie cup is the conventional container. There is one young Negro on the Seventh Avenue line who used to get on at 42nd Street and start singing a song, "I Wish That I Were Married." He was young and looked perfectly healthy. But he would get on and sing this song, "I Wish That I Were Married," at the top of his lungs and then pull a Dixie cup out from under the windbreaker he always wore and walk up and down the car waiting for contributions. I never saw him get a cent. Lately, however, life has improved for him because he has begun to understand status competition. Now he gets on and sings "I Wish That I Were Married," only when he opens up his windbreaker, he not only takes out a Dixie cup but reveals a cardboard sign, on which is written: "MY MOTHER HAS MULTIPLE SCHLERROSSIS AND I AM BLIND IN ONE EYE." His best touch is sclerosis, which he has added every conceivable consonant to, creating a good, intimidating German physiology-textbook solidity. So today he does much better. He seems to make a living. He is no idler, lollygagger or bum. He can look with condescension upon the states to which men fall.

On the East Side IRT subway line, for example, at 86th Street, the train stops and everyone comes squeezing out of the cars in clots and there on a bench in the gray-green gloom, under the girders and 1905 tiles, is an old man slouched back fast asleep, wearing a cotton windbreaker with the sleeves pulled off. That is all he is wearing. His skin is the color of congealed Wheatena laced with pocket lint. His legs are crossed in a gentlemanly fashion and his kindly juice-head face is slopped over on the back of the bench. Apparently, other winos, who are notorious thieves among one another, had stripped him of all his clothes except his windbreaker, which they had tried to pull off him, but only managed to rip the sleeves off, and left him there passed out on the bench and naked, but in a gentlemanly posture. Everyone stares at him briefly, at his congealed Wheatena-and-lint carcass, but no one breaks stride; and who knows how long it will be before finally two policemen have to come in and hold their breath and scrape him up out of the gloom and into the bosom of the law, from which he will emerge with a set of green fatigues, at least, and an honorable seat at night on the subway bench.

Stranger in the Village

JAMES BALDWIN

From all available evidence no black man had ever set foot in this tiny Swiss village before I came. I was told before arriving that I would probably be a "sight" for the village; I took this to mean that people of my complexion were rarely seen in Switzerland, and also that city people are always something of a "sight" outside of the city. It did not occur to me—possibly because I am an American—that there could be people anywhere who had never seen a Negro.

It is a fact that cannot be explained on the basis of the inaccessibility of the village. The village is very high, but it is only four hours from Milan and three hours from Lausanne. It is true that it is virtually unknown. Few people making plans for a holiday would elect to come here. On the other hand, the villagers are able, presumably, to come and go as they please—which they do: to another town at the foot of the mountain, with a population of approximately five thousand, the nearest place to see a movie or go to the bank. In the village there is no movie house, no bank, no library, no theater; very few radios, one jeep, one station wagon; and at the moment, one typewriter, mine, an invention which the woman next door to me here had never seen. There are about six hundred people living here, all Catholic—I conclude this from the fact that the Catholic church is open all year round, whereas the Protestant chapel, set off on a hill a little removed from the village, is open only in the summertime when the tourists arrive. There are four or five hotels, all closed now, and four or five *bistros*, of which, however, only two do any business during the winter. These two do not do a great deal, for life in the village seems to end around nine or ten o'clock. There are a few stores, butcher, baker, *épicerie*, a hardware store, and a money-changer—who cannot change travelers' checks, but must send them down to the bank, an operation which takes two or three days. There is something called the *Ballet Haus,* closed in the winter and used for God knows what, certainly not ballet, during the summer. There seems to be only one schoolhouse in the village, and this for the quite young children; I suppose this to mean that their older brothers and sisters at some point descend from these mountains in order to complete their education—possibly, again, to the town just below. The landscape is absolutely forbidding, mountains towering on all four sides, ice and snow as far as the eye can reach. In this white wilderness, men and women and children move all day, carrying washing, wood, buckets of milk or water, sometimes skiing on Sunday afternoons. All week long boys and young men are to be seen shoveling snow off the rooftops, or dragging wood down from the forest in sleds.

The village's only real attraction, which explains the tourist 3 season, is the hot spring water. A disquietingly high proportion of these tourists are cripples, or semi-cripples, who come year after year—from other parts of Switzerland, usually—to take the waters. This lends the village, at the height of the season, a rather terrifying air of sanctity, as though it were a lesser Lourdes. There is often something beautiful, there is always something awful, in the spectacle of a person who has lost one of his faculties, a faculty he never questioned until it was gone, and who struggles to recover it. Yet people remain people, on crutches or indeed on deathbeds; and wherever I passed, the first summer I was here, among the native villagers or among the lame, a wind passed with me—of astonishment, curiosity, amusement, and outrage. That first summer I stayed two weeks and never intended to return. But I did return in the winter, to work; the village offers, obviously, no distractions whatever and has the further advantage of being extremely cheap. Now it is winter again, a year later, and I am here again. Everyone in the village knows my name, though they scarcely ever use it, knows that I come from America—though, this, apparently, they will never really believe: black men come from Africa—and everyone knows that I am the friend of the son of a woman who was born here, and that I am staying in their chalet. But I remain as much a stranger today as I was the first day I arrived, and the children shout *Neger! Neger!* as I walk along the streets.

It must be admitted that in the beginning I was far too shocked to have any real reaction. In so far as I reacted at all, I reacted by trying to be pleasant—it being a great part of the American Negro's education (long before he goes to school) that he must make people "like" him. This smile-and-the-world-smiles-with-you routine worked about as well in this situation as it had in the situation for which it was designed, which is to say that it did not work at all. No one, after all, can be liked whose human weight and complexity cannot be, or has not been, admitted. My smile was simply another unheard-of phenomenon which allowed them to see my teeth— they did not, really, see my smile and I began to think that, should I take to snarling, no one would notice any difference. All of the physical characteristics of the Negro which had caused me, in America, a very different and almost forgotten pain were nothing less than miraculous—or infernal—in the eyes of the village people. Some thought my hair was the color of tar, that it had the texture of wire, or the texture of cotton. It was jocularly suggested that I might let it all grow long and make myself a winter coat. If I sat in the sun for more than five minutes some daring creature was certain to come along and gingerly put his fingers on my hair, as though he were afraid of an electric shock, or put his hand on my hand, astonished that the color did not rub off. In all of this, in which it must be conceded there was the charm of genuine wonder and in which there were certainly no element of intentional unkindness, there was yet no suggestion that I was human: I was simply a living wonder.

I knew that they did not mean to be unkind, and I know it now; it is necessary, nevertheless, for me to repeat this to myself each time that I walk out of the chalet. The children who shout *Neger!* have no way of knowing the echoes this sound raises in me. They are brimming with good humor and the more daring swell with pride when I stop to speak with them. Just the same, there are days when I cannot pause and smile, when I have no heart to play with them; when, indeed, I mutter sourly to myself, exactly as I muttered on the streets of a city these children have never seen, when I was no bigger than these children are now: *Your* mother *was a nigger.* Joyce is right about history being a nightmare—but it may be the nightmare from which no one *can* awaken. People are trapped in history and history is trapped in them.

There is a custom in the village—I am told it is repeated in 6 many villages—of "buying" African natives for the purpose of converting them to Christianity. There stands in the church all year round a small box with a slot for money, decorated with a black figurine, and into this box the villagers drop their francs. During the *carnaval* which precedes Lent, two village children have their faces blackened—out of which bloodless darkness their blue eyes shine like ice—and fantastic horsehair wigs are placed on their blond heads; thus disguised, they solicit among the villagers for money for the missionaries in Africa. Between the box in the church and the blackened children, the village "bought" last year six or eight African natives. This was reported to me with pride by the wife of one of the *bistro* owners and I was careful to express astonishment and pleasure at the solicitude shown by the village for the souls of black folks. The *bistro* owner's wife beamed with a pleasure far more genuine than my own and seemed to feel that I might now breathe more easily concerning the souls of at least six of my kinsmen.

I tried not to think of these so lately baptized kinsmen, of 7 the price paid for them, or the peculiar price they themselves would pay, and said nothing about my father, who having taken his own conversion too literally never, at bottom, forgave the white world (which he described as heathen) for having saddled him with a Christ in whom, to judge at least from their treatment of him, they themselves no longer believed. I thought of white men arriving for the first time in an African village, strangers there, as I am a stranger here, and tried to imagine the astounded populace touching their hair and marveling at the color of their skin. But there is a great difference between being the first white man to be seen by Africans and being the first black man to be seen by whites. The white man takes the astonishment as tribute, for he arrives to conquer and to convert the natives, whose inferiority in relation to himself is not even to be questioned; whereas I, without a thought of conquest, find myself among a people whose culture controls me, has even, in a sense, created me, people who have cost me more in anguish and rage than they will ever know, who yet do not even know of my existence. The astonishment with which I might have greeted them, should they have stumbled into my African village a few hundred years ago, might have rejoiced their hearts. But the astonishment with which they greet me today can only poison mine.

And this is so despite everything I may do to feel differently, despite my friendly conversations with the *bistro* owner's wife, despite their three-year-old son who has at last become my friend, despite the *saluts* and *bonsoirs* which I exchange with people as I walk, despite the fact that I know that no individual can be taken to task for what history is doing, or has done. I say that the culture of these people controls me—but they can scarcely be held responsible for European culture. America comes out of Europe, but these people have never seen America, nor have most of them seen more of Europe than the hamlet at the foot of their mountain. Yet they move with an authority which I shall never have; and they regard me, quite rightly, not only as a stranger in their village but as a suspect latecomer, bearing no credentials, to everything they have—however unconsciously—inherited.

For this village, even were it incomparably more remote and incredibly more primitive, is the West, the West onto which I have been so strangely grafted. These people cannot be, from the point of view of power, strangers anywhere in the world; they have made the modern world, in effect, even if they do not know it. The most illiterate among them is related, in a way that I am not, to Dante, Shakespeare, Michelangelo, Aeschylus, Da Vinci, Rembrandt, and Racine; the cathedral at Chartres says something to them which it cannot say to me, as indeed would New York's Empire State Building, should anyone here ever see it. Out of their hymns and dances come Beethoven and Bach. Go back a few centuries and they are in their full glory—but I am in Africa, watching the conquerors arrive.

The rage of the disesteemed is personally fruitless, but it is also absolutely inevitable; this rage, so generally discounted, so little understood even among the people whose daily bread it is, is one of the things that makes history. Rage can only with difficulty, and never entirely, be brought under the domination of the intelligence and is therefore not susceptible to any arguments whatever. This is a fact which ordinary representatives of the *Herrenvolk*,[1] having never felt this rage and being unable to imagine, quite fail to understand. Also, rage cannot be hidden, it can only be dissembled. This dissembling deludes the thoughtless, and strengthens rage and adds, to rage, contempt. There are, no doubt, as many ways of coping with the resulting complex of tensions as there are black men in the world, but no black man can hope ever to be entirely liberated from this internal warfare—rage, dissembling, and contempt having inevitably accompanied his first realization of the power of white men. What is crucial here is that, since white men represent in the black man's world so heavy a weight, white men have for black men a reality which is far from being reciprocal; and hence all black men have toward all white men an attitude which is designed, really, either to rob the white man of the jewel of his naïveté, or else to make it cost him dear.

The black man insists, by whatever means he finds at his disposal, that the white man cease to regard him as an exotic rarity and recognize him as a human being. This is a very charged and difficult moment, for there is a great deal of will power involved in the white man's naïveté. Most people are not naturally reflective any more than they are naturally malicious, and the white man prefers to keep the black man at a certain human remove because it is easier for him thus to preserve his simplicity and avoid being called to account for crimes committed by his forefathers, or his neighbors. He is inescapably aware, nevertheless, that he is in a better position in the world than black men are, nor can he quite put to death the suspicion that he is hated by black men therefore. He does not wish to be hated, neither does he wish to change places, and at this point in his uneasiness he can scarcely avoid having

[1] Master race.

recourse to those legends which white men have created about black men, the most usual effect of which is that the white man finds himself enmeshed, so to speak, in his own language which describes hell, as well as the attributes which lead one to hell, as being as black as night.

Every legend, moreover, contains its residuum of truth, and the root function of language is to control the universe by describing it. It is of quite considerable significance that black men remain, in the imagination, and in overwhelming numbers in fact, beyond the disciplines of salvation; and this despite the fact that the West has been "buying" African natives for centuries. There is, I should hazard, an instantaneous necessity to be divorced from this so visibly unsaved stranger, in whose heart, moreover, one cannot guess what dreams of vengeance are being nourished; and, at the same time, there are few things on earth more attractive than the idea of the unspeakable liberty which is allowed the unredeemed. When, beneath the black mask, a human being begins to make himself felt one cannot escape a certain awful wonder as to what kind of human being it is. What one's imagination makes of other people is dictated, of course, by the laws of one's own personality and it is one of the ironies of black-white relations that, by means of what the white man imagines the black man to be, the black man is enabled to know who the white man is.

I have said, for example, that I am as much a stranger in this village today as I was the first summer I arrived, but this is not quite true. The villagers wonder less about the texture of my hair than they did then, and wonder rather more about me. And the fact that their wonder now exists on another level is reflected in their attitudes and in their eyes. There are the children who make those delightful, hilarious, sometimes astonishingly grave overtures of friendship in the unpredictable fashion of children; other children, having been taught that the devil is a black man, scream in genuine anguish as I approach. Some of the older women never pass without a friendly greeting, never pass, indeed, if it seems that they will be able to engage me in conversation; other women look down or look away or rather contemptuously smirk. Some of the men drink with me and suggest that I learn how to ski—partly, I gather, because they cannot imagine what I would look like on skis—and want to know if I am married, and ask questions about my *métier*. But some of the men have accused *le sale nègre*—behind my back—of stealing wood and there is already in the eyes of some of them that peculiar, intent, paranoiac malevolence which one sometimes surprises in the eyes of American white men when, out walking with their Sunday girl, they see a Negro male approach.

There is a dreadful abyss between the streets of this village and the streets of the city in which I was born, between the children who shout *Neger!* today and those who shouted *Nigger!* yesterday—the abyss is experience, the American experience. The syllable hurled behind me today expresses, above all, wonder: I am a stranger here. But I am not a stranger in America and the same syllable riding on the American air expresses the war my presence has occasioned in the American soul.

For this village brings home to me this fact: that there was a day, and not really a very distant day, when Americans were scarcely Americans at all but discontented Europeans, facing a great unconquered continent and strolling, say, into a marketplace and seeing black men for the first time. The shock this spectacle afforded is suggested, surely, by the promptness with which they decided that these black men were not really men but cattle. It is true that the necessity on the part of the settlers of the New World of reconciling their moral assumptions with the fact—and the necessity—of slavery enhanced immensely the charm of this idea, and it is also true that this idea expresses, with a truly American bluntness, the attitude which to varying extents all masters have had toward all slaves.

But between all former slaves and slave-owners and the drama which begins for Americans over three hundred years ago at Jamestown, there are at least two differences to be observed. The American Negro slave could not suppose, for one thing, as slaves in past epochs had supposed and often done, that he would ever be able to wrest the power from his master's hands. This was a supposition which the modern era, which was to bring about such vast changes in the aims and dimensions of power, put to death; it only begins, in unprecedented fashion, and with dreadful implications, to be resurrected today. But even had this supposition persisted with undiminished force, the American Negro slave could not have used it to lend his condition dignity, for the reason that this supposition rests on another: that the slave in exile yet remains related to his past, has some means—if only in memory—of revering and sustaining the forms of his former life, is able, in short, to maintain his identity.

This was not the case with the American Negro slave. He is unique among the black men of the world in that his past was taken from him, almost literally, at one blow. One wonders what on earth the first slave found to say to the first dark child he bore. I am told that there are Haitians able to trace their ancestry back to African kings, but any American Negro wishing to go back so far will find his journey through time abruptly arrested by the signature on the bill of sale which served as the entrance paper for his ancestor. At the time—to say nothing of the circumstances—of the enslavement of the captive black man who was to become the American Negro, there was not the remotest possibility that he would ever take power from his master's hands. There was no reason to suppose that his situation would ever change, nor was there, shortly, anything to indicate that his situation had ever been different. It was his necessity, in the words of E. Franklin Frazier, to find a "motive for living under American culture or die." The identity of the American Negro comes out of this extreme situation, and the evolution of this identity was a source of the most intolerable anxiety in the minds and the lives of his masters.

For the history of the American Negro is unique also in this: that the question of his humanity, and of his rights therefore as a human being, became a burning one for several generations of Americans, so burning a question that it ultimately became one of those used to divide the nation. It is out of this argument that the venom of the epithet *Nigger!* is derived. It is an argument which Europe has never had, and hence Europe quite sincerely fails to understand how or why the argument arose in the first place, why its effects are frequently disastrous and always so unpredictable, why it refuses until today to be entirely settled. Europe's black possessions remained—and do remain—in Europe's colonies, at which remove they represented no threat whatever to European identity. If they posed any problem at all for the European conscience, it was a problem which remained comfortingly abstract: in effect, the black man, as a *man*, did not exist for Europe. But in America, even as a slave, he was an inescapable part of the general social fabric and no American could escape having an attitude toward him. Americans attempt until today to make an abstraction of the Negro, but the very nature of these abstractions reveals the tremendous effects the presence of the Negro has had on the American character.

When one considers the history of the Negro in America it is of the greatest importance to recognize that the moral beliefs of a person, or a people, are never really as tenuous as life—which is not moral—very often causes them to appear; these create for them a frame of reference and a necessary hope, the hope being that when life has done its worst they will be enabled to rise above themselves and to triumph over life. Life would scarcely be bearable if this hope did not exist. Again, even when the worst has been said, to betray a belief is not by any means to have put oneself beyond its power; the betrayal of a belief is not the same thing as ceasing to believe. If this were not so there would be no moral standards in the world at all. Yet one must also recognize that mortality is based on ideas and that all ideas are dangerous—dangerous because ideas can only lead to action and where the action leads no man can say. And dangerous in this respect: that confronted with the impossibility of remaining faithful to one's beliefs, and the equal impossibility of becoming free of them, one can be driven to the most inhuman excesses. The ideas on which American beliefs are based are not, though Americans often seem to think so, ideas which originated in America. They came out of Europe. And the establishment of democracy on the American continent was scarcely as radical a break with the past as was the necessity, which Americans faced, of broadening this concept to include black men.

This was, literally, a hard necessity. It was impossible, for one thing, for Americans to abandon their beliefs, not only because these beliefs alone seemed able to justify the sacrifices they had endured and the blood that they had spilled, but also because these beliefs afforded them their only bulwark against a moral chaos as absolute as the physical chaos of the continent it was their destiny to conquer. But in the situation in which Americans found themselves, these beliefs threatened an idea which, whether or not one likes to think so, is the very warp and woof of the heritage of the West, the idea of white supremacy.

Americans have made themselves notorious by the shrillness and the brutality with which they have insisted on this idea, but they did not invent it; and it has escaped the world's notice that those very excesses of which Americans have been guilty imply a certain, unprecedented uneasiness over the idea's life and power, if not, indeed, the idea's validity. The idea of white supremacy rests simply on the fact that white men are the creators of civilization (the present civilization, which is the only one that matters; all previous civilizations are simply "contributions" to our own) and are therefore civilization's guardians and defenders. Thus it was impossible for Americans to accept the black man as one of themselves, for to do so was to jeopardize their status as white men. But not so to accept him was to deny his human reality, his human weight and complexity, and the strain of denying the over-whelmingly undeniable forced Americans into rationalizations so fantastic that they approached the pathological.

At the root of the American Negro problem is the necessity of the American white man to find a way of living with the Negro in order to be able to live with himself. And the history of this problem can be reduced to the means used by Americans—lynch law and law, segregation and legal acceptance, terrorization and concession—either to come to terms with this necessity, or to find a way around it, or (most usually) to find a way of doing both these things at once. The resulting spectacle, at once foolish and dreadful, led someone to make the quite accurate observation that "the Negro-in-America is a form of insanity which overtakes white men."

In this long battle, a battle by no means finished, the unforeseeable effects of which will be felt by many future generations, the white man's motive was the protection of his identity; the black man was motivated by the need to establish an identity. And despite the terrorization which the Negro in America endured and endures sporadically until today, despite the cruel and totally inescapable ambivalence of his status in his country, the battle for his identity has long ago been won. He is not a visitor to the West, but a citizen there, an American; as American as the Americans who despise him, the Americans who fear him, the Americans who love him—the Americans who became less than themselves, or rose to be greater than themselves by virtue of the fact that the challenge he represented was inescapable. He is perhaps the only black man in the world whose relationship to white men is more terrible, more subtle, and more meaningful than the relationship of bitter possessed to uncertain possessors. His survival depended, and his development depends, on his ability to turn his peculiar status in the Western world to his own advantage and, it may be, to the very great advantage of that world. It remains for him to fashion out of his experience that which will give him sustenance, and a voice.

The cathedral at Chartres, I have said, says something to 24 the people of this village which it cannot say to me; but it is important to understand that this cathedral says something to me which it cannot say to them. Perhaps they are struck by the power of the spires, the glory of the windows; but they have known God, after all, longer than I have known him, and in a different way, and I am terrified by the slippery bottomless well to be found in the crypt, down which heretics were hurled to death, and by the obscene, inescapable gargoyles jutting out of the stone and seeming to say that God and the devil can never be divorced. I doubt that the villagers think of the devil when they face a cathedral because they have never been identified with the devil. But I must accept the status which myth, if nothing else, gives me in the West before I can hope to change the myth.

Yet, if the American Negro has arrived at his identity by 25 virtue of the absoluteness of his estrangement from his past, American white men still nourish the illusion that there is some means of recovering the European innocence, of returning to a state in which black men do not exist. This is one of the greatest errors Americans can make. The identity they fought so hard to protect has, by virtue of that battle, undergone a change: Americans are as unlike any other white people in the world as it is possible to be. I do not think, for example, that it is too much to suggest that the American vision of the world—which allows so little reality, generally speaking, for any of the darker forces in human life, which tends until today to paint moral issues in glaring black and white—owes a great deal to the battle waged by Americans to maintain between themselves and black men a human separation which could not be bridged. It is only now beginning to be borne in on us—very faintly, it must be admitted, very slowly, and very much against our will—that this vision of the world is dangerously inaccurate, and perfectly useless. For it protects our moral high-mindedness at the terrible expense of weakening our grasp of reality. People who shut their eyes to reality simply invite their own destruction, and anyone who insists on remaining in a state of innocence long after that innocence is dead turns himself into a monster.

The time has come to realize that the interracial drama acted out on the American continent has not only created a new black man, it has created a new white man, too. No road whatever will lead Americans back to the simplicity of this European village where white men still have the luxury of looking on me as a stranger. I am not, really, a stranger any longer for any American alive. One of the things that distinguishes Americans from other people is that no other people has ever been so deeply involved in the lives of black men, and vice versa. This fact faced, with all its implications, it can be seen that the history of the American Negro problem is not merely shameful, it is also something of an achievement. For even when the worst has been said, it must also be added that the perpetual challenge posed by this problem was always, somehow, perpetually met. It is precisely this black-white experience which may prove of indispensable value to us in the world we face today. This world is white no longer, and it will never be white again.

10
POSTSCRIPT: FOUR WRITERS ON WRITING

The Qualities of Good Writing

JACQUELINE BERKE

Jacqueline Berke teaches writing at Drew University in New Jersey. She has written a textbook, Twenty Questions for the Writer, *in which she approaches the writing process from the standpoint of the basic questions writers need to ask themselves when writing. In this selection from the second edition of her text, she looks at those qualities of good writing that make it "pungent, vital, moving, memorable."*

Even before you set out, you come prepared by instinct and intuition to make certain judgments about what is "good." Take the following familiar sentence, for example: "I know not what course others may take, but as for me, give me liberty or give me death." Do you suppose this thought of Patrick Henry's would have come ringing down through the centuries if he had expressed this sentiment not in one tight, rhythmical sentence but as follows:

It would be difficult, if not impossible, to predict on the basis of my limited information as to the predilections of the public, what the citizenry at large will regard as action commensurate with the present provocation, but after arduous consideration I personally feel so intensely and irrevocably committed to the position of social, political, and economic independence, that rather than submit to foreign and despotic control which is anathema to me, I will make the ultimate sacrifice of which humanity is capable—under the aegis of personal honor, ideological conviction, and existential commitment, I will sacrifice my own mortal existence.

How does this rambling, "high-flown" paraphrase measure up to the bold "Give me liberty or give me death"? Who will deny that something is "happening" in Patrick Henry's rousing challenge that not only fails to happen in the paraphrase but is actually negated there? Would you bear with this long-winded, pompous speaker to the end? If you were to judge this statement strictly on its rhetoric (its choice and arrangement of words), you might aptly call it more boring than brave. Perhaps a plainer version will work better:

> Liberty is a very important thing for a person to have. Most people—at least the people I've talked to or that other people have told me about—know this and therefore are very anxious to preserve their liberty. Of course I can't be absolutely sure about what other folks are going to do in this present crisis, what with all these threats and everything, but I've made up my mind that I'm going to fight because liberty is really a very important thing to me; at least that's the way I feel about it.

This flat, "homely" prose, weighted down with what Flaubert called "fatty deposits," is grammatical enough. As in the pompous paraphrase, every verb agrees with its subject, every comma is in its proper place; nonetheless it lacks the qualities that make a statement—of one sentence or one hundred pages—pungent, vital, moving, memorable.

Let us isolate these qualities and describe them briefly. . . . The first quality of good writing is *economy*. In an appropriately slender volume entitled *The Elements of Style,* authors William Strunk and E. B. White stated concisely the case for economy: "A sentence should contain no unnecessary words, a paragraph no unnecessary sentences, for the same reason that a drawing should have no unnecessay lines and a machine no unnecessary parts. This requires not that the writer make all his sentences short or that he avoid all detail . . . but that every word tell." In other words, economical writing is *efficient* and *aesthetically satisfying.* While it makes a minimum demand on the energy and patience of readers, it returns to them a maximum of sharply compressed meaning. You should accept this as your basic responsibility as a writer: that you inflict no unnecessary words on your readers—just as a dentist inflicts no unnecessary pain, a lawyer no unnecessary risk. Economical writing avoids strain and at the same time promotes pleasure by producing a sense of form and right proportion, a sense of words that fit the ideas that they embody—with not a line of "deadwood" to dull the reader's attention, not an extra, useless phrase to clog the free flow of ideas, one following swiftly and clearly upon another.

Another basic quality of good writing is *simplicity*. Here again this does not require that you make all your sentences primerlike or that you reduce complexities to bare bone, but rather that you avoid embellishment or embroidery. The natural, unpretentious style is best. But, paradoxically, simplicity or naturalness does not come naturally. By the time we are old enough to write, most of us have grown so self-conscious that we stiffen, sometimes to the point of rigidity, when we are called upon to make a statement in speech or in writing. It is easy to offer the kindly advice "Be yourself," but many people do not feel like themselves when they take a pencil in hand or sit down at a typewriter. Thus during the early days of the Second World War, when air raids were feared in New York City and blackouts were instituted, an anonymous writer— probably a young civil service worker at City Hall—produced and distributed to stores throughout the city the following poster:

Illumination
Is Required
to be
Extinguished
on These Premises
After Nightfall

What this meant, of course, was simply "Lights Out After Dark"; but apparently that direct imperative—clear and to the point—did not sound "official" enough; so the writer resorted to long Latinate words and involved syntax (note the awkward passives *"is* Required" and *"to be* Extinguished") to establish a tone of dignity and authority. In contrast, how beautifully simple are the words of the translators of the King James Version of the Bible, who felt no need for flourish, flamboyance, or grandiloquence. The Lord did not loftily or bombastically proclaim that universal illumination was required to be instantaneously installed. Simply but majestically "God said, Let there be light: and there was light. . . . And God called the light Day, and the darkness he called Night."

Most memorable declarations have been spare and direct. Abraham Lincoln and John Kennedy seemed to "speak to each other across the span of a century," notes French author André Maurois, for both men embodied noble themes in eloquently simple terms. Said Lincoln in his second Inaugural Address: "With malice towards none, with charity for all, with firmness in the right as God gives us the right, let us strive on to finish the work we are in. . . ." One hundred years later President Kennedy made his Inaugural dedication: "With a good conscience our only sure reward, with history the final judge of our deeds, let us go forth to lead the land we love. . . ."

A third fundamental element of good writing is *clarity*. Some people question whether it is always possible to be clear; after all, certain ideas are inherently complicated and inescapably difficult. True enough. But the responsible writer recognizes that writing should not add to the complications nor increase the difficulty; it should not set up an additional roadblock to understanding. Indeed, the German philosopher Wittgenstein went so far as to say that "whatever can be said can be said clearly." If you understand your own idea and want to convey it to others, you are obliged to render it in clear, orderly, readable, understandable prose—else why bother writing in the first place? Actually, obscure writers are usually confused, uncertain of what they want to say or what they mean; they have not yet completed that process of thinking through and reasoning into the heart of the subject.

Suffice it to say here that whatever the topic, whatever the occasion, expository writing should be readable, informative, and, wherever possible, engaging. At its best it may even be poetic, as Nikos Kazantzakis suggests in *Zorba the Greek,* where he draws an analogy between good prose and a beautiful landscape:

> To my mind the Cretan countryside resembled good prose, carefully ordered, sober, free from superfluous ornament, powerful and restrained. It expressed all that was necessary with the greatest economy. It had no flippancy nor artifice about it. It said what it had to say with a manly austerity. But between the severe lines one could discern an unexpected sensitiveness and tenderness; in the sheltered hollows the lemon and orange trees perfumed the air, and from the vastness of the sea emanated an inexhaustible poetry.

Even in technical writing, where the range of styles is necessarily limited (and poetry is neither possible nor appropriate), you must always be aware of "the reader over your shoulder." Take such topics as how to follow postal regulations for overseas mail, how to change oil in an engine, how to produce aspirin from salicylic acid. Here are technical expository descriptions that defy a memorable turn of phrase; here is writing that is of necessity cut and dried, dispassionate, and bloodless. But it need not be difficult, tedious, confusing, or dull to those who want to find out about mailing letters, changing oil, or making aspirin. Those who seek such information should have reasonably easy access to it, which means that written instructions should be clear, simple, spare, direct, and most of all, *human*: for no matter how technical a subject, all writing is done *for* human beings *by* human beings. Writing, in other words, like language itself, is a strictly human enterprise. Machines may stamp letters, measure oil, and convert acids, but only human beings talk and write about these procedures so that other human beings may better understand them. It is always appropriate, therefore, to be human in one's statement.

Part of this humanity must stem from your sense of who your readers are. You must assume a "rhetorical stance." Indeed this is a fundamental principle of rhetoric: *nothing should ever be written in a vacuum.* You should identify your audience, hypothetical or real, so that you may speak to them in an appropriate voice. A student, for example, should never "just write," without visualizing a definite group of readers—fellow students, perhaps, or the educated community at large (intelligent nonspecialists). Without such definite readers in mind, you cannot assume a suitable and appropriate relationship to your material, your purpose, and your audience. A proper rhetorical stance, in other words, requires that you have an active sense of the following:

1. Who you are as a writer.
2. Who your readers are.
3. Why you are addressing them and on what occasion.
4. Your relationship to your subject matter.
5. How you want your readers to relate to the subject matter.

Starting to Write: Some Practical Advice

WILLIAM ZINSSER

William Zinsser was born in New York City in 1922. After graduating from Princeton University, he worked for the New York Herald Tribune, *first as a feature writer and later as its drama editor and film critic. Zinsser's books include* The City Dwellers, Pop Goes America, *and* The Lunacy Boom *as well as other social and cultural commentaries. He currently teaches a course in writing nonfiction at Yale University.*

In this selection from his book On Writing Well *(2nd edition, 1980), Zinsser tells the writer to "be yourself" and gives some practical advice on just how to do this.*

Few people realize how badly they write. Nobody has shown them how much excess or murkiness has crept into their style and how it obstructs what they are trying to say. If you give me an article that runs to eight pages and I tell you to cut it to four, you'll howl and say it can't be done. Then you will go home and do it, and it will be infinitely better. After that comes the hard part: cutting it to three.

The point is that you have to strip down your writing before you can build it back up. You must know what the essential tools are and what job they were designed to do. If I may labor the metaphor of carpentry, it is first necessary to be able to saw wood neatly and to drive nails. Later you can bevel the edges or add elegant finials, if that is your taste. But you can never forget that you are practicing a craft that is based on certain principles. If the nails are weak, your house will collapse. If your verbs are weak and your syntax is rickety, your sentences will fall apart.

I'll admit that various nonfiction writers like Tom Wolfe and Norman Mailer and Hunter Thompson have built some remarkable houses. But these are writers who spent years learning their craft, and when at last they raised their fanciful turrets and hanging gardens, to the surprise of all of us who never dreamed of such ornamentation, they knew what they were doing. Nobody becomes Tom Wolfe overnight, not even Tom Wolfe.

First, then, learn to hammer in the nails, and if what you build is sturdy and serviceable, take satisfaction in its plain strength.

But you will be impatient to find a "style"—to embellish the plain words so that readers will recognize you as someone special. You will reach for gaudy similes and tinseled adjectives, as if "style" were something you could buy at a style store and drape onto your words in bright decorator colors. (Decorator colors are the colors that decorators come in.) Resist this shopping expedition: there is no style store.

Style is organic to the person doing the writing, as much a part of him as his hair, or, if he is bald, his lack of it. Trying to add style is like adding a toupee. At first glance the formerly bald man looks young and even handsome. But at second glance—and with a toupee there is always a second glance—he doesn't look quite right. The problem is not that he doesn't look well groomed; he does, and we can only admire the wigmaker's almost perfect skill. The point is that he doesn't look like himself.

This is the problem of the writer who sets out deliberately to garnish his prose. You lose whatever it is that makes you unique. The reader will usually notice if you are putting on airs. He wants the person who is talking to him to sound genuine. Therefore a fundamental rule is: be yourself.

No rule, however, is harder to follow. It requires the writer to do two things which by his metabolism are impossible. He must relax and he must have confidence.

Telling a writer to relax is like telling a man to relax while being prodded for a possible hernia, and, as for confidence, he is a bundle of anxieties. See how stiffly he sits at his typewriter, glaring at the paper that awaits his words, chewing the eraser on the pencil that is so sharp because he has sharpened it so many times. A writer will do anything to avoid the act of writing. I can testify from my newspaper days that the number of trips made to the water cooler per reporter-hour far exceeds the body's known need for fluids.

What can be done to put the writer out of these miseries? Unfortunately, no cure has yet been found. I can only offer the consoling thought that you are not alone. Some days will go better than others; some will go so badly that you will despair of ever writing again. We have all had many of these days and will have many more.

Still, it would be nice to keep the bad days to a minimum, which brings me back to the matter of trying to relax.

As I said earlier, the average writer sets out to commit an act of literature. He thinks that his article must be of a certain length or it won't seem important. He thinks how august it will look in print. He thinks of all the people who will read it. He thinks that it must have the solid weight of authority. He thinks that its style must dazzle. No wonder he tightens: he is so busy thinking of his awesome responsibility to the finished article that he can't even start. Yet he vows to be worthy of the task. He will do it—by God!—and, casting about for heavy phrases that would never occur to him if he weren't trying so hard to make an impression, he plunges in.

Paragraph 1 is a disaster—a tissue of ponderous generalities that seem to have come out of a machine. No *person* could have written them. Paragraph 2 is not much better. But Paragraph 3 begins to have a somewhat human quality, and by Paragraph 4 the writer begins to sound like himself. He has started to relax.

It is amazing how often an editor can simply throw away the first three or four paragraphs of an article and start with the paragraph where the writer begins to sound like himself. Not only are the first few paragraphs hopelessly impersonal and ornate; they also don't really say anything. They are a self-conscious attempt at a fancy introduction, and none is necessary.

A writer is obviously at his most natural and relaxed when

he writes in the first person. Writing is, after all, a personal transaction between two people, even if it is conducted on paper, and the transaction will go well to the extent that it retains its humanity. Therefore I almost always urge people to write in the first person—to use "I" and "me" and "us." They usually put up a fight.

"Who am I to say what *I* think?" they ask. "Or what *I* feel?"

"Who are you *not* to say what you think?" I reply. "There's only one you. Nobody else thinks or feels in exactly the same way."

"But no one cares about my opinions," they say. "It would make me feel conspicuous."

"They'll care if you tell them something interesting," I say, "and tell them in words that come naturally."

Nevertheless, getting writers to use "I" is seldom easy. They think they must somehow earn the right to reveal their emotions or their deepest thoughts. Or that it is egotistical. Or that it is undignified—a fear that hobbles the academic world. Hence the professorial use of "one" ("One finds oneself not wholly in accord with Dr. Maltby's view of the human condition") and of the impersonal "it is" ("It is to be hoped that Professor Felt's essay will find the wider audience that it most assuredly deserves"). These are arid constructions. "One" is a pedantic fellow—I've never wanted to meet him. I want a professor with a passion for his subject to tell me why it fascinates *him*.

I realize that there are vast regions of writing where "I" is not allowed. Newspapers don't want "I" in their news stories; many magazines don't want it in their articles and features; businesses and institutions don't want it in the annual reports and pamphlets that they send so profusely into the American home. Colleges don't want "I" in their term papers or dissertations, and English teachers in elementary and high schools have been taught to discourage any first-person pronoun except the literary "we" ("We see in Melville's symbolic use of the white whale . . .").

Many of these prohibitions are valid. Newspaper articles should consist of news, reported as objectively as possible. And I sympathize with schoolteachers who don't want to give students an easy escape into opinion—"I think Hamlet was stupid"—before the students have grappled with the discipline of assessing a work on its merits and on external sources. "I" can be a self-indulgence and a cop-out.

Still, we have become a society fearful of revealing who we are. We have evolved a national language of impersonality. The institutions that seek our support by sending us their brochures tend to sound remarkably alike, though surely all of them—hospitals, schools, libraries, museums—were founded and are still sustained by men and women with different dreams and visions. Where are these people? It is hard to glimpse them among all the passive sentences that say "initiatives were undertaken" and "priorities have been identified."

Even when "I" is not permitted, it's still possible to convey a sense of I-ness. James Reston and Red Smith, for instance, don't use "I" in their columns; yet I have a good idea of what kind of people they are, and I could say the same of other essayists and reporters. Good writers are always visible just behind their words. If you aren't allowed to use "I," at least think "I" while you write, or write the first draft in the first person and then take the "I"s out. It will warm up your impersonal style.

Style, of course, is ultimately tied to the psyche, and writing has deep psychological roots. The reasons why we express ourselves as we do, or fail to express ourselves because of "writer's block," are buried partly in the subconscious mind. There are as many different kinds of writer's block as there are kinds of writers, and I have no intention of trying to untangle them here. This is a short book, and my name isn't Sigmund Freud.

But I'm struck by what seems to be a new reason for avoiding "I" that runs even deeper than what is not allowed or what is undignified. Americans are suddenly uncertain of what they think and unwilling to go out on a limb—an odd turn of events for a nation famous for the "rugged individualist." A generation ago our leaders told us where they stood and what they believed. Today they perform the most strenuous verbal feats to escape this fate. Watch them wriggle through *Meet the Press* or *Face the Nation* without committing themselves on a single issue.

President Ford, trying to assure a group of visiting businessmen that his fiscal policies would work, said: "We see nothing but increasingly brighter clouds every month." I took this to mean that the clouds were still fairly dark. Ford's sentence, however, was just misty enough to say nothing and still sedate his constituents.

But the true champ is Elliot Richardson, who held four major Cabinet positions in the 1970s—Attorney General and Secretary of Defense, Commerce and H.E.W. It's hard to know even where to begin picking from his vast trove of equivocal statements, but consider this one: "And yet, on balance, affirmative action has, I think, been a qualified success." A thirteen-word sentence with five hedging words. I give it first prize as the most wishy-washy sentence of the decade, though a close rival would be Richardson's analysis of how to ease boredom among assembly-line workers: "And so, at last, I come to the one firm conviction that I mentioned at the beginning: it is that the subject is too new for final judgments."

That's a firm conviction? Leaders who bob and weave like aging boxers don't inspire confidence—or deserve it. The same thing is true of writers. Sell yourself, and your subject will exert its own appeal. Believe in your own identity and your own opinions. Proceed with confidence, generating it, if necessary, by pure willpower. Writing is an act of ego and you might as well admit it. Use its energy to keep yourself going.

The Maker's Eye: Revising Your Own Manuscripts

DONALD M. MURRAY

Donald M. Murray is a writer, and he currently teaches writing at the University of New Hampshire. Among his published works are novels, books of nonfiction, short stories, and poetry. He served as an editor at Time *and won the Pulitzer Prize in 1954 for editorials he wrote for the* Boston Herald. *In his textbook for teachers of writing,* A Writer Teaches Writing, *Murray explores the writing process.*

In this essay, first published in a different form in The Writer *(October 1973), Murray discusses the importance of the process of revision.*

When students complete a first draft, they consider the job of writing done—and their teachers too often agree. When professional writers complete a first draft, they usually feel that they are at the start of the writing process. When a draft is completed, the job of writing can begin.

That difference in attitude is the difference between amateur and professional, inexperience and experience, journeyman and craftsman. Peter F. Drucker, the prolific business writer, calls his first draft "the zero draft"—after that he can start counting. Most writers share the feeling that the first draft, and all of those which follow, are opportunities to discover what they have to say and how best they can say it.

To produce a progression of drafts, each of which says more

and says it more clearly, the writer has to develop a special kind of reading skill. In school we are taught to decode what appears on the page as finished writing. Writers, however, face a different category of possibility and responsibility when they read their own drafts. To them the words on the page are never finished. Each can be changed and rearranged, can set off a chain reaction of confusion or clarified meaning. This is a different kind of reading which is possibly more difficult and certainly more exciting.

Writers must learn to be their own best enemy. They must accept the criticism of others and be suspicious of it; they must accept the praise of others and be even more suspicious of it. Writers cannot depend on others. They must detach themselves from their own pages so that they can apply both their caring and their craft to their own work.

Such detachment is not easy. Science fiction writer Ray Bradbury supposedly puts each manuscript away for a year to the day and then rereads it as a stranger. Not many writers have the discipline or the time to do this. We must read when our judgment may be at its worst, when we are close to the euphoric moment of creation.

Then the writer, counsels novelist Nancy Hale, "should be critical of everything that seems to him most delightful in his style. He should excise what he most admires, because he wouldn't thus admire it if he weren't . . . in a sense protecting it from criticism." John Ciardi, the poet, adds, "The last act of the writing must be to become one's own reader. It is, I suppose, a schizophrenic process, to begin passionately and to end critically, to begin hot and to end cold; and, more important, to be passion-hot and critic-cold at the same time."

Most people think that the principal problem is that writers are too proud of what they have written. Actually, a greater problem for most professional writers is one shared by the majority of students. They are overly critical, think everything is dreadful, tear up page after page, never complete a draft, see the task as hopeless.

The writer must learn to read critically but constructively, to cut what is bad, to reveal what is good. Eleanor Estes, the children's book author, explains: "The writer must survey his work critically, cooly, as though he were a stranger to it. He must be willing to prune, expertly and hard-heartedly. At the end of each revision, a manuscript may look . . . worked over, torn apart, pinned together, added to, deleted from, words changed and words changed back. Yet the book must maintain its original freshness and spontaneity."

Most readers underestimate the amount of rewriting it usually takes to produce spontaneous reading. This is a great disadvantage to the student writer, who sees only a finished product and never watches the craftsman who takes the necessary step back, studies the work carefully, returns to the task, steps back, returns, steps back, again and again. Anthony Burgess, one of the most prolific writers in the English-speaking world, admits, "I might revise a page twenty times." Roald Dahl, the popular children's writer, states, "By the time I'm nearing the end of a story, the first part will have been reread and altered and corrected at least 150 times. . . . Good writing is essentially rewriting. I am positive of this."

Rewriting isn't virtuous. It isn't something that ought to be done. It is simply something that most writers find they have to do to discover what they have to say and how to say it. It is a condition of the writer's life.

There are, however, a few writers who do little formal rewriting, primarily because they have the capacity and experience to create and review a large number of invisible drafts in their minds before they approach the page. And some writers slowly produce finished pages, performing all the tasks of revision simultaneously, page by page, rather than draft by draft. But it is still possible to see the sequence followed by most writers most of the time in rereading their own work.

Most writers scan their drafts first, reading as quickly as possible to catch the larger problems of subject and form, then move in closer and closer as they read and write, reread and rewrite.

The first thing writers look for in their drafts is *information*. They know that a good piece of writing is built from specific, accurate, and interesting information. The writer must have an abundance of information from which to construct a readable piece of writing.

Next writers look for *meaning* in the information. The specifics must build to a pattern of significance. Each piece of specific information must carry the reader toward meaning.

Writers reading their own drafts are aware of *audience*. They put themselves in the reader's situation and make sure that they deliver information which a reader wants to know or needs to know in a manner which is easily digested. Writers try to be sure that they anticipate and answer the questions a critical reader will ask when reading the piece of writing.

Writers make sure that the *form* is appropriate to the subject and the audience. Form, or genre, is the vehicle which carries meaning to the reader, but form cannot be selected until the writer has adequate information to discover its significance and an audience which needs or wants that meaning.

Once writers are sure the form is appropriate, they must then look at the *structure*, the order of what they have written. Good writing is built on a solid framework of logic, argument, narrative, or motivation which runs through the entire piece of writing and holds it together. This is the time when many writers find it most effective to outline as a way of visualizing the hidden spine by which the piece of writing is supported.

The element on which writers may spend a majority of their time is *development*. Each section of a piece of writing must be adequately developed. It must give readers enough information so that they are satisfied. How much information is enough? That's as difficult as asking how much garlic belongs in a salad. It must be done to taste, but most beginning writers underdevelop, underestimating the reader's hunger for information.

As writers solve development problems, they often have to consider questions of *dimension*. There must be a pleasing and effective proportion among all the parts of the piece of writing. There is a continual process of subtracting and adding to keep the piece of writing in balance.

Finally, writers have to listen to their own voices. *Voice* is the force which drives a piece of writing forward. It is an expression of the writer's authority and concern. It is what is between the words on the page, what glues the piece of writing together. A good piece of writing is always marked by a consistent, individual voice.

As writers read and reread, write and rewrite, they move

closer and closer to the page until they are doing line-by-line editing. Writers read their own pages with infinite care. Each sentence, each line, each clause, each phrase, each word, each mark of punctuation, each section of white space between the type has to contribute to the clarification of meaning.

Slowly the writer moves from word to word, looking through language to see the subject. As a word is changed, cut, or added, as a construction is rearranged, all the words used before that moment and all those that follow that moment must be considered and reconsidered.

Writers often read aloud at this stage of the editing process, muttering or whispering to themselves, calling on the ear's experience with language. Does this sound right—or that? Writers edit, shifting back and forth from eye to page to ear to page. I find I must do this careful editing in short runs, no more than fifteen or twenty minutes at a stretch, or I become too kind with myself. I begin to see what I hope is on the page, not what actually is on the page.

This sounds tedious if you haven't done it, but actually it is fun. Making something right is immensely satisfying, for writers begin to learn what they are writing about by writing. Language leads them to meaning, and there is the joy of discovery, of understanding, of making meaning clear as the writer employs the technical skills of language.

Words have double meanings, even triple and quadruple meanings. Each word has its own potential for connotation and denotation. And when writers rub one word against the other, they are often rewarded with a sudden insight, an unexpected clarification.

The maker's eye moves back and forth from word to phrase to sentence to paragraph to sentence to phrase to word. The maker's eye sees the need for variety and balance, for a firmer structure, for a more appropriate form. It peers into the interior of the paragraph, looking for coherence, unity, and emphasis, which make meaning clear.

I learned something about this process when my first bifocals were prescribed. I had ordered a larger section of the reading portion of the glass because of my work, but even so, I could not contain my eyes within this new limit of vision. And I still find myself taking off my glasses and bending my nose towards the page, for my eyes unconsciously flick back and forth across the page, back to another page, forward to still another, as I try to see each evolving line in relation to every other line.

When does this process end? Most writers agree with the great Russian writer Tolstoy, who said, "I scarcely ever reread my published writings, if by chance I come across a page, it always strikes me: all this must be rewritten; this is how I should have written it."

The maker's eye is never satisfied, for each word has the potential to ignite new meaning. This article has been twice written all the way through the writing process, and it was published four years ago. Now it is to be republished in a book. The editors made a few small suggestions, and then I read it with my maker's eye. Now it has been re-edited, re-revised, re-read, re-re-edited, for each piece of writing to the writer is full of potential and alternatives.

A piece of writing is never finished. It is delivered to a deadline, torn out of the typewriter on demand, sent off with a sense of accomplishment and shame and pride and frustration. If only there were a couple more days, time for just another run at it, perhaps then . . .

Notes on Punctuation

LEWIS THOMAS

Lewis Thomas was born in 1913 in New York and attended Princeton and the Harvard Medical School. Thomas has had a distinguished career as a physician, administrator, researcher, teacher, and writer. Having been affiliated with the University of Minnesota Medical School, the New York University-Bellevue Medical Center, and the Yale University Medical School, Thomas is currently the president of the Memorial Sloan-Kettering Cancer Center. In 1971 he started writing a series of essays for The New England Journal of Medicine, *many of which were collected in* The Lives of a Cell: Notes of a Biology Watcher, *which won a National Book Award in 1974. A second collection of essays,* The Medusa and the Snail: More Notes of a Biology Watcher, *appeared in 1979.*

"Notes on Punctuation" is taken from The Medusa and the Snail. *In this selection Thomas discusses the meaning and practical value of various marks of punctuation.*

There are no precise rules about punctuation (Fowler lays out some general advice (as best he can under the complex circumstances of English prose (he points out, for example, that we possess only four stops (the comma, the semicolon, the colon and the period (the question mark and exclamation point are not, strictly speaking, stops; they are indicators of tone (oddly enough, the Greeks employed the semicolon for their question mark (it produces a strange sensation to read a Greek sentence which is a straightforward question: Why weepest thou; (instead of Why weepest thou? (and, of course, there are parentheses (which are surely a kind of punctuation making this whole matter much more complicated by having to count up the left-handed parentheses in order to be sure of closing with the right number (but if the parentheses were left out, with nothing to work with but the stops, we would have considerably more flexibility in the deploying of layers of meaning than if we tried to separate all the clauses by physical barriers (and in the latter case, while we might have more precision and exactitude for our meaning, we would lose the essential flavor of language, which is its wonderful ambiguity)))))))))))).

The commas are the most useful and usable of all the stops. It is highly important to put them in place as you go along. If you try to come back after doing a paragraph and stick them in the various spots that tempt you you will discover that they tend to swarm like minnows into all sorts of crevices whose existence you hadn't realized and before you know it the whole long sentence becomes immobilized and lashed up squirming in commas. Better to use them sparingly, and with affection, precisely when the need for each one arises, nicely, by itself.

I have grown fond of semicolons in recent years. The semicolon tells you that there is still some question about the preceding full sentence; something needs to be added; it reminds you sometimes of the Greek usage. It is almost always a greater pleasure to come across a semicolon than a period. The period tells you that that is that; if you didn't get all the meaning you wanted or expected, anyway you got all the writer intended to parcel out and now you have to move along. But with a semicolon there you get a pleasant little feeling of expectancy; there is more to come; read on; it will get clearer.

Colons are a lot less attractive, for several reasons: firstly, they give you the feeling of being rather ordered around, or at least having your nose pointed in a direction you might not be inclined to take if left to yourself, and, secondly, you suspect you're in for one of those sentences that will be labeling the points to be made: firstly, secondly and so forth, with the implication that you haven't sense enough to keep track of a sequence of notions without having them numbered. Also, many writers use this system loosely and incompletely, starting out with number one and number two as though counting off on their fingers but then going on and on without the succession of labels you've been led to expect, leaving you floundering about searching for the ninethly or seventeenthly that ought to be there but isn't.

Exclamation points are the most irritating of all. Look! they say, look at what I just said! How amazing is my thought! It is like being forced to watch someone else's small child jumping up and down crazily in the center of the living room shouting to attract attention. If a sentence really has something of importance to say, something quite remarkable, it doesn't need a mark to point it out. And if it is really, after all, a banal sentence needing more zing, the exclamation point simply emphasizes its banality!

Quotation marks should be used honestly and sparingly, when there is a genuine quotation at hand, and it is necessary to be very rigorous about the words enclosed by the marks. If something is to be quoted, the *exact* words must be used. If part of it must be left out because of space limitations, it is good manners to insert three dots to indicate the omission, but it is unethical to do this if it means connecting two thoughts which the original author did not intend to have tied together. Above all, quotation marks should not be used for ideas that you'd like to disown, things in the air so to speak. Nor should they be put in place around clichés; if you want to use a cliché you must take full responsibility for it yourself and not try to fob it off on anon., or on society. The most objectionable misuse of quotation marks, but one which illustrates the dangers of misuse in ordinary prose, is seen in advertising, especially in advertisements for small restaurants, for example "just around the corner," or "a good place to eat." No single, identifiable, citable person ever really said, for the record, "just around the corner," much less "a good place to eat," least likely of all for restaurants of the type that use this type of prose.

The dash is a handy device, informal and essentially playful, telling you that you're about to take off on a different tack but still in some way connected with the present course—only you have to remember that the dash is there, and either put a second dash at the end of the notion to let the reader know that he's back on course, or else end the sentence, as here, with a period.

The greatest danger in punctuation is for poetry. Here it is necessary to be as economical and parsimonious with commas and periods as with the words themselves, and any marks that seem to carry their own subtle meanings, like dashes and little rows of periods, even semicolons and question marks, should be left out altogether rather than inserted to clog up the thing with ambiguity. A single exclamation point in a poem, no matter what else the poem has to say, is enough to destroy the whole work.

The things I like best in T. S. Eliot's poetry, especially in the *Four Quartets,* are the semicolons. You cannot hear them, but they are there, laying out the connections between the images and the ideas. Sometimes you get a glimpse of a semicolon coming, a few lines farther on, and it is like climbing a steep path through woods and seeing a wooden bench just at a bend in the road ahead, a place where you can expect to sit for a moment, catching your breath.

Commas can't do this sort of thing; they can only tell you how the different parts of a complicated thought are to be fitted together, but you can't sit, not even take a breath, just because of a comma,

Glossary of Rhetorical Terms

Abstract See *Concrete/Abstract*.

Allusion An allusion is a passing reference to a familiar person, place, or thing drawn from history, the Bible, mythology, or literature. An allusion is an economical way for a writer to capture the essence of an idea, atmosphere, emotion, or historical era, as in "The scandal was his Watergate," or "He saw himself as a modern Job," or "Everyone there held those truths to be self-evident." An allusion should be familiar to the reader for if it is not, it will add nothing to the meaning.

Analogy Analogy is a special form of comparison in which the writer explains something unfamiliar by comparing it to something familiar: "A transmission line is simply a pipeline for electricity. In the case of a water pipeline, more water will flow through the pipe as water pressure increases. The same is true of a transmission line for electricity." See also the discussion of analogy in the introduction to Section 6 (pp. 176–179).

Appropriateness See *Diction*.

Argumentation Argumentation is one of the four basic types of prose. (Narration, description, and exposition are the other three.) To argue is to attempt to convince a reader to agree with

367

a point of view, to make a given decision, or to pursue a particular course of action. Argumentation is based upon logical explanations and appeals to the reader's intelligence. See the introduction to Section 8 (pp. 250–252) for further discussion of argumentation. See also *Persuasion* and *Logical Fallacies*.

Attitude   A writer's attitude reflects his or her opinion of a subject. For example, a writer can think very positively or very negatively about a subject. In most cases the writer's attitude falls somewhere between these two extremes. See also *Tone*.

Audience   An audience is the intended readership for a piece of writing. For example, the readers of a national weekly newsmagazine come from all walks of life and have diverse opinions, attitudes, and educational experiences. In contrast, the readership for an organic chemistry journal is made up of people whose interests and educations are quite similar. The essays in this book are intended for general readers, intelligent people who may lack specific information about the subject being discussed.

Beginnings   See *Beginnings/Endings*.

Beginnings/Endings   A *beginning* is that sentence, group of sentences, or section that introduces an essay. Good beginnings usually identify the thesis or controlling idea, attempt to interest the reader, and establish a tone. Some effective ways in which writers begin essays include (1) telling an anecdote that illustrates the thesis, (2) providing a controversial statement or opinion which engages the reader's interest, (3) presenting startling statistics or facts, (4) defining a term that is central to the discussion that follows, (5) asking thought-provoking questions, (6) providing a quotation that illustrates the thesis, (7) referring to a current event that helps to establish the thesis, or (8) showing the significance of the subject or stressing its importance to the reader.

An *ending* is that sentence or group of sentences which brings an essay to closure. Good endings are purposeful and well planned. Endings satisfy readers when they are the natural outgrowths of the essays themselves and give the readers a sense of finality or completion. Good essays do not simply stop; they conclude.

Cause and Effect   Cause and effect is one of the types of exposition. (Process analysis, definition, classification, and comparison and contrast are the others.) Cause-and-effect analysis answers the question *why*. It explains the reasons for an occurrence or the consequences of an action. See the introduction to Section 7 (pp. 206–208) for a detailed discussion of cause and effect. See also *Exposition*.

Classification   Classification is one of the types of exposition. (Process analysis, definition, comparison and contrast, and cause and effect are the others.) When classifying, the writer arranges and sorts people, places, or things into categories according to their differing characteristics, thus making them more manageable for the writer and more understandable for the reader. See the introduction to Section 5 (pp. 135–138) for a detailed discussion of classification. See also *Exposition*.

Cliché   A cliché is an expression that has become ineffective through overuse. Expressions such as *quick as a flash, dry as dust, jump for joy,* and *slow as molasses* are all clichés. Writers normally avoid such trite expressions and seek instead to express themselves in fresh and forceful language.

Coherence   Coherence is a quality of good writing that results when all sentences, paragraphs, and longer divisions of an essay are naturally connected. Coherent writing is achieved through (1) a logical sequence of ideas (arranged in chronological order, spatial order, order of importance, or some other appropriate order), (2) the thoughtful repetition of key words and ideas, (3) a pace suitable for your topic and your reader, and (4) the use of transitional words and expressions. Coherence should not be confused with unity. (See *Unity*.) Also see *Transitions*.

Colloquial Expressions   A colloquial expression is characteristic of or appropriate to spoken language or to writing that seeks its effect. Colloquial expressions are informal, as *chem, gym, come up with, be at loose ends, won't,* and *photo* illustrate.

Thus, colloquial expressions are acceptable in formal writing only if they are used purposefully.

Comparison and Contrast   Comparison and contrast is one of the types of exposition. (Process analysis, definition, classification, and cause and effect are the others.) In comparison and contrast, the writer points out the similarities and differences between two or more subjects in the same class or category. The function of any comparison and contrast is to clarify—to reach some conclusion about the items being compared and contrasted. See the introduction to Section 6 (pp. 176–179) for a detailed discussion of comparison and contrast. See also *Exposition*.

Conclusions   See *Beginnings/Endings*.

Concrete   See *Concrete/Abstract*.

Concrete/Abstract   A concrete word names a specific object, person, place, or action that can be directly perceived by the senses: *car, bread, building, book, John F. Kennedy, Chicago,* or *hiking*. An abstract word, in contrast, refers to general qualities, conditions, ideas, actions, or relationships which cannot be directly perceived by the senses: *bravery, dedication, excellence, anxiety, stress, thinking,* or *hatred*.

Although writers must use both concrete and abstract language, good writers avoid too many abstract words. Instead, they rely on concrete words to define and illustrate abstractions. Because concrete words affect the senses, they are easily comprehended by a reader.

Connotation   See *Connotation/Denotation*.

Connotation/Denotation   Both connotation and denotation refer to the meanings of words. Denotation is the dictionary meaning of a word, the literal meaning. Connotation, on the other hand, is the implied or suggested meaning of a word. For example, the denotation of *lamb* is "a young sheep." The connotations of lamb are numerous: *gentle, docile, weak, peaceful, blessed, sacrificial, blood, spring, frisky, pure, innocent,* and so on. Good writers are sensitive to both the denotations and the connotations of words and use these meanings to advantage in their writing.

Controlling Idea   See *Thesis*.

Deduction   Deduction is the process of reasoning from stated premises to a conclusion which follows necessarily. This form of reasoning moves from the general to the specific. See the introduction to Section 8 (pp. 250–252) for a discussion of deductive reasoning and its relation to argumentation. See also *Syllogism*.

Definition   Definition is one of the types of exposition. (Process analysis, classification, comparison and contrast, and cause and effect are the others.) Definition is a statement of the meaning of a word. A definition may be either brief or extended, part of an essay or an entire essay itself. See the introduction to Section 4 (pp. 96–98) for a detailed discussion of definition. See also *Exposition*.

Denotation   See *Connotation/Denotation*.

Description   Description is one of the four basic types of prose. (Narration, exposition, and argumentation are the other three.) Description tells how a person, place, or thing is perceived by the five senses. Objective description reports these sensory qualities factually, whereas subjective description gives the writer's interpretation of them. See the introduction to Section 2 (pp. 35–36) for a detailed discussion of description.

Diction   Diction refers to a writer's choice and use of words. Good diction is precise and appropriate—the words mean exactly what the writer intends, and the words are well suited to the writer's subject, intended audience, and purpose in writing. The word-conscious writer knows that there are differences among *aged, old,* and *elderly; blue, navy,* and *azure;* and *disturbed, angry,* and *irritated.* Furthermore, this writer knows in which situation to use each word. See also *Connotation/ Denotation*.

Dominant Impression   A dominant impression is the single mood, atmosphere, or quality a writer emphasizes in a piece of descriptive writing. The dominant impression is created through the careful selection of details and is, of course, influenced by the writer's subject, audience, and purpose. See also the introduction to Section 2 (pp. 35–36).

Endings See *Beginnings/Endings.*

Essay An essay is a relatively short piece of nonfiction in which the writer attempts to make one or more closely related points. A good essay is purposeful, informative, and well organized.

Evaluation An evaluation of a piece of writing is an assessment of its effectiveness or merit. In evaluating a piece of writing, one should ask the following questions: What is the writer's purpose? Is it a worthwhile purpose? Does the writer achieve the purpose? Is the writer's information sufficient and accurate? What are the strengths of the essay? What are its weaknesses? Depending on the type of writing and the purpose, more specific questions can also be asked. For example, with an argument one could ask: Does the writer follow the principles of logical thinking? Is the writer's evidence convincing?

Evidence Evidence is the data on which a judgment or argument is based or by which proof or probability is established. Evidence usually takes the form of statistics, facts, names, examples or illustrations, and opinions of authorities.

Example An example illustrates a larger idea or represents something of which it is a part. An example is a basic means of developing or clarifying an idea. Furthermore, examples enable writers to show and not simply to tell readers what they mean. The terms *example* and *illustration* are sometimes used interchangeably.

Exposition Exposition is one of the four basic types of prose. (Narration, description, and argumentation are the other three.) The purpose of exposition is to clarify, explain, and inform. The methods of exposition presented in this text are process analysis, definition, classification, comparison and contrast, and cause and effect. For a detailed discussion of each of these methods of exposition, see the appropriate section introduction.

Fallacy See *Logical Fallacies.*

Figures of Speech Figures of speech are brief, imaginative comparisons which highlight the similarities between things that are basically dissimilar. They make writing vivid and interesting and therefore more memorable. The most common figures of speech are:

> *Simile:* An implicit comparison introduced by *like* or *as.* "The fighter's hands were like stone."
>
> *Metaphor:* An implied comparison which uses one thing as the equivalent of another. "All the world's a stage."
>
> *Personification:* A special kind of simile or metaphor in which human traits are assigned to an inanimate object. "The engine coughed and then stopped."

Focus Focus is the limitation that a writer gives his or her subject. The writer's task is to select a manageable topic given the constraints of time, space, and purpose. For example, within the general subject of sports, a writer could focus on government support of amateur athletes or narrow the focus further to government support of Olympic athletes.

General See *Specific/General.*

Idiom An idiom is a word or phrase that is used habitually with a particular meaning in a language. The meaning of an idiom is not always readily apparent to nonnative speakers of that language. For example, *catch cold, hold a job, make up your mind,* and *give them a hand* are all idioms in English.

Illustration See *Example.*

Induction Induction is the process of reasoning to a conclusion about all members of a class through an examination of only a few members of the class. This form of reasoning moves from the particular to the general. See the introduction to Section 8 (pp. 250–252) for a discussion of inductive reasoning and its relation to argumentation.

Introductions See *Beginnings/Endings.*

Irony The use of words to suggest something different from their literal meaning. For example, when Jonathan Swift proposes in *A Modest Proposal* that Ireland's problems could be solved if the people of Ireland fattened their babies and sold them to the English landlords for food, he meant that almost any other solution would be preferable. A writer can use irony to establish a special relationship with the reader and to add an extra dimension or twist to the meaning.

Jargon   See *Technical Language*.

Logical Fallacies   A logical fallacy is an error in reasoning that renders an argument invalid. Some of the more common logical fallacies are:

> *Oversimplification:* The tendency to provide simple solutions to complex problems. "The reason we have inflation today is that OPEC has unreasonably raised the price of oil."
>
> *Non sequitur* ("It does not follow"): An inference or conclusion that does not follow from established premises or evidence. "It was the best movie I saw this year, and it should get an Academy Award."
>
> *Post hoc, ergo propter hoc* ("After this, therefore because of this"): Confusing chance or coincidence with causation. Because one event comes after another one, it does not necessarily mean that the first event caused the second. "I won't say I caught cold at the hockey game, but I certainly didn't have it before I went there."
>
> *Begging the question:* Assuming in a premise that which needs to be proven. "If American autoworkers built a better product, foreign auto sales would not be so high."
>
> *False analogy:* Making a misleading analogy between logically unconnected ideas. "He was a brilliant basketball player; therefore, there's no question in my mind that he will be a fine coach."
>
> *Either/or thinking:* The tendency to see an issue as having only two sides. "Used car salesmen are either honest or crooked."

Logical Reasoning   See *Deduction* and *Induction*.

Metaphor   See *Figures of Speech*.

Narration   One of the four basic types of prose. (Description, exposition, and argumentation are the other three.) To narrate is to tell a story, to tell what happened. While narration is most often used in fiction, it is also important in nonfiction, either by itself or in conjunction with other types of prose. See the introduction to Section 1 (pp. 1–3) for a detailed discussion of narration.

Objective/Subjective Objective writing is factual and impersonal, whereas subjective writing, sometimes called impressionistic, relies heavily on personal interpretation. For a discussion of *objective description* and *subjective description*, see the introduction to Section 2 (pp. 35–36).

Opinion An opinion is a belief or conclusion not substantiated by positive knowledge or proof. An opinion reveals personal feelings or attitudes or states a position. Opinion should not be confused with argument.

Paradox A paradox is a seemingly contradictory statement that may nonetheless be true. For example, *we little know what we have until we lose it* is a paradoxical statement. For a detailed discussion of paradox which includes additional examples, see Laurence Perrine's "Paradox," pp. 99–100.

Paragraph The paragraph, the single most important unit of thought in an essay, is a series of closely related sentences. These sentences adequately develop the central or controlling idea of the paragraph. This central or controlling idea, usually stated in a topic sentence, is necessarily related to the purpose of the whole composition. A well-written paragraph has several distinguishing characteristics: a clearly stated or implied topic sentence, adequate development, unity, coherence, and an appropriate organizational strategy.

Parallelism Parallel structure is the repetition of word order or form either within a single sentence or in several sentences that develop the same central idea. As a rhetorical device, parallelism can aid coherence and add emphasis. Roosevelt's statement, "I see one third of the nation ill-housed, ill-clad, and ill-nourished," illustrates effective parallelism.

Personification See *Figures of Speech*.

Persuasion Persuasion is an attempt to convince readers to agree with a point of view, to make a given decision, or to pursue a particular course of action. Persuasion heavily appeals to the emotions whereas argumentation does not. For the distinction between *logical argument* and *persuasive argument*, see the introduction to Section 8 (pp. 250–252).

Point of View Point of view refers to the grammatical person of the speaker in an essay. For example, a first-person point of view uses the pronoun *I* and is commonly found in autobiography and the personal essay; a third-person point of view uses the pronouns *he, she,* or *it* and is commonly found in objective writing. See the introduction to Section 1 (pp. 1–3) for a discussion of point of view in narration.

Process Analysis Process analysis is a type of exposition. (Definition, classification, comparison and contrast, and cause and effect are others.) Process analysis answers the question *how* and explains how something works or gives step-by-step directions for doing something. See the introduction to Section 3 (pp. 63–65) for a detailed discussion of process analysis. See also *Exposition*.

Purpose Purpose is what the writer wants to accomplish in a particular piece of writing. Purposeful writing seeks to *relate* (narration), to *describe* (description), to *explain* (process analysis, definition, classification, comparison and contrast, and cause and effect), or to *convince* (argumentation).

Rhetorical Question A rhetorical question is asked but requires no answer from the reader. "When will nuclear proliferation end?" is such a question. Writers use rhetorical questions to introduce topics they plan to discuss or to emphasize important points.

Sequence Sequence refers to the order in which a writer presents information. Writers commonly select chronological order, spatial order, order of importance, or order of complexity to arrange their points.

Simile See *Figures of Speech*.

Slang   Slang is the unconventional, very informal language of particular subgroups in our culture. Slang, such as *zonk, coke, split, rap, cop,* and *stoned,* is acceptable in formal writing only if it is used purposefully.

Specific/General   General words name groups or classes of objects, qualities, or actions. Specific words, on the other hand, name individual objects, qualities, or actions within a class or group. To some extent the terms *general* and *specific* are relative. For example, *dessert* is a class of things. *Pie,* however, is more specific than *dessert* but more general than *pecan pie* or *chocolate cream pie.*

Good writing judiciously balances the general with the specific. Writing with too many general words is likely to be dull and lifeless. General words do not create vivid responses in the reader's mind as concrete specific words can. On the other hand, writing that relies exclusively on specific words may lack focus and direction, the control that more general statements provide.

Strategy   A strategy is a means by which a writer achieves his or her purpose. Strategy includes the many rhetorical decisions that the writer makes about organization, paragraph structure, syntax, and diction. In terms of the whole essay, strategy refers to the principal rhetorical mode that a writer uses. If, for example, a writer wishes to show how to make chocolate chip cookies, the most effective strategy would be process analysis. If it is the writer's purpose to show why sales of American cars have declined in recent years, the most effective strategy would be cause-and-effect analysis.

Style   Style is the individual manner in which a writer expresses his or her ideas. Style is created by the author's particular selection of words, construction of sentences, and arrangement of ideas.

Subject   The subject of an essay is its content, what the essay is about. Depending on the author's purpose and the constraints of space, a subject may range from one that is broadly conceived to one that is narrowly defined.

Supporting Evidence   See *Evidence*.

Syllogism   A syllogism is an argument that utilizes deductive reasoning and consists of a major premise, a minor premise, and a conclusion. For example,

All trees that lose leaves are deciduous. (major premise)
Maple trees lose their leaves. (minor premise)
Therefore, maple trees are deciduous. (conclusion)

See also *Deduction*.

Symbol   A symbol is a person, place, or thing that represents something beyond itself. For example, the eagle is a symbol of America, and the bear, a symbol of Russia.

Syntax   Syntax refers to the way in which words are arranged to form phrases, clauses, and sentences as well as to the grammatical relationship among the words themselves.

Technical Language   Technical language, or jargon, is the special vocabulary of a trade or profession. Writers who use technical language do so with an awareness of their audience. If the audience is a group of peers, technical language may be used freely. If the audience is a more general one, technical language should be used sparingly and carefully so as not to sacrifice clarity. See also *Diction*.

Thesis   A thesis is a statement of the main idea of an essay. Also known as the controlling idea, a thesis may sometimes be implied rather than stated directly.

Title   A title is a word or phrase set off at the beginning of an essay to identify the subject, to capture the main idea of the essay, or to attract the reader's attention. A title may be explicit or suggestive. A subtitle, when used, extends or restricts the meaning of the main title.

Tone   Tone is the manner in which a writer relates to an audience, the "tone of voice" used to address readers. Tone may be described as friendly, serious, distant, angry, cheerful, bitter, cynical, enthusiastic, morbid, resentful, warm, playful, and so forth. A particular tone results from a writer's diction, sentence structure, purpose, and attitude toward the subject. See *Attitude*.

Topic Sentence The topic sentence states the central idea of a paragraph and thus limits and controls the subject of the paragraph. Although the topic sentence normally appears at the beginning of the paragraph, it may appear at any other point, particularly if the writer is trying to create a special effect. Also see *Paragraph*.

Transitions Transitions are words or phrases that link sentences, paragraphs, and larger units of a composition in order to achieve coherence. These devices include parallelism, pronoun references, conjunctions, and the repetition of key ideas, as well as the many conventional transitional expressions such as *moreover, on the other hand, in addition, in contrast,* and *therefore*. Also see *Coherence*.

Unity Unity is achieved in an essay when all the words, sentences, and paragraphs contribute to its thesis. The elements of a unified essay do not distract the reader. Instead, they all harmoniously support a single idea or purpose.

Didion. Reprinted by permission of Simon and Schuster, a Division of Gulf & Western Corporation.

5. Classification

"Name-Calling" from *Word Play: What Happens When People Talk,* by Peter Farb. Copyright © 1973 by Peter Farb. Reprinted by permission of Alfred A. Knopf, Inc.

"Weasel Words: God's Little Helpers" by Paul Stevens (pseudonym, Carl P. Wrighter). From *I Can Sell You Anything* by Carl P. Wrighter. Copyright © 1972 by Ballantine Books, Inc. Reprinted by permission of Ballantine Books, a Division of Random House, Inc.

"Can People Be Judged by Their Appearance?" by Eric Berne from *A Layman's Guide to Psychiatry and Psychoanalysis.* Copyright © 1947, 1957, 1968 by Eric Berne. Reprinted by permission of Simon and Schuster, a Division of Gulf & Western Corporation.

"Sexism in English: A Feminist View" by Alleen Pace Nilsen from *Female Studies VI: Closer to the Ground,* pp. 102–109; copyright © 1972 by Nancy Hoffman, Cynthia Secor, Adrian Tinsley. Reprinted by permission of The Feminist Press, Old Westbury, New York.

6. Comparison and Contrast

"From Song to Sound: Bing and Elvis" by Russell Baker. © 1977 by The New York Times Company. Reprinted by permission.

"Grant and Lee: A Study in Contrasts" by Bruce Catton from *The American Story,* ed. by Earl Schenck Miers, © 1956 by Broadcast Music, Inc. Used by permission of the copyright holder.

"The Death of Silence" by Robert Paul Dye. From *The Journal of Broadcasting,* vol. 12, no. 3 (Summer 1968). Copyright 1968 by the Broadcast Education Association. Reprinted by permission of the Broadcast Education Association.

"Good Morning" by Michael J. Arlen. Reprinted with the permission of Farrar, Straus and Giroux, Inc. From *The View from Highway 1* by Michael J. Arlen. Copyright © 1974, 1975, 1976 by Michael J. Arlen.

"The Base Stealer" by Robert Francis. Copyright © 1948 by Robert Francis. Reprinted from *The Orb Weaver* by permission of Wesleyan University Press.

"Foul Shot" by Edwin A. Hoey. Special permission granted by *Read* Magazine, published by Xerox Corp.

7. Cause and Effect

"The Thin Grey Line" by Marya Mannes. Reprinted by permission of the author.

"Confessions of a Working Stiff" by Patrick Fenton. Copyright © 1973 by News Group Publications, Inc. Reprinted with the permission of *New York* Magazine.

"How TV Violence Damages Your Children" by Victor B. Cline. © 1975 LHJ Publishing, Inc. Reprinted by permission of Ladies' Home Journal.

"Three Mile Island" from *The Politics of Energy* by Barry Commoner. Copyright © 1979 by Barry Commoner. Reprinted by permission of Alfred A. Knopf, Inc. Portions of this book have previously appeared in *The New Yorker*.

"Marriage as a Wretched Institution" by Mervyn Cadwallader. Copyright © 1966 by The Atlantic Monthly Company, Boston, Massachusetts. Reprinted with permission.

8. Argumentation

"The Obligation to Endure" from *Silent Spring* by Rachel Carson, published by Houghton Mifflin Company. Copyright © 1962 by Rachel L. Carson. Reprinted by permission of the publisher.

"The Right to Die" by Norman Cousins. In *Saturday Review,* June 14, 1975. Reprinted by permission of the author.

"Health and High Voltage" by Kelly Davis. "Health and High Voltage: 765 kV Lines" by Kelly Davis, from the July/August 1978 issue of *Sierra*. Reprinted by permission of the Sierra Club.

"Taming Technology" from *Future Shock* by Alvin Toffler. Copyright © 1970 by Alvin Toffler. Reprinted by permission of Random House, Inc.

"Uncritical Inference Test, Story B" by William V. Haney. Copyright 1979 by William V. Haney and reprinted with his permission.

9. Essays for Further Analysis

"Let's Suppose . . ." by Isaac Asimov. An adaptation of the text of Chapter 5, "Limits," from *Earth: Our Crowded Spaceship* by Isaac Asimov. Copyright © 1974 by Isaac Asimov. A John Day Book. By permission of Thomas Y. Crowell, Publishers.

"An 18-Year-Old Looks Back on Life" by Joyce Maynard. © 1972 by The New York Times Company. Reprinted by permission.

"Once More to the Lake" from *Essays of E. B. White* by E. B. White. Copyright 1941 by E. B. White. Reprinted by permission of Harper & Row, Publishers, Inc.

"The Subway" by Tom Wolfe from *New York, New York*. Copyright © 1964 by The New York Herald Tribune, Inc. Reprinted by permission of The Dial Press.

"Stranger in the Village" from *Notes of a Native Son* by James Baldwin. Copyright © 1953, 1955 by James Baldwin. Reprinted by permission of Beacon Press.

10. Postscript: Four Writers on Writing

"The Qualities of Good Writing" by Jacqueline Berke. Abridged and adapted from "The Qualities of Good Writing" in *Twenty Questions for the Writer: A*